Writing & Speaking at Work

FOURTH EDITION

WRITING & SPEAKING AT WORK

A Practical Guide for Business Communication

Edward P. Bailey

PEARSON

Prentice
Hall

Upper Saddle River, New Jersey 07458

Library of Congress Cataloging-in-Publication Data

Bailey, Edward P.
  Writing & speaking at work : a practical guide for business communication/
Edward P. Bailey.—4th ed.
    p. cm.
  Includes indexes.
  ISBN 0-13-188130-2
  1. Business communication—Handbooks, manuals, etc.   2. Business
writing—Handbooks, manuals, etc.   3. Public speaking—Handbooks, manuals,
etc.   I. Title.   II. Title: Writing and speaking at work.
HF5718.B343 2008
658.4'5—dc22   2007001602

Editor-in-Chief: David Parker
VP/Editorial Director: Jeff Shelstad
Product Development Manager: Ashley Santora
Assistant Editor: Keri Molinari
Editorial Assistant: Kristen Varina
Marketing Manager: Anne Howard
Marketing Assistant: Susan Osterlitz
Associate Director, Production Editorial: Judy Leale
Managing Editor: Renata Butera
Production Editor: Kelly Warsak
Permissions Coordinator: Charles Morris
Associate Director, Manufacturing: Vinnie Scelta
Manufacturing Buyer: Michelle Klein
Director of Design: Christy Mahon
Cover Design: Bruce Kenselaar
Cover Photo: Getty Images
Illustration (Interior): ICC Macmillan Inc.
Composition: ICC Macmillan Inc.
Full-Service Project Management: ICC Macmillan Inc.
Printer/Binder: R.R.D./Harrisonburg
Cover Printer: Lehigh Press
Typeface: 10/12 Times Ten Roman

Credits and acknowledgments borrowed from other sources and reproduced, with permission, in this textbook
appear on appropriate page within text.

Pearson Education LTD.   Pearson Education Australia PTY, Limited
Pearson Education Singapore, Pte. Ltd   Pearson Education North Asia Ltd
Pearson Education, Canada, Ltd   Pearson Educación de Mexico, S.A. de C.V.
Pearson Education–Japan   Pearson Education Malaysia, Pte. Ltd.

10 9 8 7 6 5 4 3 2 1
ISBN-13: 978-0-13-188130-3
ISBN-10: 0-13-188130-2

For my wife, Janet

Brief Contents

Contents

ix

Preface

A famous adventure writer once said, "When I write, I try to leave out the parts people skip."

I've tried to do the same thing in this book. You'll find this book is shorter than most other business communication texts, but it's full of practical advice. That advice comes from my years as a college teacher and as a frequent consultant to business and government.

Instead of dealing with various theories of communication, this book focuses directly on the two most important communication skills that people in business need: writing and speaking. The first half of the book covers writing; the second half, speaking.

While writing this book, I've pictured myself talking to my readers, as though they are my students in the classroom. As a result, I've adopted a straightforward, spoken style with—I hope—an accessible tone.

What's New?

This new edition has been a general update: adding examples, revising some of the exercises, and—especially—keeping up with today's technology.

Also, I've (cheerfully) deleted the chapter on using transparencies and added a new appendix on commonly confused words.

My goal is to help students dramatically improve their ability to write and speak—so they can be confident rather than self-conscious or embarrassed. The target audience is anybody in college at whatever level. The majority of my students have been graduate students in our MBA program. They're successful adults who want practical help they can apply today and every day in the future. Most of the examples in the book are from their work.

But undergraduate students want the same thing graduate students do, and this book aims to help them too.

If you want a quick overview of the book, Chapter 1 is a short introduction to writing and Chapter 13 is a short introduction to speaking. They're good places to start.

Edward P. Bailey
Wilmington, North Carolina

Acknowledgments

I want to express my deep thanks to the people at Prentice Hall and ICC Macmillan Inc.—especially David Parker, Ashley Santora, and Keri Molinari.

I also owe thanks to these people:

- My friends at Marymount: Professor Jim Ryerson, Professor Charlie Miller, Dr. Charles Hurst, Dr. Steve Knode, Professor Don Lavanty, Dr. Art Meiners, Dr. Ed Parks, Dr. Thomas Lee, and Dr. Bob Sigethy.
- My reviewers (who gave me excellent advice):

Lynnea Brumbaugh	Washington University–St. Louis
Timothy Flood	University of North Carolina–Chapel Hill
Virginia Garrison	Covenant College
Becky Kellam	Reedley College
Robert Saba	Florida International University
Judy Jones Tisdale	University of North Carolina–Chapel Hill

Finally, I thank my students (both academic and consulting), especially the ones who have given me permission to use their work in this book. I've listed them by the chapter their work appears in:

Chapter 3	Kristen Doles, Julia Kramer, Carmen Ross, Shawn Morris, Min Jing Bookbinder, Joanna Hartis, Mary Scohera, and Alyson Bartol
Chapter 4	Mary Scohera
Chapter 6	Terri Lamb, Robert Turner, Aleksandra Regulski, Kent C. Engdahl, Amy E. Wiley, Aida Gregory, and Sandy Niese
Chapter 14	Arleen Courtney
Chapter 16	Lisa Janssen and Gus Creedon
Chapter 17	Lisa Janssen (again!)
Appendix D	Nattawat Sattaworakul, Michael Day, and Liz Wood

PART I
Writing

CHAPTER I

What Is Good Writing?

Good writing is . . . Plain English!

A number of years ago, there was a standard for business writing that most people accepted but few liked—a formal style with a stiff tone. Writers sounded as distant and impersonal as the buildings they worked in. Worse, their writing was hard to read—using big words, long sentences, and huge paragraphs.

The name for that kind of writing? Bureaucratese.

Believe me, bureaucratese still exists in too many places even today. But in most places, Plain English is now the standard. Who has time to struggle with a piece of writing just to figure out what it says?

Boiled down to its essentials, Plain English means the following:

- *Making your main point easy to find.* Usually you should start with your main point. For example, most companies write important reports. Believe me, almost everyone who picks up those reports wants to know—in the first few *seconds*— What does the report look into? And what does it find? Readers don't want to struggle through lots of pages—or go on a hunting expedition—just to find the most important point in the report.
- *Writing the way you talk.* Most of you are perfectly articulate when talking face-to-face with someone. You probably feel you can manage your tone well in talking and capture nuances of meaning. Why not use those words when you write? Writing the way you talk will not make you sound simplistic.
- *Using good layout.* Headings and bullets help readers *see* the underlying structure of your writing. And graphics—such as tables, flow charts, and decision trees— turn paragraphs full of words into what you wanted your readers to picture in the first place!

So Plain English doesn't mean dumbing things down. It just means getting to your point, being comfortable with everyday language, and using good layout to show the structure and content of your writing.

This book shows you how to write Plain English.

 The Web site for this book is http://www.professorbailey.com. It quickly teaches a key point from each chapter (including this one). Be sure to look at it!

AN EXAMPLE OF PLAIN ENGLISH

Let's look at an example. Suppose you make computers and want to sell some to the government. You send in a bid and then wonder what the competition has proposed. Here's an excerpt from a government regulation that tells you when you can look at a competitor's bid:

> Examination of bids by interested persons shall be permitted if it does not interfere unduly with the conduct of Government business. Original bids shall not be allowed to pass out of the hands of Government officials unless a duplicate bid is not available for public inspection. The original bid may be examined by the public only under the immediate supervision of a Government official and under conditions that preclude possibility of substitution, addition, deletion, or alteration in the bid.

Unfortunately, that example isn't unusual at all. It's typical writing B.P.E. (Before Plain English). Now let's translate it into ordinary language:

> Can you look at a copy of another company's bid? Yes—if there's no undue interference with government business.
>
> If a copy isn't available, you can look at an original bid. In that case, a government official must be present to make sure no one tampers with it.

Which version would you rather read? (The second version, I hope!)

Plain English is a straightforward way of writing. It sounds more like talking. It looks more inviting. And it's much easier to understand.

SO . . . WHAT IS GOOD WRITING?

Good writing was easy to define under the old standard. It was terribly correct. In fact, the rules were so involved, I'm not sure any one person knew them all.

So to decide whether Plain English is appropriate (don't worry—it is!), let's consider the definition of good writing. Here are some possibilities:

- *Is good writing something that simply follows all the rules?* In other words, if you could actually memorize a grammar handbook and apply everything in it, would your writing necessarily be good?

  I don't think so. We've all seen writing that's correct—semicolons in the right places and no misspelled words—but nearly impossible to read. Also, there's considerable disagreement as to what the rules actually are. Is it all right to begin sentences with *and* or *but*? Are dashes all right in formal writing? (Yes and yes.)

  A key goal of this book is to help you "unlearn" old-fashioned rules and learn commonsense ones. Once you learn a good set of rules, however, you're still only part way to good writing.

- *Is good writing something that's easy to read?* Yes—clarity is a key part of good business writing. Clarity doesn't mean being simple-minded. Business people often deal with complex matters. Many of my students, for example, work with computers, telecommunications, accounting, auditing, physics, medicine, law, or operations research. Plain English is *especially* important for complex content.

- *Finally, is good writing something people actually pick up to read?* Again, yes! Lots of people think that what's in their in-box or e-mail is optional reading. The memo you wrote is halfway to the trash can as your reader skims it for anything of value. Or her index finger hovers impatiently over the delete key as she reads the e-mail you sent her. One more goal of the book is to show you how to get people to pick up your writing in the first place.

There you have it. In my opinion, good writing:

- follows commonsense rules,
- is easy to read, and
- attracts the reader in the first place.

That's a lot to demand of today's business writing. But there's some good news: Plain English does all those things.

Writing Plain English is not that hard. It's an eminently learnable skill. And once you learn how to write Plain English, you should feel as though a burden has lifted from your shoulders.

CHAPTER 2

Developing a Good Style

*Learn to write more the way you talk. This is a powerful metaphor
that can revolutionize your writing.*

This is the most important chapter in the book. For most people, it involves a lot of "unlearning."

The main message of the chapter is to write more the way you talk. For example:

- Should you prefer common words like *help* and *send* when you write? Or *assist* and *forward?*
- Should you use contractions like *here's* and *don't* when you write? Or *here is* and *do not?*
- Should you use pronouns like *I* and *you* when you write? Or should you avoid them entirely?

These fundamental choices have a huge impact. The reason has to do with a term linguists use, *fluency. Fluency* means "flowing," and that's what happens when you're talking to someone. You don't plan each word, each sentence, each idea. You just talk. The words come. The words flow. We all have fluency to varying degrees in talking.

But what if, when you write, you avoid standard characteristics of talking such as common words, contractions, pronouns? How would you like to try talking for even a few minutes without them? What would happen? You'd lose fluency, wouldn't you? Words, sentences, ideas would be painfully slow in coming and awkward sounding when they did come.

Write the Way You Talk!

As you write to someone, think, "What words would I actually *say* to that person?" Then use those words.

Some people think the result will sound like a kindergartner. Nope—only if you talk like a kindergartner! If you can express complex ideas with a nuanced tone in talking, then you can do the same thing in writing by talking on paper. And your readers will be grateful.

As I write this book, I imagine I'm talking to you. You should be able to look on just about any page, and the writing should sound like talking. Take a look!

What if, when you write, you use common words, contractions, pronouns? And all the techniques of spoken writing? Then you could tap into the same fluency when you write as when you speak. That's a big benefit, and that's one important reason most businesses today are rejecting the old, painful, overly formal style of writing. Why make employees struggle to communicate even simple ideas in writing? Is that the way to good business?

You may be wondering if you can have a professional tone when you write the way you talk. Yes, you can. Don't think of Plain English as the sloppiest, chattiest, most informal type of talking. You can sound chillingly distant when you talk, can't you? Or pretty formal? Or deadly serious? Or firm of purpose? You can have a large range of tones in talking. The same for writing. Imagine talking to your reader about your subject, and you should get the tone right.

These are my suggestions for writing the way you talk:

- Use common words.
- Use contractions.
- Use pronouns.
- Use active voice.
- Use proper tone.

We'll finish by looking at grammar checkers. They tell you whether your sentences are easy or hard to read.

USE COMMON WORDS

For years, there's been the mistaken belief that writers must use big words to sound educated. That's probably the main reason that people don't use *help* when they write; they use *assist*. They don't *want* something; they *request* it. And they never *need* anything; they *desire* it (see Fig. 2.1).

On the other hand, early courses in Plain English took the opposite (and, I believe, also mistaken) approach: They recommended that you use only the common words and never the less common substitutes.

My advice is different: I recommend that you use common words commonly. Use less common words sparingly. Common words are common for a reason. They're common because they usually work well, because they usually capture your meaning well.

No two words mean quite the same thing. Each word has its own denotations and connotations. We can all tell the difference between "wanting" something and "requesting" it, can't we? So it didn't make sense for the old, formal style of writing to use "request" all the time. No wonder formal writing often sounded artificial and pompous! Yet many people today—students and business people alike—still struggle unnecessarily to write without their most accessible vocabulary.

Let me show you one of my favorite paragraphs. It's the first paragraph of *Growing Up* by Russell Baker, and the book won the Pulitzer Prize:

At the age of eighty my mother had her last bad fall, and after that her mind wandered free through time. Some days she went to weddings and funerals that

---

Oaks Telecommunications
1212 Spruce Street • Pine City, MN 22222
(999) 999-9999 • oaks@tree.com

November 13, 2008

Mr. Joseph K. Elm
3434 Snowy Branch Parkway
Cold River, NY 33333

Dear Joe:

We'd like your help in preparing for this year's Board meeting.
Our focus for the meeting will be the new telecommunications law
and what changes we'll need to make as a result. We want the Board
members to understand the implications of the law—and the *big*
impact it has on us.

You're the expert! I'll be sending you a contract next week.
Briefly, we'll need you for about a month, full-time, in our
Honolulu office in January. We'll pay your usual fee and all
expenses.

Looking forward to working with you again!

Best wishes,

Elizabeth

Elizabeth Oaks
Chief Executive Officer

FIGURE 2.1 Sample Letter Demonstrating Plain English Vocabulary

---

had taken place half a century earlier. On others she presided over family dinners cooked on Sunday afternoons for children who were now gray with age. Through all this, she lay in bed but moved across time, traveling among the dead decades with a speed and an ease beyond the gift of physical science.[1]

You can see why it won a Pulitzer Prize, can't you? Every phrase hits home.

---

[1]Russell Baker, *Growing Up* (New York: New American Library, 1982), p. 1.

Now examine the paragraph carefully for word choice. Can you find the one word that's not a common, everyday one? How about *presided?* That's a less common word, but it's an excellent word choice. It connotes the matriarch, the woman who was in charge of her life but no longer is. Now she spends her life in bed, her body in the present but her mind in the past. So there's no problem with using a less common word like *presided*. It's a good word choice—a good time to reach onto the upper shelf.

Now examine that paragraph for one-syllable words. There are 17 out of 21 in the first sentence. And all 21 are ordinary words. Yet the sentence is far from being simple-minded or unintelligent.

My point? We sound intelligent not by the words we choose but by what we do with them. Russell Baker surely has a vast vocabulary. He's a top-notch professional writer. Yet he uses common words most of the time and uncommon words (like *presided*) only occasionally, when they carry just the right meaning.

If you go to the bookstore and browse through books, magazines, newspapers, you'll find that almost all of them are in Plain English. You may not find many paragraphs with the impact of Baker's, but you'll find that most professionals have the same approach to choosing words: They use common words most of the time; they use less common words when appropriate, which is sparingly.

My message is not whether to use "big words" but how often. The next time you write, don't click on the thesaurus. Trust your day-to-day vocabulary. Chances are, it's the same vocabulary as your reader's!

Check your own writing for word choice. Figure 2.2 shows you 50 common substitutes for formal words bureaucrats often choose.

USE CONTRACTIONS

Contractions (words like *I've, here's, don't*) scare the heck out of hard-core bureaucrats! Yet, if you're a supervisor and tell your people to use contractions, they'll have trouble writing anything that sounds bureaucratic. It's as though there's a switch in our heads: old style/Plain English.

If you use contractions, you automatically set the switch to Plain English. As a result, you'll almost certainly choose common words, use pronouns, write in the active voice—in other words, without even thinking about it, you'll almost certainly write in Plain English. The contraction is a little thing that does a big thing: It's a tiny mark on the page that opens the door to Plain English.

What about tone? Contractions make the tone real, adding credibility, as though the writer is really saying those words and really means them. Writing without contractions too often makes the tone distant, artificial. Your readers may not feel they're hearing from the real you.

I have often looked at the top 10 books on the *New York Times* best seller list. Here's what I find almost every time:

- nonfiction: 10 of 10 best sellers use contractions
- fiction: 10 of 10 best sellers use contractions

Bureaucratic	Common	Bureaucratic	Common
afford an opportunity	let	insufficient	not enough
approximately	about	locate	find
assist	help	modify	change
at the present time	now	monitor	check, watch
attached herewith is	here's	notify	tell
close proximity	near	numerous	many, most
commence	begin	permit	let
complete	fill out	prior to	before
concur	agree	provide	give
demonstrate	show, prove	provided that	if
desire	want	request	ask
determine	find out	retain	keep
endeavor	try	reveal	show
facilitate	help	review	check, go over
forward	send	state	say
furnish	send	submit	send
furthermore	also	subsequent	later, next
has the capability	can	sufficient	enough
however	but	terminate	stop
implement	carry out, do	therefore	so
in addition	also	this office	we, us
in the event that	if	transmit	send
in the near future	soon	undersigned	me
incumbent upon	must	utilize	use
initiate	start	witnessed	saw

FIGURE 2.2 Common Substitutes for Bureaucratic Words

Professional writers use contractions. They have for years. Why should business writing be any different?

USE PRONOUNS

Pronouns—like *I, we, you*—are some of the most common words in the language. Can you imagine trying to go all day without using them when you talk? Yet some people have tried to go their entire professional careers without using them in their writing. If you haven't done much business writing, you may think I'm exaggerating. But if you have, you know that many business writers avoid pronouns. The result is terrible:

- When people try to avoid such common words, their fluency disappears. Simply getting anything on paper becomes a major struggle. You can see why writer's block is common.
- Also, when people avoid pronouns, their sentence structure changes for the worse: They have to write with such verbal contortions that simply getting an idea into a sentence is success—never mind if that sentence flows nicely from the previous one or into the next.

- Finally—and worst of all—when people avoid pronouns, they almost automatically write in passive voice. As you'll see in the next section, passive voice isn't just some grammar to learn. Passive voice often creates major problems of readability.

You should be comfortable using all pronouns. Here are the ones people used to avoid:

- First-person singular: *I, me, my, mine, myself*
- First-person plural: *we, us, our, ours, ourselves*
- Second-person singular and plural: *you, your, yours, yourself, yourselves*

E-mail has helped with pronouns. For some reason, people almost automatically use pronouns when typing e-mail into their computers. In the past, many of the same people would have been very uncomfortable putting pronouns on paper.

That brings me to a comment that General Jim Monroe, then a leader in the U.S. Army, said to his people: "When you write to me on paper, make it sound like e-mail."

Great advice!

USE ACTIVE VOICE

The section you just read was about pronouns. I'm going to make a strong statement: I've never worked with an organization that avoided pronouns and wrote clearly. The reason is that people avoiding pronouns are, as I said earlier, almost automatically writing in passive voice. Passive voice isn't wrong, but it often causes big problems with readability and tone.

This section on passive voice is important. I tell my students that passive voice is going to come up during almost every class for the entire semester. I'm going to organize the discussion by answering these questions:

- What is passive voice?
- Is there another way to identify passive voice?
- Is passive voice really that simple to identify?
- What problems does passive voice cause?
- When is passive voice all right?

Let's look more closely at these.

What Is Passive Voice?

The best way to explain passive voice is to give an example and then convert it to active voice. Here's a sentence in passive voice:

The car is washed by Fred.

Now let's make it active voice:

Fred washes the car.

Do you see the difference?

- In the first sentence, the subject (*car*) is *passive*. That is, the car isn't doing anything.
- In the second sentence, the subject (*Fred*) is *active*. Fred is doing something (washing).

In active voice, the subject of the sentence is doing something.

And in passive voice, the subject of the sentence isn't doing anything. It's, well . . . passive!

Here's a diagram:

	Actor
Active voice	Fred washes the car.
	Subject

	Actor
Passive voice	The car is washed by Fred.
	Subject

So the name "passive voice" makes sense: The subject is passive when the verb is in the passive voice.

Is There Another Way to Identify Passive Voice?

Yes. You'll probably find this much easier, too. Passive voice has these three identifiers:

- a form of the verb *to be* (*am, are, is, was, were, be, been, being*), *and*
- a past participle (which normally ends in *-ed* or *-en*), *and*
- a prepositional phrase beginning with *by*.

Here's how our example has those three identifiers:

Form of verb to be   *"by" phrase*

Passive voice   The car is washed by Fred.

past participle

Here are some other examples of sentences in the passive voice:

The meeting <u>was</u> supervis<u>ed</u> <u>by the new president</u> of the company.
The lamp <u>was</u> brok<u>en</u> <u>by the movers</u>.
The Web site <u>was</u> updat<u>ed</u> <u>by the graphics designers</u>.

 For a quick lesson on this topic, go to http://www.professorbailey.com.

Notice that each of these examples has a form of the verb *to be*, a past participle, and a prepositional phrase beginning with *by*. And, in each case, the subject isn't doing the action. That is:

- the meeting isn't doing the supervising,
- the lamp isn't breaking itself, and
- the Web site isn't updating itself.

The subjects are all passive.

Is Passive Voice Really That Simple to Identify?

Yes and no. Many passives have the three identifiers I just showed you, but there are complications. Let's look more closely at two of the identifiers:

- A past participle (which normally ends in -*ed* or -*en*). The past participle will always be there, but it doesn't always end in -*ed* or -*en*. Sometimes the verb is irregular, so the past participle will look different. Examples: *held, made, kept, sent,* and other mainly common words. You'll quickly get the hang of spotting irregular past participles.
- A prepositional phrase beginning with *by*. Actually, this phrase doesn't have to be there. There only has to be a place to put one. Both of these sentences are passive: "The condominium was constructed by a new company" and "The condominium was constructed." This last sentence has a slot for the "by" phrase. So every passive sentence either has a prepositional phrase beginning with *by,* OR it has a place where you could put one.

Important Note on Passive Voice

Passive voice needs a form of the verb *to be* as well as a past participle. Simply having a form of the verb *to be* isn't enough to make a verb passive!

Can you see that both of these sentences have passive verbs?

> The roof was replaced by workers during a cold winter month.
> The roof was replaced during a cold winter month.

What Problems Does Passive Voice Cause?

There are two problems:

- Passive voice usually has a bureaucratic tone (costing the writer credibility).
- Worse, passive voice lets the writer accidentally, unconsciously leave out information that active voice automatically includes. In other words, the sentence actually has less information in it than the writer realizes!

The first problem with passive voice is subjective: It usually has a bureaucratic tone. As a result, it often sounds as though the writer isn't really looking us in the eye and isn't entirely credible. Most old-fashioned business and government writing used a great deal of passive voice and, therefore, usually had an artificial and distant tone.

For example, in the first chapter, I quoted a difficult passage from a government regulation. It has three sentences, all passive:

> Examination of bids by interested persons <u>shall be permitted</u> if it does not interfere unduly with the conduct of Government business. Original bids <u>shall not be allowed</u> to pass out of the hands of Government officials unless a duplicate bid is not available for public inspection. The original bid <u>may be</u>

<u>examined</u> by the public only under the immediate supervision of a Government official and under conditions that preclude possibility of substitution, addition, deletion, or alteration in the bid.

The tone of that passage is terrible, isn't it? It's terrible for a number of reasons, and one significant culprit is the passive voice.

The second problem with passive voice is that the prepositional phrase beginning with *by* often isn't there—but needs to be!

This is very, very important. Passive voice lets a writer leave out the prepositional phrase beginning with *by*. In fact, many passages of bureaucratic writing don't have the *by* phrase. That means that the writer—accidentally and unintentionally, most of the time—leaves out the actor (the person or thing doing the action). You, as the reader, then have to figure things out!

This isn't just theory. It's a major problem. For example, let's look at that bad passage again:

Examination of bids by interested persons <u>shall be permitted</u> [by ?] if it does not interfere unduly with the conduct of Government business. Original bids <u>shall not be allowed</u> [by ?] to pass out of the hands of Government officials unless a duplicate bid is not available for public inspection. The original bid <u>may be examined</u> by the public only under the immediate supervision of a Government official and under conditions that preclude possibility of substitution, addition, deletion, or alteration in the bid.

For two of the three sentences, the prepositional phrase beginning with *by* isn't there. You, the reader, now have to try to figure out who the actor is in each sentence. This problem happens in sentence after sentence, paragraph after paragraph, page after page in typical old-fashioned business writing.

So the two main problems with passive voice are that

- it has a bureaucratic tone (costing the writer credibility);
- it leaves out information (making the reader guess).

Those are two good reasons to cut back on passive voice.

When Is Passive Voice All Right?

Passive voice isn't wrong. All good writers use it occasionally. Here are good times to use passive voice:

- You don't know who did the action: "The candy store was robbed last night."
- Everybody knows who did the action: "The senator was barely reelected."
- You don't want the emphasis on the actor, and nobody will become confused: "The new policy was recently signed."

That said, I use passive voice only sparingly, clearly less than 5 percent of the time. In fact, most professional writing rarely uses over 10 percent passives. Neither should you.

USE SHORT SENTENCES

The message here may not be what you think. It's not to write a lot of short, choppy sentences. Actually, short, choppy sentences are often hard to read because they don't connect ideas well. I have two messages about sentence length:

- Don't write sentences that are too long (that happens all the time).
- Do have some short sentences. By short, I mean nine words or fewer.

Let's look at these points more closely.

Don't Write Sentences That Are Too Long

What's too long? There's no easy answer because there are so many ways to put together sentences. We've all seen short sentences, full of jargon, that were too much for us. And professionals can put together an occasional long sentence—30, 40, even 50 words—that is easy to read.

For example, if a sentence has a semicolon, colon, or dash in the middle, it may not seem like a very long sentence. That's because it's in distinct parts that the reader's short-term memory can handle. On the other hand, sentences relying only on commas and a period can seem long with fewer words. Here's an example of a sentence that is too long for most people the first time they read it:

> This instability is especially true now that we have expanded the agency's field of membership to include industrial and manufacturing groups that are generally not as stable as the agency's traditional field of membership.

It's 34 words long. Now let's turn that one sentence into three sentences:

> This instability is especially true now that we have expanded the agency's field of membership. It now includes industrial and manufacturing groups. These groups are generally not as stable as the agency's traditional field of membership.

Those three sentences average 12 words long—a good average. And the passage is much easier to understand, isn't it?

My suggestion is that your average sentence length should almost never exceed 17 words for business writing. And an average sentence length of 15 or even a little less is just fine!

However, typical bureaucratic writing often averages about 23 words a sentence or more. Remember this piece of bad writing?

> Examination of bids by interested persons shall be permitted if it does not interfere unduly with the conduct of Government business. Original bids shall not be allowed to pass out of the hands of Government officials unless a duplicate bid is not available for public inspection. The original bid may be examined by the public only under the immediate supervision of a Government official and under conditions that preclude possibility of substitution, addition, deletion, or alteration in the bid.

Hard to read, isn't it? Well, a big reason is that the average sentence length is over 26 words per sentence—far too long.

My rule of thumb is this: Whenever you have a sentence longer than two lines of type, think about it. It may be a good sentence. If so, keep it. But look at every sentence longer than two lines and consciously evaluate its readability. You should rarely keep more than a couple per page.

Do Have Some Short Sentences

Short sentences have impact.

I don't believe in artificially worrying about sentence variety. I don't say, "I just wrote a long sentence. Now I'd better write a short one." Short sentences aren't there just for variety. They emphasize an idea, make your point. Check your writing. You should have several sentences per page with nine words or fewer.

Here's a short sentence I really like from one of GE's annual reports—summing up GE's performance in the twentieth century: "Edison would be pleased." Gets your attention, doesn't it? (Note: Edison was a founder of GE.)

USE THE PROPER TONE

At the beginning of the chapter, I said that you can have a variety of tones when you write the way you talk. Now I want to give you three examples:

- First, I'll show you some typical bureaucratic writing. It's hard to read, and it has a formal tone. (I'm sure you'll be excited to read this.)
- Second, I'll translate the bureaucratic writing into Plain English—but I'll use a tone that's way too informal (inappropriate for most business writing). You should find this passage easy to read, but the tone will surely distract you.
- Finally, I'll keep the readability easy (Plain English), but I'll make the tone less informal. You should find the readability and tone good in this passage.

My purpose? To show that you can have a variety of tones in Plain English, including a tone perfectly appropriate for most business writing situations.

> **BUREAUCRATIC STYLE, FORMAL TONE**
> Enclosed is the data printout listing all of the accounts that are to be considered for purchase. Those accounts that are not to be purchased are to be lined off entirely. On those accounts that are approved for purchase, the following must be verified: the balance due, the interest rate, and the payment amount which is reflected on the data printout with the records which are maintained by the seller. This is most important as the entire pricing report is dependent on correct information concerning payments and balances. Additionally, appraisal sheet signatures must be obtained for all appraisal sheets; initials will not be accepted.

PLAIN ENGLISH STYLE, OVERLY INFORMAL TONE

OK guys—time to get to those DATA PRINTOUTS AGAIN!!!! Mary and the folks have put together all the accounts we're thinking about picking up. Whaddya think—should we get 'em or not?? So to keep the old ball rollin', how about helping us out: If you don't want 'em, line 'em out. And if you do want 'em:

- Check all this stuff with the seller: balance due, interest rate, payment amount. (DO IT!! VERY, VERY, VERY IMPORTANT!!!).
- Get those appraiser fellows to sign (initials are a no-no!!) EACH sheet of the appraisal (Got that, Fred??)!!

PLAIN ENGLISH STYLE, APPROPRIATE TONE

I've attached a list of all the accounts we're thinking about purchasing. If you don't want to purchase any of these, please line them off. For those accounts you do want to purchase, take these steps:

- Verify this information with the seller: balance due, interest rate, payment amount. (This is very important because the entire pricing report depends on this information.)
- Be sure appraisers sign—not just initial—each sheet of the appraisal.

The message is that you can write in Plain English and vary your tone according to your audience. Your tone can be just as professional in writing as it can be when you're talking face-to-face.

Your tone can also be friendly or unfriendly when you talk, can't it? Same thing in writing. Figures 2.3 and 2.4 are two letters, both written in Plain English. One has a friendly tone and the other an unfriendly tone—each appropriate for the situation.

USE GRAMMAR CHECKERS

I'm sure you know what a grammar checker is. It's a menu item on your computer's word processing program. Instead of just checking your spelling, though, it checks your grammar . . . well, sort of. Actually, it checks some grammar, some style, and some other things. If you use it properly, it can help check your sentences to see if they're hard or easy to read.

I'm going to recommend you use your grammar checker. But I have a caution: The worst thing you can do is follow all of its advice.

This section will help you understand which parts of a grammar checker's advice to ignore and which parts to accept. Grammar checkers do good things, bad things, and stupid things.

Bad things? Grammar checkers usually tell you not to use contractions and many of the other techniques I've been showing you in this chapter. But you can fix that—just change the options. For example, in Microsoft Word, go to Tools > Options > Spelling & Grammar. Then choose Settings and remove the checkmark for contractions. Then Word will stop flagging all of your contractions. While you're there, set all the options the way you want them.

Elm Consulting Company
3434 Snowy Branch Parkway
Cold River, NY 33333
(333) 333-3333 • elm@tree.com

November 21, 2008

Ms. Elizabeth Oaks
Chief Executive Officer
Oaks Telecommunications
1212 Spruce Street
Pine City, MN 22222

Dear Elizabeth:

I'd be glad to help with your Board meeting. I'm tied up the first week of
January, but I can be in Honolulu for the four weeks after that.

I'm sending you a summary of the key points of the new telecommunications
law—just for your background. Could you have your folks send me a copy of the
recent report they wrote on the implications of the law for your company?

Thanks!

        Sincerely,

        Joe

        Joseph K. Elm
        Consultant

FIGURE 2.3   Sample Letter in Plain English with *Friendly* Tone

Stupid things? Grammar checkers are much smarter today than even a few years ago.
Still, grammar checkers aren't as bright about some parts of the language as a typical
five-year-old. That's not because grammar checkers are really stupid; that's because a
typical five-year-old has already internalized an amazing amount of knowledge of language. For example, a grammar checker may tell you something isn't a sentence when
you know quite well it is. Once again, ignore any advice from a grammar checker that
doesn't make sense to you.

Birch Debt Collectors
Overnight Computers
5656 Plywood Street
Knothole, MN 22222
(333) 444-5555 • birch@tree.com

June 23, 2008

Dear Ms. Pixel:

Your company's check bounced. I'm returning it and asking for a certified check by Friday. If I don't hear from you by then, you'll be hearing from our lawyers.

Sincerely,

Cameron Melton

Cameron Melton
Chief Financial Officer

FIGURE 2.4 Sample Letter in Plain English with *Unfriendly* Tone

Good things? Yes—and that's why I strongly recommend you use a grammar checker as you move to Plain English. Here are four good things grammar checkers do:

- Tell you your average sentence length (words per sentence)
- Tell you how hard your words are to read (characters per word)
- Tell you the percent of your sentences that use passive voice
- Give you a number that rates the overall readability of your writing (readability index)

I've had my students check their writing for these four items for many years. The numbers almost always confirm our own subjective view of whether a piece of writing is hard or easy to read. Let's look more closely at these four items.

Average Sentence Length

Computers are good at counting things. This simple number—average sentence length—is a good indicator of whether your readers are struggling to understand your sentences. To give you a feel for the numbers, I've run four items through a grammar checker:

- the excerpt from the government regulation I quoted in Chapter 1 (typical bureaucratic writing)
- the Plain English revision of that excerpt
- Russell Baker's description of his mother in the nursing home (Pulitzer-Prize-winning writing)
- Chapter 1 of this book

Here are the results for sentence length:

Document length	Average sentence
Government regulation (bureaucratic)	26.3
Government regulation (Plain English)	12.0
Excerpt from Russell Baker	21.0
Chapter 1 of this book	11.1

My recommendation, you'll remember, is that you stay under an average of 17 words per sentence.

How about Russell Baker's writing? His average sentence length is slightly high, but all of his other numbers I'm about to show you are terrific. And remember, I checked only one short paragraph of his writing.

How Hard Your Words Are to Read

Grammar checkers try to show you how hard your words are to read. The most common measure is characters per word—in other words, what's the average number of letters in your words.

Here are the results for the four items we're following:

Document	Characters per word
Government regulation (bureaucratic)	5.2
Government regulation (Plain English)	4.3
Excerpt from Russell Baker	4.3
Chapter 1 of this book	4.6

The differences among the numbers in the table may seem small, but they can make a big difference. My recommendation is that you try to stay at 5.0 characters per word or lower. I need to qualify that, though. Sometimes a longer word, like *unconstitutional,* is also an easy word, one we all know. But *unconstitutional* would give you a higher average from the grammar checker. That's where your judgment must come in.

The key indicator of whether your words are hard to read is how common they are. The more common the word, the easier it is for us to read. Personal computers can't tell us how common a word is, but they can count how many letters are in it. And the length of a word is a rough approximation of how common it is—but only a rough approximation.

Still, notice that there's a big difference between the characters per word for the bureaucratic regulation (5.2) and Russell Baker's paragraph (4.3). So the number does have some value.

Sentences Using Passive Voice

Linguists and grammarians would have trouble telling you what percent of your sentences use passive voice. Does a passive infinitive count as a passive verb? And what if you have two passive verbs in the same sentence? You get the idea.

I don't have much faith that the number from the grammar checker is completely accurate. But I do have faith, from the hundreds and hundreds of documents I've checked, that the number is an excellent *indicator*.

Here's the table comparing the percent of passives in various documents:

Document (%)	Passive sentences
Government regulation (bureaucratic)	100
Government regulation (Plain English)	0
Excerpt from Russell Baker	0
Chapter 1 of this book	2

You may wonder why I had as high as 2 percent passives in Chapter 1. Easy—I included an excerpt of bad writing from a government regulation. The grammar checker included that excerpt when it counted passive verbs. Without that excerpt, my number was zero.

What are good numbers? You definitely need to stay under 10 percent. Is the optimum zero? No. Remember, there are a few times you'll prefer passive voice.

Readability Indexes

Grammar checkers include, as part of the statistics they show, the results of readability indexes. Microsoft Word shows the results of two: the Flesch-Kincaid Grade Level and the Flesch Reading Ease.

What do all those numbers mean? The first thing to understand about the Flesch-Kincaid Grade Level is that a lower number is a better number. You want to be somewhere below 12, and a number in the single digits is even better. About the highest you'll see (terrifically dense writing!) is 19 or so.

So the term *grade level* is a tremendous misnomer. You definitely don't want to be at fourteenth or sixteenth grade level, even if that reflects your education.

> ### How Accurate are Grammar Checkers?
>
> Getting better! However, if you run the same document through different versions of your word processing program, you may get different numbers. But the numbers are almost always close and certainly give a very good indication of how readable your writing is.
>
> For the statistics in this book, I used the same version of Microsoft Word at all times.

How did the term *grade level* come about? In the early days of readability indexes, researchers were trying to figure out if a piece of writing was within the capability of third, or fourth, or fifth graders. They developed formulas to predict the readability for those students. Rudolf Flesch, a pioneer in the Plain English movement, then developed formulas to predict readability for businesspeople. He kept the terminology *grade level*—but he shouldn't have.

I'm reluctant to criticize Flesch because I love his books, one of which converted me to Plain English. Still, you should ignore the term *grade level* and strive for a lower number.

How low? Anywhere in the single digits is fine. About the highest number I've seen is 19 and the lowest 5. One of my students kept trying to move from an 8.4 to an 8.3 to an 8.2. That's wasted effort. The indexes are not that precise. Here's what Flesch said in *The Art of Plain Talk* about one of his indexes: "What I hope for are readers who won't take the formula too seriously and won't expect from it more than a rough estimate."

Flesch is too modest. His index is an estimate, but it's a good one. Bad bureaucratic writing never gets as low as the single digits; Plain English usually does.

Here are the numbers for the writing we've been looking at:

Document	Flesch-Kincaid Grade Level (lower is better)
Government regulation (bureaucratic)	17.2
Government regulation (Plain English)	7.5
Excerpt from Russell Baker	8.6
Chapter 1 of this book	6.5

So if you get a number like 8.6, don't think you're in there with ninth graders. Instead, you're in there with a Pulitzer Prize-winning writer!

Microsoft Word gives you a second readability index: Flesch Reading Ease. With this index—which goes from 1 to 100—higher is better! I've found that about 40 or higher usually translates to Plain English.

Here are the Flesch Reading Ease numbers for the writing we've been looking at:

Document	Flesch Reading Ease (higher is better)
Government regulation (bureaucratic)	18.4
Government regulation (Plain English)	62.4
Excerpt from Russell Baker	70.7
Chapter 1 of this book	68.5

EXERCISES

A. Simplify all the words you can in these passages (in some cases, you'll need to do some rephrasing):

1. Subsequent to the passage of subject legislation, it is incumbent upon you to advise your staff to comply with it.
2. Approximately 15 people replied that they would forward their applications to this office.
3. Request you furnish your Social Security number to the undersigned in the immediate future.
4. Furthermore, this office will afford you the opportunity to complete your application prior to your interview.
5. In the event that we determine to interview you, it is incumbent on you to arrive subsequent to the end of the month.

B. Find the passive verbs in these sentences (some sentences may not have any). Then rewrite any sentences with passive verbs into active voice.

1. The movie was viewed by many people.
2. The movie was seen by many people.
3. The movie was left early by many people.
4. The committee has finished on time.
5. The reporter could have attended the meeting.
6. The reporter could have been attending the meeting.
7. The reporter was attending the meeting.
8. The meeting was attended by the reporter.
9. The artificial tree was losing its leaves.
10. The artificial tree was thrown out.

C. Find the passive verbs in this passage:

Although a review of the appeal has been conducted, the results are not available. In fact, the results to be released were kept temporarily pending a second review. The board is deciding now when the second review will be held. However, the appeals authority could have decided to delay that review.

D. Rewrite this memo into Plain English, making it as clear and spoken as possible. Keep all the information in it. (Nothing sneaky allowed: "Well, the boss doesn't really need to know all that!") Use everything. I suggest you not try to paraphrase line by line. Instead, imagine you're actually talking to your boss. What would you say?

To: The Boss
Subject: Interviews

Reference verbal request for an update memo regarding the assignment interview process with reference to analyst replacement. Personnel interviews have recently been conducted by this office with two applicants, Brian Cooper and Arthur Kantlin. Evaluation results of these people appear satisfactory; however, Kantlin has experience qualifications that exceed the experience qualifications of Cooper. Interview arrangements have been completed for Susanne Frank. Frank is scheduled to be interviewed tomorrow. A final memo will be furnished immediately thereafter.

E. Bring a copy of an annual report to class. Be prepared to discuss whether the letter from the chairman of the board uses Plain English.

F. Bring the editorial page of any newspaper to class. Be prepared to discuss which techniques of Plain English it uses.

G. Go to a bookstore and look at the best seller list for fiction and nonfiction books. Look for the characteristics of Plain English and report to the class what you find.

H. For this exercise, write a memo that describes your job—or part of it—*so everybody in class can understand every word you write*. Be sure to use the techniques of Plain English that you read about in this chapter. Even if you feel uncomfortable with these techniques, use them for this assignment.

When you've finished writing your paper, run it through a grammar checker and attach a list of the important statistics this chapter discusses. Special requirement: Use no passive verbs at all.

What if you don't have a job (or if your current job isn't appropriate to this exercise)? You may describe a previous job, or you may interview someone who has a substantial job and explain that job to the class. Be sure you get detailed information during the interview and try to have a way to get answers to questions you may think of later as you write your paper. (Relatives are normally understanding and good people to interview for this assignment!)

Length? About two pages. Single-space your paper and double-space between paragraphs (that's standard for business writing and will help you learn proper layout for business writing).

Where do people go wrong on this assignment?

- They try to tell the class everything they do on their job instead of emphasizing the two or three most important responsibilities.
- They don't use any examples.
- They use jargon the class isn't familiar with.

Note: Appendix D has sample good papers in response to this exercise. I recommend you look at them before you write your paper.

I. If your class uses course software (such as Blackboard), see if your instructor will try this:

- Divide the class into groups of three or four students.
- Set up a discussion forum (on the discussion board) for each group.
- Have students post their papers within each discussion forum and critique each other's. For example, if you're a member of a group of four students, all four of you will post your drafts in the same forum. And all four of you will critique each other.
- If you're persuasive, get your instructor to then critique all of your drafts.
- Look at everybody's paper (not just the ones in your group), everybody's comments, and your instructor's comments on everybody's paper.
- Then revise your paper before handing it in. At this point—after all the critiquing and after looking at everybody else's papers—your paper should be great!

Note: In revising your paper, should you accept all of your classmates' suggestions for revision? It's your paper—not theirs. You decide what to accept! (But if your instructor makes a suggestion—do it!)

CHAPTER 3

Using Examples and Comparisons

Examples and comparisons help your readers understand—
and remember*—your point.*

This chapter gives you advice on an indispensable writing technique: using examples and comparisons. Examples and comparisons are so important—so fundamental to good writing—that it's hard to overemphasize them. Virtually all professionals depend on them. Yet nonprofessional writers seldom use them.

Hardly anybody can become a good writer without understanding their immense value. For example, many writers assume their readers understand something when they don't. If you use an example or a comparison to explain your idea, then you can be more confident that your readers understand it.

Can you use examples and comparisons in e-mail? Business reports? Executive summaries? Web sites? Letters? Memos? Of course. Format is irrelevant. What's relevant is whether a reader needs an example or comparison to understand something.

The rest of this chapter shows you a number of good examples and comparisons.

EXAMPLES

If you're writing about something complicated or unfamiliar, your readers will probably understand you better if your writing is concrete rather than abstract. One of the best ways to make your writing concrete is to use examples.

What do the terms *concrete* and *abstract* mean? *Abstract* means general, hard to picture. *Concrete* means the opposite: specific, easy to picture.

Here's an abstract term: *transportation.*

Here's a concrete term: *black Ford Mustang* (a much more specific type of transportation).

The term *transportation* is abstract because it's general and hard to picture. The term *black Ford Mustang*, an example of transportation, is concrete because it's specific and easy to picture . . . well, easy if you know something about cars. The point is that people often understand abstract points better when you add concrete examples to explain them.

For example, here's an abstract sentence from a paper describing someone's job:

I helped my boss remember things.

We understand that. It's okay. But it's still rather general and abstract. Let's add some concrete examples and see what happens:

> I helped my boss remember things. In fact, I was Dan's walking, talking Blackberry. I was his *Who do we have at two thirty? Who's that guy with the short hair and glasses in Legal? What is Bob's home number? Where are my glasses?*

> In short, I was an extension of his memory. I was in charge of the details that he had no room left to remember—quite an undertaking. My typical day found me asking him things like, "Do we want to send your wife's birthday flowers on time this year?" As you can see, I had a lot to keep track of!

Adding examples makes a huge difference, doesn't it?

So if you want people to really understand an abstract point, the key is to add some examples. It's hard (possible, of course, but hard) to overuse them. Professional writers depend on them.

Let's look at:

- brief examples
- narrative examples
- combination of a brief and narrative example

Brief Examples

You should use brief examples in almost everything you write.

A woman describing her job said that she loved the employee relations part of her job. If she'd stopped there, we would have understood her to some degree. But her point wouldn't have really found a home in our brains, would it? It's a bit abstract. But she didn't stop with just that sentence. She added these brief examples:

> I love the employee relations part of my job. On a typical day, I might help an abused single parent find safety and shelter, get an employee into a detox program for alcohol or drug abuse, help an angry manager and hurt employee talk to each other, and work with an attorney to process an immigrant's work visa.

The brief examples help us understand her point: why she loves the employee relations part of her job. How much would we have learned if she hadn't continued with the brief examples?

 For a quick lesson on this topic, go to http://www.professorbailey.com.

Another woman describing her job—a very different type of job than the one you just read about—also makes excellent use of examples:

> I'm a Correctional Treatment Specialist. My most important responsibility is classifying inmates. Here are two examples showing the importance of classification:
>
> - Imagine committing a minor crime in Washington, D.C.—shoplifting, for instance. You may get six months in jail. Now imagine that your cellmate is

the man a jury convicted of the Starbucks murders. If I do my job, that won't happen.
- Now imagine that I, as a Correctional Treatment Specialist, improperly classified the Starbucks murderer as a minimum custody inmate, and now he is living in a halfway house—in *your* neighborhood.

What if the job description had stopped before the bullets? Without the examples?

Finally, notice how helpful the brief examples are in an article from the *Journal of Marketing*. The authors, Brian Wasink and Michael Ray, describe "expansion advertising opportunities"—that is, having advertisers suggest creative new uses for their products. Here are some of the brief examples the authors give:[1]

Alpha-Bits Cereal	Spell your name on pudding, cookies, or jelly sandwiches
Milk (American Dairy Council)	Drink after exercising
Clorox Bleach	Clean counters and sinks
Special K Cereal	Eat as afternoon snack or midnight snack

The examples make the point, don't they?

The value of brief examples clearly extends to many types of business writing. Suppose, for example, you're naming the problems with your current computer system. Your goal is to convince a decision maker to buy new computers for your division. Simply saying the computer has failed during crucial projects won't be very effective, will it? But what if you name a few projects and the clients who were not well served? That would more likely get the decision maker's attention—and get your division the new computers.

Or suppose you're trying to convince a prospective client that your company has the right kind of experience to do the job. Examples!

Can you use examples in typical business correspondence, such as a letter? Of course. Figure 3.1 is a sample of such a letter.

Narrative Examples

A narrative example is simply a story. Narrative examples are longer than brief examples but not necessarily longer than a paragraph. They can really get your reader's attention. Use them for your most important points.

Suppose you want to communicate a great principle you've learned for motivating sales people. You could be abstract and simply say, "It's important for salespeople to set realistic goals and then work to achieve them." Ho hum! We all understand the words, but we forget them before we get to the period at the end of the sentence.

---

[1]Brian Wasink and Michael Ray, "Advertising Strategies to Increase Usage Frequency," *Journal of Marketing, 60*(31), 1996.

Technical Support, Inc.
5454 Beltway Road
Warm Springs, NY 33333
(333) 444-3333 • sprucea@spruce.com

February 28, 2008

Ms. Tina Pixel
Overnight Computers
5656 Plywood Street
Knothole, MN 22222

Dear Ms. Pixel:

We're having trouble again with the five computers you recently installed. As a result, we're returning them to you today and requesting our money back—as you agreed today on the telephone. You asked for brief documentation of the problems we're having so you can tell your suppliers. Here are the main problems we had:

- Two notebook computers wouldn't boot up. Your technicians suspected a problem with the motherboards but never could solve the problem.

- One monitor made a continuous, high-pitched whining sound.

- Two desktop computers came infected with viruses.

Because of the number of problems, we don't have confidence in any of the equipment you installed.

Sincerely,

Alfred

Alfred Spruce
Assistant to the President

FIGURE 3.1 Sample Letter Using Examples

But what if that's a really important point you want to make? Then a narrative example may be the solution:

> When I first got into sales, my manager told me that successful sales people set goals for themselves—realistic goals, goals they can achieve if they work hard.
>
> To make her point, she asked me, "What do you really want for yourself, more than anything else?" Having just graduated from college and never having had any money, the choice was easy. I told her I wanted a new car. She asked, "What kind of car?" After thinking about it, I came back to her and said that I liked the new Ford Mustang.

She followed up with me again and said, "What color?" I told her the color didn't matter (I would take any color). She disagreed and made me think about it again. I finally came back to her and said that I liked black. She said, "Great! That's one of the colors I have." She then opened up her brief case and pulled out a color picture of a brand new black Ford Mustang. I was stunned! I couldn't figure out why this was so important to her. Then she told me.

"It's not important to me. It's important to you!" I was puzzled. She walked over to my cubicle and posted the picture above my telephone. She said, "Every time you pick up that phone to talk with a prospect, I want you to think about that Mustang. Before you prepare for a meeting, look at that Mustang. First thing each day, think about that Mustang." She was trying to motivate me by making me work for that Mustang. It worked! That Mustang became more than just a car; it became a symbol of success. Six months later, after a great deal of hard work—I bought that Mustang.

That's a story with a point. A narrative example is usually the highlight of a piece of writing *and* the most memorable part.

When you use narrative examples—and who doesn't like a good story?—readers perk up, and you get your message across.

Combination of a Brief and Narrative Example

Can you combine a brief and a narrative example? Of course! Look at this nice paragraph by a woman who served as an American Consular Officer in Chengdu, China. She wants to make the point that she had to deal with a variety of problems.

> During any time of the day, a problem with an American citizen could come up. We helped to solve the nonemergency problems, such as replacing a lost or stolen passport, notarizing documents or issuing Consular reports of birth for American citizens, during business hours.
>
> However, we also had to deal with emergency problems whenever they occurred. For example, one evening the local police found an American citizen dead next to the bathtub in his hotel. They called the Consulate right away and wanted to conduct an autopsy. To do so, we needed to contact the family. We checked our U.S. citizen registration records and found no record of this individual. I then went to his apartment and searched through his belongings and found a letter from his daughter—a key to contacting the family.

The *brief example* comes in the second sentence: "We helped to solve the nonemergency problems, *such as replacing a lost or stolen passport, notarizing documents or issuing Consular reports of birth for American citizens,* during business hours." The second paragraph is a *narrative example* about solving the emergency problems—and really makes the point, doesn't it?

Let's finish by looking at a nice paper that uses both brief and narrative examples very well. The author has the task of describing her job clearly and interestingly. Notice that if you removed the examples, there would be very little left. Yet with the examples, the paper is effective (Fig. 3.2).

Medical Technologist

I enjoy telling people what I do for a living because most people have no idea what a medical technologist is. Do you know? If you do, then you are among a small number of folks. If not, then be prepared to enter briefly the world that I have lived in for many years.

A Medical Technologist is the person who performs laboratory tests on blood, urine, and other samples from the human body. The reason most people don't know who we are is because they rarely see us. We spend most of our time in the laboratory, normally located in the basement of a medical facility. And don't confuse us with the person who takes your blood specimen. We rarely do that task in these days of specialization. Our main duty is to actually run the tests—quickly and accurately.

There are three descriptions that help to sum up the duties of a medical technologist:
- Detective
- Sentry
- Mechanic

I'll describe these using examples of what I do on a typical day.

Detective

The work of a detective occurs in these ways:
- Performing laboratory tests
- Considering abnormal results
- Using our knowledge of theory to further investigate an abnormality

Here's an example. Let's say I'm running a test on a blood sample and the results show that the patient has some type of anemia. (That means that the person doesn't have enough iron in his or her blood.) The next thing that I will do is to take a drop of that blood, smear it on a slide, and stain it. Then I will use a microscope to examine the actual red blood cells from that patient to see if they look abnormal. Providing the doctor with specific information about how the red cells look can be very helpful in determining what kind of medical treatment the doctor orders for that person.

Sentry

In this role, the technologist acts as a *watchdog* on behalf of her customer—the doctor. We accomplish this by doing these three things:

- Making the test results accessible by entering them into a computer network
- Noting if there are any significant abnormal results
- Contacting the doctor to alert him or her to these significant abnormal results

This happens more often than you might think. In the lab where I worked, we had a number of patients who had AIDS. They were on numerous medications to help keep their bodies functional. Many times, however, the number of white blood cells

FIGURE 3.2 Sample Paper with Good Examples

in their bloodstream would drop to a dramatic degree. This was significant because white cells are the cells in the blood that act like soldiers to fight bacteria and viruses. If their level got too low, the patient would be unable to fight back an infection. It was not uncommon for me to frequently see results that were significantly abnormal. It would be my responsibility to contact the doctor. Armed with that information, the doctor could change the medication so that the patient's body would start producing more of these valued white cells.

Mechanic

The last role of a technologist is not unlike that of a mechanic. We must be sure that the instrumentation that we are using is working properly by doing the following:

- Running samples with known ranges of values on the equipment
- Performing routine calibrations to adjust the output of values on the instruments
- Troubleshooting and doing minor repairs on the equipment

This is a less dramatic part of the job, but no less important. If the technologists didn't routinely do this work, there would be no reason to trust the information that is coming out of the instruments. For instance, a normal range for blood sugar levels is 70 to 120. One time when I was running a chemistry analyzer, I got a blood sugar result of 4. That is a number that I just could not believe because it would be incompatible with life! So I checked the instrument and found that, sure enough, there was a clog in one of the lines. I fixed the problem and confirmed it by running samples with known values. Then, when I reran the patient, I got a value that made a lot more sense!

FIGURE 3.2 *(Continued)*

COMPARISONS

The problem with comparisons is they're hard to think of! But when you think of a good one, you can really make your point. Let's look at a couple brief comparisons and then a longer (and very famous) one.

Brief Comparisons

A comparison doesn't have to be long to be effective. This writer is responsible for planning large meetings for her association. Here's the comparison she uses:

> A lot of what meeting planners do is behind the scenes. It's like planning a dinner party. Your guests don't see all the hard work and preparation you put into the dinner, and you probably don't want them to. You want them to have a great time and leave feeling good. Me, too! It's my job to "sweat the details"—not yours.

Simple—and effective, isn't it?

The next brief comparison—by William Bernstein in *The Four Pillars of Investing*—makes the point that you should avoid dealing with stockbrokers:

> The stockbroker services his clients in the same way that Bonnie and Clyde serviced banks. A broker's only hope of making a good living is to milk your account dry with commissions and spreads.[2]

Whoa! That's pretty strong! Bonnie and Clyde!? Is the point he makes a valid one? I have no idea—that's not my expertise. *My* point is that by using a comparison, Bernstein makes *his* point even more powerfully.

A Longer (and Famous) Comparison

And here's one of the most famous comparisons in the field of investing. It comes from Fred Schwed's classic book about Wall Street, *Where Are the Customers' Yachts?* Schwed believes that successful speculation in the stock market is simply good luck. In other words:

- successful speculators are lucky,
- very successful speculators are *very* lucky,
- and extraordinarily successful speculators are *extraordinarily* lucky.

If Schwed had stopped there, we'd probably agree or disagree and then move on. But he doesn't stop there. He gives us this memorable comparison showing not only that there *might* be some extraordinarily lucky speculators—but there *must* be:

> Let us have 400,000 men (and women) engage in this contest at one time. . . . We line them up, facing each other in pairs, across a refectory table miles long. Each player is going to play the person facing him a series of games, the game chosen being a matter of pure luck, say matching coins. Two hundred thousand on one side of the table face 200,000 on the other side.
>
> The referee gives a signal for the first game and 400,000 coins flash in the sun as they are tossed. The scorers make their tabulations, and discover that 200,000 are winners and 200,000 are losers. Then the second game is played. Of the original 200,000 winners, about half of them win again. . . .
>
> The third game is played, and of the 100,000 who have won both games, half of them are again successful. These 50,000, in the fourth game, are reduced to 25,000, and in the fifth to 12,500. These 12,500 have now won five straight without a loss and are no doubt beginning to fancy themselves as coin flippers. They feel they have an "instinct" for it. . . .

---

[2]William Bernstein, *The Four Pillars of Investing* (New York: McGraw-Hill, 2002), p. 297.

Eventually there are about a dozen men who have won every single time for about fifteen games. These are regarded as the experts, the greatest coin flippers in history, the men who never lose, and they have their biographies written.[3]

Great, isn't it? We'll probably remember the comparison a long, long time—and the statement it's supporting, too!

EXAMPLES AND COMPARISONS

Can you use both an example and a comparison to make a point? Of course. Suppose someone writes this abstract sentence:

My job is to try to negotiate the best deal for government contracts.

Well, that's okay. But here's what she really wrote (the comparison is in the first paragraph and the example in the second one):

My job is to try to negotiate the best deal for government contracts. You do the same kind of thing when you buy a car. You don't settle for what the dealer tells you. The dealer makes an offer—then you make an offer. You negotiate the price of the car.

That's what I do with government contracts. I try to negotiate the best deal. For example, last year when I negotiated the contract for training services, the representative for the company argued about the profit rate. I offered him 7.5%, which is the rate his company usually receives. He offered 8.5%. He had reasons for offering 8.5%—but not good reasons. After going back and forth, he finally agreed to 7.5%.

The comparison is how negotiating for a car and for a government contract have similarities. The paragraph that follows is a real-life example about one particular negotiation. Very effective, isn't it?

EXERCISES

A. For each sentence, make up a *brief example* (just a sentence or two).
1. Pop-up ads on Web pages are a nuisance.
2. A new style of clothes is becoming popular.
3. The news is often depressing.
4. Computer games aren't always a waste of time.
5. Cable television can provide a valuable service.

---

[3]Fred Schwed, *Where Are the Customers' Yachts?* (Hoboken, NJ: Wiley, 2006) (original copyright: 1940), pp. 126–127.

B. Find a good *narrative example* in some published writing—magazines, newspapers, books. Bring it to class.

C. Find a good *comparison* in some published writing—magazines, newspapers, books. Bring it to class.

D. Keep the first sentence of this paragraph and replace the rest (which is dull and overly general) with an *interesting narrative example*:

Changing a tire on a car isn't always as easy as the instruction books tell us. For example, sometimes the weather isn't good. Other times, the place you need to change the tire can cause problems. And sometimes your companions are more a problem than a help.

E. Look at any other papers you've written for this class:

- Choose one sentence you wrote, and add two or three brief examples to illustrate it.
- Choose another sentence you wrote, and write a narrative example to illustrate it.

CHAPTER 4

Making Your Page Look Inviting

Use headings, indented lists, appropriate typefaces, and other techniques of good layout.

"Layout" means the overall look of your page—from the typeface you choose to how much space you put above and below your headings. Making good choices can make all the difference!

Here are some of the advantages of good layout:

- If your document looks good, people will more likely pick it up.
- Good layout helps your document look professional. The right typefaces, the right spacing, and all the other small choices *working together* add up to a professional image.
- Good layout helps readers *see* the parts of a document—and know where they are in it.

Those are all reasons to have a good layout, but there's a more important advantage: When you learn the value of headings and lists, you begin to use them. That means you bring structure to your writing and it becomes better organized.

So good layout doesn't just mean showing your reader the parts of your paper; it also means *creating* a document with parts in the first place! Good layout, then, helps your page look good—and more.

Figure 4.1 is a memo with good layout (it follows the advice in this chapter). Some people wonder if you should use headings and indented lists in letters, memos, e-mail, and Web pages. Of course you can! Headings and indented lists don't care if they are in letters or not—and neither do most readers. Readers don't think about formats ("Oh, this is a letter. It shouldn't have headings!"). Readers just read for content, trying to find out what the writer is saying. So if headings serve to label parts of a report, they can also label parts of a letter, a memo, e-mail, or Web page. The same value to the reader is there.

The techniques of layout in this chapter are useful regardless of your format. Here's what this chapter suggests:

- Choose your typefaces carefully.
- Use block paragraphing (don't indent first lines).
- Create good headings.
- Use good layout for lists.

From: Sophia Hiller
To: Mackenzie Melton
Subject: Is accurate stock forecasting possible?
Date: May 26, 2008

You asked me to look into the subject of *stock forecasting* and let you know what I found out. The issue is whether investors can forecast whether a particular stock is likely to go up or down. For example, is it possible to predict whether Techronics stock is likely to go up during the next month? Or year? Or five years?

Many experts believe the answer is "probably not." To see why, let's look at two prominent types of stock forecasting:

- Technical analysis
- Fundamental analysis

Technical analysis

Technical analysis means looking at stock charts. Suppose a stock has gone up every day for the past 30 days. Can we assume it *will* go up again tomorrow? The answer is "no." Well, can we assume it's *likely* to go up tomorrow? The answer is "probably not."

Or suppose that every time Techronics has dropped from 45 to 30, it has bottomed out and begun climbing again. Can we assume that when it drops to 30 again, it will rise? No.

Lots of research shows that past performance is not a reliable indicator of future performance. According to Burton Malkiel in *A Random Walk through Wall Street*, "The stock market has little, if any, memory."

Fundamental analysis

Fundamental analysis means looking at a company's value and trying to determine its future earnings. To do that, analysts consider the management of a company, the future demand for its product, the possible risks involved, the dividends it's paying, etc.

For example, suppose an analyst spends time at Techronics and believes the company has a great product, great financing, a great management team, and tremendous growth potential. He also believes the market has undervalued the Techronics stock. Does that mean the stock is likely to go up? Some experts would say, "Buy!" Others would say, "Hmmmm ... I think I'll just put my money in index funds."

In other words, experts are more inclined to accept fundamental analysis than technical analysis; however, there's still lots of controversy and disagreement about its practical effectiveness.

Malkiel hedges on whether fundamental analysis can work, though he's skeptical. Here's his summary: "Security analysts have enormous difficulty in performing their basic function of forecasting company earnings prospects. Investors who put blind faith in such forecasts in making their investment selections are in for some rude disappointments."

Tellingly, the section in Malkiel's book immediately after that quotation is "Why the Crystal Ball Is Clouded"!

FIGURE 4.1   Sample Memo with Good Layout

CHOOSE YOUR TYPEFACES CAREFULLY

Before you put a word on a page, you should decide what typefaces you want to use. Here are my suggestions.

Use a Typeface with Serifs for Body Text

Most publications in the United States—well over 95%—use a typeface with serifs for the body text. Body text means, essentially, all of the paragraphs but not the titles, headings, illustrations, and so forth.

What does the term *serif* mean? A serif is a small stroke at the ends of many characters. For example:

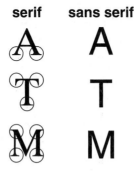

The typeface on the left is Times New Roman. It has serifs, which I've circled. The typeface on the right, without serifs, is Arial. *Sans serif* means "without serifs."

Times New Roman is by far the most common typeface for body text in business writing—and it's a great choice. If you use Times New Roman for your body text, the standard size is 12 points. That's a good size most of the time. (By the way, Georgia is a common font with serifs for Web pages. It was designed with Web pages in mind.)

Notice the typefaces in this book. Can you tell which have serifs?

Use a Sans Serif Typeface for Headings and Illustrations

The standard for years has been to use a typeface with serifs for body text but a sans serif typeface for most headings. "Standard" doesn't mean the right way or the only way—just the most common way.

If you look at publications in a bookstore, you'll find that a clear majority—not all, a *majority*—of headings use a sans serif typeface. Sans serif works well as a heading because:

- sans serif is clearly different from the body text
- sans serif has a clean, uncluttered look in boldface (and you want to make most of your headings bold)

Sans serif is also a good choice for your text for tables, illustrations, indented quotations, sidebars, and so forth. That's because these items normally need a smaller size (usually 2 points). A typeface with serifs in a small size can look cluttered and busy. A sans serif typeface doesn't.

Good Choices

Most people in business use 12-point Times New Roman for all of their body text.

They use Arial for headings (there's no standard size because headings can vary so much).

They use Arial for labels (such as for graphs) and for illustrations (such as for the text in a table or in a flowchart). The most common type size for these is 10 points.

And they use Georgia (a font with serifs) and Verdana (a sans serif font) for Web pages. They were designed with Web pages in mind.

Arial is the most popular sans serif typeface for business writing. Verdana is a common choice for Web pages.

Use Typesetting—Not Typewriting—Conventions

Typewriters had limited capability, yet some people still use the conventions of type-writing (such as improvised dashes) while using a computer. But computers have more capability today than entire print shops did several decades ago.

I recommend you use the conventions that typesetters use. That will give your document a professional look, and it's as easy to do it one way as another.

Here are the main differences between typewriting and typesetting conventions:

TYPEWRITING	TYPESETTING (PREFERRED)
2 spaces after periods, etc.	1 space after all punctuation
improvised dash (- -)	em dash (—)
improvised ellipsis (. . .)	typeset ellipsis (...)
underline	italic

You can find the em dash and the typeset ellipsis in word processing programs under different menus. Go to Insert > Symbol if you're using Microsoft Word.

Once you start using typesetting conventions, typewriting conventions will look outdated.

A caution: You may want to underline sans serif type instead of italicizing it. That's because sans serif type only slants the characters when making them italic; serif type

---

Italic Versus Bold

When you want to emphasize a word or a phrase within a paragraph, use italic instead of bold. Bold stands out too much, from several feet away. Reserve bold for headings and titles. Italic type, on the other hand, stands out *as you read it*—perfect for words and phrases within paragraphs.

---

slants and redesigns its italic characters. As a result, when you italicize a word or phrase in sans serif type, it may not stand out enough from the rest of the text for your reader to notice. Compare these letters in serif and sans serif type:

	upright	italic
serif type	a f	*a f*
sans serif type	a f	*a f*

Quite a difference for the serif type; not much change for the sans serif.

USE BLOCK PARAGRAPHING

By block paragraphing, I mean:

- don't indent the first line of your paragraphs, and
- do put space between all paragraphs.

Does that advice seem strange? In the past, the preference was to indent the first lines of paragraphs. What's changed? The answer: Layout has changed. More and more business documents use headings, lists, and illustrations of all sorts. So much is happening on the left margin that indenting first lines adds confusion—making the page look disorganized.

So I recommend you use block paragraphing because it helps your reader better *see* the organization of your page.

Figure 4.2 is a sample memo with poor paragraph layout. Notice that the indented first lines create a confusing left margin.

Now look at the good sample again (Fig. 4.1). That memo uses block paragraphing. Notice that the headings stand out a little more and the page, visually, is more organized.

You may wonder if you should *justify* your paragraphs. That is, should both the right and left margins be squared off like the paragraphs in this book? Or should you use a ragged right margin, as in Figure 4.1? Either way is fine; it's your choice. Virtually all typefaces today are proportional and do a good job with full justification.

DESIGN GOOD HEADINGS

Whenever you write anything longer than a page, you'll probably want to use headings (and they work fine in documents less than a page, too). You already know to choose a sans serif typeface for most headings. This section will give you other tips so your headings will be efficient and attractive.

Use at Least Two Headings of Each Type

Headings label the parts of your document. Look at Figure 4.1 again. Notice that it has two headings (not just one heading).

From: Sophia Hiller
To: Mackenzie Melton
Subject: Is accurate stock forecasting possible?
Date: May 26, 2008

You asked me to look into the subject of *stock forecasting* and let you know what I found out. The issue is whether investors can forecast whether a particular stock is likely to go up or down. For example, is it possible to predict whether Techronics stock is likely to go up during the next month? Or year? Or five years?

Many experts believe the answer is "probably not." To see why, let's look at two prominent types of stock forecasting:

- Technical analysis
- Fundamental analysis

Technical analysis

Technical analysis means looking at stock charts. Suppose a stock has gone up every day for the past 30 days. Can we assume it *will* go up again tomorrow? The answer is "no." Well, can we assume it's *likely* to go up tomorrow? The answer is "probably not."

Or suppose that every time Techronics has dropped from 45 to 30, it has bottomed out and begun climbing again. Can we assume that when it drops to 30 again, it will rise? No.

Lots of research shows that past performance is not a reliable indicator of future performance. According to Burton Malkiel in *A Random Walk through Wall Street*, "The stock market has little, if any, memory."

Fundamental analysis

Fundamental analysis means looking at a company's value and trying to determine its future earnings. To do that, analysts consider the management of a company, the future demand for its product, the possible risks involved, the dividends it's paying, etc.

For example, suppose an analyst spends time at Techronics and believes the company has a great product, great financing, a great management team, and tremendous growth potential. He also believes the market has undervalued the Techronics stock. Does that mean the stock is likely to go up? Some experts would say, "Buy!" Others would say, "Hmmmm … I think I'll just put my money in index funds."

In other words, experts are more inclined to accept fundamental analysis than technical analysis; however, there's still lots of controversy and disagreement about its practical effectiveness.

FIGURE 4.2   Indented First Lines Cause a Confusing Left Margin

A heading isn't a title. It's a label for one of *several* parts. If you have only one part, skip the heading and (for a report) use a title. For a memo or e-mail, rely on the subject line. For a letter, which has neither a title nor a subject line, rely on a strong beginning.

Consider Informative Headings

Sometimes simple headings such as "Technical Analysis" and "Fundamental Analysis" are clear enough. Too often, though, writers use overly brief headings when something longer would be better. For example, instead of saying "Results," consider saying, "Our sales are improving." That way, readers who are skimming still get the most important information just by reading your headings.

You might also want to consider headings that engage your readers. For example, instead of saying, "Our sales are improving," you could make your heading a question: "How are our sales this quarter?" Questions usually draw your readers into the content of your section. Hint: If your heading asks a question, give the answer right away—usually with the first sentence after the heading. So the first sentence after "How are our sales this quarter?" might say this: "Not very good."

Finally, it's possible to have good headings that don't carry much information at all about the subject matter but are still effective because they pique the reader's interest. In other words, they are uninformative but engaging headings. Here are two examples:

INFORMATIVE HEADING	ENGAGING HEADING
What does an association do?	The big picture
Handling all the details	Soup to nuts

I prefer informative headings whenever readers (like you) are trying to get information as quickly as possible. I use engaging headings for more optional reading—marketing material, for instance.

Put More Space Above Than Below Your Headings

One of the most common design mistakes with headings is putting the same space above and below them. Notice that the headings seem jammed in on Figure 4.3 (which has the same space above as below) and don't seem connected to the part below them.

 For a quick lesson on this topic, go to http://www.professorbailey.com.

Now review Figure 4.1, the sample good memo, again. This time notice there is more space above the headings than below them. The headings seem connected with the parts below them, the parts they label, don't they? They are clearly part of what they label, becoming a unit with the text below. So always put more space above than below your headings.

Consider a Down-Style Heading

Lots of people today still use typewriter techniques when writing on computers. Most typewriters couldn't do bold or italic or larger type sizes. So one way to differentiate headings from body text was to use initial capital letters for each important word: "Our

From: Sophia Hiller
To: Mackenzie Melton
Subject: Is accurate stock forecasting possible?
Date: May 26, 2008

You asked me to look into the subject of *stock forecasting* and let you know what I found out. The issue is whether investors can forecast whether a particular stock is likely to go up or down. For example, is it possible to predict whether Techronics stock is likely to go up during the next month? Or year? Or five years?

Many experts believe the answer is "probably not." To see why, let's look at two prominent types of stock forecasting:

- Technical analysis
- Fundamental analysis

Technical analysis

Technical analysis means looking at stock charts. Suppose a stock has gone up every day for the past 30 days. Can we assume it *will* go up again tomorrow? The answer is "no." Well, can we assume it's *likely* to go up tomorrow? The answer is "probably not."

Or suppose that every time Techronics has dropped from 45 to 30, it has bottomed out and begun climbing again. Can we assume that when it drops to 30 again, it will rise? No.

Lots of research shows that past performance is not a reliable indicator of future performance. According to Burton Malkiel in *A Random Walk through Wall Street*, "The stock market has little, if any, memory."

Fundamental analysis

Fundamental analysis means looking at a company's value and trying to determine its future earnings. To do that, analysts consider the management of a company, the future demand for its product, the possible risks involved, the dividends it's paying, etc.

For example, suppose an analyst spends time at Techronics and believes the company has a great product, great financing, a great management team, and tremendous growth potential. He also believes the market has undervalued the Techronics stock. Does that mean the stock is likely to go up? Some experts would say, "Buy!" Others would say, "Hmmmm … I think I'll just put my money in index funds."

In other words, experts are more inclined to accept fundamental analysis than technical analysis; however, there's still lots of controversy and disagreement about its practical effectiveness.

FIGURE 4.3   Poor Headings: Same Space Above and Below Them

Sales Are Improving." Graphics designers call that an "up-style" heading. That's okay to use, but don't feel you have to use the up style.

Many graphics designers today prefer the down style: "Our sales are improving." Boldface and a larger type size then set the headings apart from body text.

Does the sample memo, Figure 4.1, use an up-style or down-style heading?

Differentiate Levels of Headings

What if you need more than one level of heading? Our sample memo (Fig. 4.1) uses two headings that are both the same level: "Technical analysis" and "Fundamental analysis."

Reasons to Use Headings

You'll want to use headings in anything longer than a page because they:

- show your reader at a glance that your document is organized,
- label the parts of your document,
- show where parts begin and end (replacing the need for strong verbal transitions),
- help your readers find the parts of your document they need to read, and
- help you organize your writing in the first place.

But what if you want to have headings to further divide the topic "fundamental analysis"? You can do that, but you'd want to be certain that a reader clearly understands that your subheadings are subordinate to your headings.

You wouldn't want your headings to be left-justified, bold, 14-point type and your subheadings to be just the same except 12-point type. Readers may not notice the difference. Instead, make sure your subheadings are subordinate in *at least* two ways. For example, consider these possible designs for two levels of headings—would they work?

POSSIBLE HEADING STYLE	POSSIBLE SUBHEADING STYLE
centered	left-justified
14-point Arial	12-point Arial
bold	bold

Yes. With this design, your readers should have no trouble telling a heading from a subheading.

USE GOOD LAYOUT FOR LISTS

Whenever you have more than one of something, consider using an indented (or "bulleted") list. For instance, consider using an indented list if you have two or more of these:

- reasons
- examples
- recommendations
- conclusions
- steps

If you're not sure what an indented list is, you've just read one. And the marks in front of the items (•) are "bullets." Bullets are commonplace in business writing because they instantly let readers see that there's more than one of something.

Whenever you make a list, you want to be sure that it's grammatically parallel. Chapter 8 tells you about parallelism. If you're not sure what parallelism is, you should turn to Chapter 8 before you write any lists. The remaining sections of this chapter will help you make your lists look good.

Choose a Good Bullet Symbol

In the old days, you saw the asterisk (*) and the hyphen (-) as bullet symbols. If you see those in business writing today, that means the writer hasn't yet found out how to make a bullet!

Here's the most common bullet symbol:

- sample item
- sample item
- sample item

When should you use numbers instead of bullet symbols? I use numbers whenever I'm listing the steps in a process. Otherwise, I stick with bullets because I want to have a consistent look to my document. For that reason, I also rarely use more than one type of bullet symbol in a document.

Use Good Spacing for Your Bulleted Lists

The defaults from your word processing program are usually just fine.

If you look around at professional publications, you'll see many, many good variations. Newspapers, for example, usually don't indent the bullets at all from the left. That's fine because, with several columns of text on the page, too much indenting would make the page look fragmented.

Now let's turn to punctuating your bulleted lists.

Use a System for Punctuating Your Bulleted Lists

There is no single system. In fact, there aren't even any standards. One company may use one system for punctuating bullets; the company next door may use another. That said, let's consider two systems, starting with the traditional system. Suppose there is a list in a paragraph, with no indenting (yet):

> Our company is about to buy new equipment: computers, printers, and fax machines.

The traditional system simply keeps all the punctuation and the word *and:*

> Our company is about to buy new equipment:
>
> - computers,
> - printers, and
> - fax machines.

That system is fine. I use a slightly different one. If the items in the indented list are not full sentences, I get rid of the punctuation and often the word *and:*

> Our company is about to buy new equipment:
>
> - computers
> - printers
> - fax machines

And if the bulleted items are all sentences, then I make them look like sentences:

> Our company is about to buy new equipment:
>
> - We're ordering five new computers.
> - We're ordering two color printers.
> - We're ordering three fax machines.

But any system is fine because there is no standard system. Just be consistent.

Learn How to Use Bulleted Paragraphs

You don't have to limit bullets to words, phrases, or even single sentences. Full paragraphs are fine. By using bulleted paragraphs, you show that those paragraphs are related.

For example, suppose you've studied the need for a new parking lot. You've led a task force that concludes your company needs a new lot and has two reasons for that conclusion. Bulleted paragraphs can effectively lay out those conclusions:

> After meeting with contractors, the task force has decided to recommend we build a new parking lot for these two reasons:
>
> - We expect to hire 200 new people in the next year. Because our parking lot is full now, with people looking for space every morning, there will be no good place for new employees to park unless we build a new lot. No other lots are available within a five-block radius.
> - This is a favorable time to finance a new parking lot. Interest rates are at the lowest point in several years. Rates may rise in the future. We can

afford a loan now, but if we wait, we may not be able to finance the parking lot.

Bulleted paragraphs look good on the page. There's a refinement you can use with them—add headings:

> After meeting with contractors, the task force has decided to recommend we build a new parking lot for these two reasons:
>
> - *New hires.* We expect to hire 200 new people in the next year. Because our parking lot is full now, with people looking for space every morning, there will be no good place for new employees to park unless we build a new lot. No other lots are available within a five-block radius.
> - *Low interest rates.* This is a favorable time to finance a new parking lot. Interest rates are at the lowest point in several years. Rates may do anything in the future. We can afford a loan now, but if we wait, we may not be able to.

Generally don't use bold for these headings because they'll stand out too much, drawing your reader's eyes to a relatively subordinate part of your page. Instead, use italic type. The technique of bulleted paragraphs with italic headings is a great one to learn— and useful time after time! Scan through the book and notice how many lists use this technique. Helpful, isn't it?

IN SUMMARY . . .

In other words:

- *Fonts.* Normally use 12-point Times New Roman for your body text. Use Arial for your headings, labels, and illustrations. And use Georgia and Verdana for your Web pages.
- *Typesetting conventions.* Use typeset dashes, italic instead of underlining, and one space after all punctuation.
- *Paragraphing.* Don't indent the first lines of your paragraphs—instead, use block paragraphing (no indented first lines).
- *Headings.* Use at least two headings. Put more space above than below them. Differentiate levels of headings. And consider informative and down-style headings.
- *Lists.* Normally accept your word processor's default for bullet symbol and spacing. Use a consistent system for punctuating your lists. And don't forget the value of bulleted paragraphs with italicized headings (like this list!).

Figure 4.4 is a graphic that shows good layout.

body text:
12-point
Times New
Roman

bullets

headings:
12-point
bold Arial,
down style

block
paragraphs

more space
above
heading
than below

From: Sophia Hiller
To: Mackenzie Melton
Subject: Is accurate stock forecasting possible?
Date: May 26, 2008

italic (not underlining)

You asked me to look into the subject of *stock forecasting* and let you know what I found out. The issue is whether investors can forecast whether a particular stock is likely to go up or down. For example, is it possible to predict whether Techronics stock is likely to go up during the next month? Or year? Or five years?

Many experts believe the answer is "probably not." To see why, let's look at two prominent types of stock forecasting:

- Technical analysis
- Fundamental analysis

one space after all
punctuation

Technical analysis

Technical analysis means looking at stock charts. Suppose a stock has gone up every day for the past 30 days. Can we assume it *will* go up again tomorrow? The answer is "no." Well, can we assume it's *likely* to go up tomorrow? The answer is "probably not."

Or suppose that every time Techronics has dropped from 45 to 30, it has bottomed out and begun climbing again. Can we assume that when it drops to 30 again, it will rise? No.

Lots of research shows that past performance is not a reliable indicator of future performance. According to Burton Malkiel in *A Random Walk through Wall Street*, "The stock market has little, if any, memory."

em dash (not
two hyphens)

Fundamental analysis

Fundamental analysis means looking at a company's value—and trying to determine its future earnings. To do that, analysts consider the management of a company, the future demand for its product, the possible risks involved, the dividends it's paying, etc.

For example, suppose an analyst spends time at Techronics and believes the company has a great product, great financing, a great management team, and tremendous growth potential. He also believes the market has undervalued the Techronics stock. Does that mean the stock is likely to go up? Some experts would say, "Buy!" Others would say, "Hmmmm … I think I'll just put my money in index funds."

In other words, experts are more inclined to accept fundamental analysis than technical analysis; however, there's still lots of controversy and disagreement about its practical effectiveness.

FIGURE 4.4   Sample Memo with Good Layout

EXERCISES

A. Improve the layout of this memo (you don't need to do any rewriting):

To: Chief Executive Officer (Tom Hiller)

From: Johnny

Subject: Update Seminar on Legal Issues for Managers

Date: August 11

Tom, we're planning a two-day training seminar on "Legal Issues for Managers." This memo updates you on the speakers. We've asked Ms. Jeannette Boot to give the keynote address, and she's trying to fit us into her schedule. We'll let you know as soon as we hear from her. We expect she will be able to give the address, but just in case she can't, we have a list of alternates. Frankly, though, Ms. Boot would be hard to top.

We have arranged for the following speakers for our other sessions: Judge Elizabeth Melton, State Supreme Court; Mr. Joseph Hiller, American Bar Association (Section of Environmental Management Issues); and Professor Gera Brown, Professor of Law at the University of Michigan. They will all give their views of important legal issues that managers must deal with today.

Because we believe it is beneficial to have fresh viewpoints on these issues, we have asked all outside speakers, including the keynote speaker, to participate in a panel at the end of the conference. They've all tentatively agreed. We haven't had such a panel before, but it seems a natural way to use our speakers' expertise and to tie things together at the end.

B. Find a page with *excellent overall layout* in some published writing—especially in magazines and books. Bring it to class. Be able to explain why you think the layout is excellent.

C. Find a page with *poor layout*. Bring it to class. Be able to explain why you think the layout is poor and how you could improve it.

D. Find a page with *excellent headings* in some published writing—especially in magazines and books. Bring it to class. Be able to explain why you think the headings are excellent.

E. Find a journal or professional magazine in your field from the past 12 months. Write a paper that analyzes the layout of the first two pages of one of the main articles. Be thorough in your analysis. Include whatever you like and don't like. Use the best layout you can for your own writing.

F. Find a news or business magazine from the past 12 months. Write a paper that analyzes the layout of the first two pages of one of the main articles. Be thorough in your analysis. Include whatever you like and don't like. (You will find plenty to write about!) As part of your analysis, explain what layout techniques in the magazine article would be appropriate or inappropriate for the first pages of chapters in a lengthy business report. Use the best layout you can for your own writing.

CHAPTER 5

Making Your Main Point Easy to Find

Start with your main point. That way your readers can hardly miss it!

How many times have you been reading something and wondered, "What's the point?" Too often, writers bury the main point of their document—the very reason they're writing it—somewhere near the end. They usually do that so they can build their case. They want to lead you step-by-step through all of their facts and logic so their conclusion at the end will make sense to you.

That sounds good, but there's a fundamental problem: Without the context the bottom line gives, most readers get lost in all of those facts.

For example, have you ever begun reading something, gotten lost, skipped to the end to find the main point, and then started over? The first part usually makes sense once you know what the main point is, doesn't it?

Once we get lost, just about all of us skip ahead. So whatever reason writers give for putting their main point at the end, it doesn't matter! Readers won't put up with it— they'll skip ahead (don't you?).

Starting with the main point is only one key to keep your readers from getting lost and skipping ahead. Specifically, this chapter urges you to:

- start with your main point,
- use a blueprint to show the structure of the body of your document,
- create "to do" lists, and
- prepare good executive summaries.

START WITH YOUR MAIN POINT

What do you suppose is the most read sentence in any document? My guess: the first sentence. If you put your main point there (or near there), you can be pretty sure your readers, no matter how busy they are, will at least see the most important thing you have to say.

Picture yourself as a reader at work. And picture yourself with plenty of work to do already and new stuff hits your e-mail. How attentive will you be to it? How carefully will you go through it? And what if your biorhythms aren't at their peak when you start to go through your new e-mail?

What Is a Bottom Line?

Not all documents have bottom lines. Some documents simply inform. Your document has a bottom line (or main point) if it contains:

- a conclusion
- a recommendation or
- a request for someone to do something

If that's not the picture of you, it may well be the picture of your reader. That's why most readers at work want to know the bottom line of any document—immediately! In fact, if the document doesn't start with it, readers may never get to it, ever. Or, if the document is something the reader obviously must read, typical busy readers start skimming almost immediately, looking for that bottom line.

Suppose this is an e-mail you're getting ready to send:

> From: James Bond, Department of Security
>
> To: Department Heads
>
> CC: Miss Moneypenny
>
> Subject: Outdated procedures
>
> We've learned that many of our procedures relating to security are out-of-date. A task force has been working on the problem. Recently, it recommended that my department should review all of the company's security directives in detail and update them as necessary. I plan to start with directives involving the people who work for me and then move on to the directives with company-wide applications. However, even the directives involving my people have implications for the entire company.
>
> As a result, I have decided to hold a meeting of department security representatives to help us gather ideas for specific changes we should make. Department security representatives can give their department's perspective to this important project. Therefore, it would be helpful if the security representative from your department would attend a meeting in our conference room at 10 a.m., Thursday. Please have your representative contact my Security Head, Mort Mole, at extension 007.

Where is the bottom line? That's right—at the end. You may think that e-mail is contrived (okay, the Mort Mole part is)—would writers really give all that background first just to ask someone to come to a meeting? Absolutely. In fact, most written requests fail just that way. Why? Because people want to tell the story of what led up to the request they're about to make. In other words, they use the chronological approach:

- First I learned something.
- Then I learned something else.
- Then I decided that I needed to do something.
- Therefore, I'd like you to do this.

That's the typical structure of a bad business e-mail. The tip-off is the word *therefore*. Notice it's near the end of the poor e-mail. *Therefore* usually follows the rationale, which means your bottom line is at the end. When you find yourself using *therefore*, see if you've fallen into the trap of delaying your main point.

"But perhaps," a writer might think, "if I explain all the reasons for something first and then make my request, my reader will more likely accept my request as reasonable." The only problem with that logic is that most readers won't read all those reasons. They'll start skimming.

Think of yourself if you have an office job. Don't you wonder, with every item in your e-mail, "Does this ask me to do anything?" And isn't that what you skim for—isn't that what you want to know before anything else?

So what would be a better structure for e-mail or memos that make a request? How about this:

- Here's what I'd like you to do.
- And here's why.

Let's see how that works with our security e-mail:

From: James Bond, Department of Security

To: Department Heads

CC: Miss Moneypenny

Subject: Outdated procedures

Could you have your security representative attend a meeting in our conference room at 10 a.m., Thursday? Please let Mort Mole, my Security Head, know. His extension is 007.

The purpose of the meeting is to review outdated security procedures and then come up with ideas for revising security directives throughout the company. Your representative can give your department's perspective to this important project.

Now your readers *can't miss* the reason you're sending the e-mail: to gather people for that meeting. With the earlier version, the readers had to hunt for the main point. Notice also that the revised e-mail is much shorter. That typically happens when you start with your main point: Irrelevant information tends to disappear because there's no place for it.

 For a quick lesson on this topic, go to http://www.professorbailey.com.

You may wonder if starting with the bottom line doesn't give your readers an excuse to stop reading. Perhaps. But remember, they'll probably stop reading and hunt for the main point if you *don't* give it to them up front!

Also, I think the bottom line often serves as a "hook" to draw your readers into your writing. It gives them a clear understanding of your point, and a clear beginning stands a much greater chance of success than a muddy one! For example, one of the most popular books on investing—Burton Malkiel's *A Random Walk Down Wall Street*—has the bottom line of the book in the first few lines of his preface! Take a look:

> It has now been over thirty years since I began writing the first edition of *A Random Walk Down Wall Street*. The message of the original edition was a very simple one: Investors would be far better off buying and holding an index fund than attempting to buy and sell individual securities or actively managed stocks. . . .
>
> Now, over thirty years later, I believe even more strongly in that original thesis.[1]

Malkiel's main point of his entire book—buy index funds—comes by the second paragraph. And it's a very successful book. Obviously readers don't just stop after Malkiel's second paragraph. If anything, it makes them want to keep reading!

Finally, let's take another look at the memo you first saw in Chapter 4. I've repeated it in this chapter (Fig. 5.1). Notice where the main point is—the first sentence of the second paragraph.

Put Your Bottom Line in the Subject Line

Memos and e-mail have one important thing in common: they both have subject lines. And almost all readers will at least read the subject line of what you write.

What if you're a busy reader and the subject line is the one I just showed you: "Outdated procedures." That'll really draw you in, won't it! In fact, it almost begs you to hit the delete button before reading any more. Wouldn't the following subject line work better than "Outdated procedures"?

> From: James Bond, Department of Security and Administrative Services
> From: James Bond, Department of Security
> To: Department Heads
> CC: Miss Moneypenny
> Subject: Meeting for security representatives
>
> Could you have your security representative attend a meeting in our conference room at 10 a.m., Thursday? Please let Mort Mole, my Security Head, know. His extension is 007.
>
> The purpose of the meeting is to review outdated security procedures and then come up with ideas for revising security directives throughout the company. Your representative can give your department's perspective to this important project.

Now if you have a security representative working for you—or if you are one—you know just from the subject line that you'd better read this message.

---

[1]Burton Malkiel, *A Random Walk Down Wall Street* (New York: Norton, 2003), p. 15. (Note: Page 15 is the first page of the preface—immediately following the table of contents.)

From: Sophia Hiller
To: Mackenzie Melton
Subject: Is accurate stock forecasting possible?
Date: May 26, 2008

You asked me to look into the subject of *stock forecasting* and let you know what I found out. The issue is whether investors can forecast whether a particular stock is likely to go up or down. For example, is it possible to predict whether Techronics stock is likely to go up during the next month? Or year? Or five years?

main point — Many experts believe the answer is "probably not." To see why, let's look at two prominent types of stock forecasting:

- Technical analysis
- Fundamental analysis

Technical analysis

Technical analysis means looking at stock charts. Suppose a stock has gone up every day for the past 30 days. Can we assume it *will* go up again tomorrow? The answer is "no." Well, can we assume it's *likely* to go up tomorrow? The answer is "probably not."

Or suppose that every time Techronics has dropped from 45 to 30, it has bottomed out and begun climbing again. Can we assume that when it drops to 30 again, it will rise? No.

Lots of research shows that past performance is not a reliable indicator of future performance. According to Burton Malkiel in *A Random Walk through Wall Street*, "The stock market has little, if any, memory."

Fundamental analysis

Fundamental analysis means looking at a company's value—and trying to determine its future earnings. To do that, analysts consider the management of a company, the future demand for its product, the possible risks involved, the dividends it's paying, etc.

For example, suppose an analyst spends time at Techronics and believes the company has a great product, great financing, a great management team, and tremendous growth potential. He also believes the market has undervalued the Techronics stock. Does that mean the stock is likely to go up? Some experts would say, "Buy!" Others would say, "Hmmmm ... I think I'll just put my money in index funds."

In other words, experts are more inclined to accept fundamental analysis than technical analysis; however, there's still lots of controversy and disagreement about its practical effectiveness.

FIGURE 5.1   Memo with Main Point Up Front

Subject lines are especially important for e-mail. "Outdated procedures" wouldn't do much for you.

So craft your subject line. Try to get bottom-line information in it. You don't have to have the entire bottom line in it (for example, you don't have to include the date and time of the meeting). But have enough so people will actually read the e-mail you send.

Now let's look at some other issues involving the bottom line.

What Are Types of "Bottom Line"?

In the sample e-mail we've been looking at, the bottom line is a request: send someone to a meeting.

Should You Always Start with Your Bottom Line?

Usually you should because readers will hunt for it if you don't. But sometimes a little delay is okay for these reasons:

- to give enough brief background so readers can understand what your bottom line means (especially important with technical documents the reader may not understand)
- to soften the tone when the reader may react negatively to your bottom line

These are reasons for only *brief* delays, though. Busy readers typically won't put up with anything longer.

A request is one of the most common types of bottom line. Whenever you ask somebody to do something—that is, whenever you make a request—start with it. It doesn't have to be the first sentence, but it can be and often should be.

Here are two other types of bottom line:

- *Recommendations.* Sometimes you aren't telling your reader to do something (send your security representative to a meeting); instead, you're suggesting something. Readers want that up front, too. For example, if you write a report recommending that your company build a new parking lot, your readers don't want the architect's design and the lawyer's opinion first. Your readers want to know that you recommend a new parking lot first. Otherwise, why should they study the architect's design and read the lawyer's opinion?
- *Conclusions.* Sometimes you aren't even suggesting something. You're simply reaching a conclusion. Suppose, for example, you write a report concluding that your company's parking lot isn't adequate. You're not recommending building a new one or firing half the workforce so the rest of the people can park easily. Again, readers want that conclusion first—and only later the details of how you conducted your survey and what method you chose to find a representative sample of people to interview.

Is There Always A Bottom Line?

Well . . . yes and no. In Chapter 4, you read a memo from a student who was describing his job as regional sales manager. He wasn't telling us to do anything, suggesting we do anything, or announcing any conclusion. He was simply *informing* us.

Lots of writing in business does the same thing—it simply informs: the board of trustees will be here next week; the network will be down for repair on Saturday; the brown bag topic this month is on how to give computer presentations; and so on.

The problem is that the reader often can't tell, without reading the entire memo, whether it's only informative. Lots of memos that ask the reader to do something begin the same way and appear to be only informative—until the hand grenade goes off somewhere near the end. So, from the reader's point of view, the fact that a memo is *only informative*—no action to take—is bottom-line material.

That's why it's often good to begin information memos by saying that's what they are: "This memo lets you know the board of trustees' schedule for next week so that you won't be surprised to see them in our office."

Where Are Other Good Places to Put the Bottom Line?

So far, I've urged you to begin with your bottom line. That, of course, doesn't mean it has to be the first sentence, but it should be way up front—before your reasons.

But the principle of putting the bottom line up front can apply in places other than correspondence. Think about business reports, usually lengthy documents involving lots of preparation. Here are some creative ways of getting the bottom line up front in them:

- *Title.* The U.S. Government Accountability Office (more commonly, GAO), which does auditing for the federal government, often puts its overall conclusion in the title:

  instead of *Review of Accounting Procedures at the Department of Agriculture*, say this: *Accounting Procedures Were Effective at the Department of Agriculture*

  That's a fast start, isn't it?

- *Table of contents.* A table of contents doesn't have to list only chapter name and page number. Look at popular magazines. Almost all of them have a brief description of each article underneath the article's title. Business reports can do the same thing for each section, and the brief description can be the section's bottom line—in a sentence or two. Readers love that technique, and it more likely gets them to turn to the sections that interest them.

- *Sidebars.* A *sidebar* is simply a short amount of information set off from the main text, often in a box or with shading or both. What if you put a sidebar with the bottom line on the first page of each section of a report? Your readers couldn't miss it! *Consumer Reports* does that for its featured topics.

- *Graphs.* Graphs are usually there for a purpose. Many professional publications make the title of the graph state its bottom line:

  Instead of: "Oil reserves"

  Say this: "Oil reserves are dropping drastically."

You can use the same technique for any illustration.

- *Side notes.* Some reports have wide outside margins, maybe 2 inches. Once or twice a page, the writer puts a sentence or so of bottom-line information in that margin. That way, a reader can skim the side notes and learn key information.
- *Executive summaries.* Longer business reports almost always begin with an executive summary. An executive summary isn't just for executives: Every reader starts with it because that's where the bottom-line information is! An executive summary should usually have the bottom line up front. I saw one from a research institute that began with this heading: "The Question." In a paragraph, the writer then briefly summarized the question his report was answering. The next heading was "The Answer." Those are two great headings to begin a long report with! There's more about executive summaries later in this chapter.

These are just a few places you can make your main point easy to find in reports. You can also use these techniques for your longer college papers, too. A sidebar, for example, explaining your bottom line would make your first page look good *and* get your reader (and you!) off to a good start.

USE A BLUEPRINT

A blueprint is simply a brief list of the topics you plan to cover. It normally comes near the beginning, just before you start your main discussion. Think of your blueprint as a list of your main headings. Figure 5.2 shows you a memo containing a blueprint.

The blueprint (the first set of bullets in the example) simply names the three headings in the memo, thereby giving its structure. You see the first heading ("Technical analysis") right after the blueprint. The second heading is ("Fundamental analysis"). For anything longer than a page, you should always consider a blueprint. But notice the blueprint works perfectly well for our sample memo—which is less than a page.

Think of Your Document as a Journey

You're taking your reader on a trip. Too many writers essentially say, "Get in the car and don't ask where we're going!" Most of us don't want to get in that car!

Instead, tell where you're going (the bottom line) and how you plan to get there (your blueprint). Your headings then serve as the road signs along the way!

Blueprints have these advantages:

- They help your reader quickly understand your document's structure. In other words, blueprints are a "road map" for your readers.
- They tell your reader that your document does have a structure and will probably be easy to read.
- They provide good places for white space, which the last chapter covered—a layout that makes your page look inviting.

From: Sophia Hiller
To: Mackenzie Melton
Subject: Is accurate stock forecasting possible?
Date: May 26, 2008

You asked me to look into the subject of *stock forecasting* and let you know what I found out. The issue is whether investors can forecast whether a particular stock is likely to go up or down. For example, is it possible to predict whether Techronics stock is likely to go up during the next month? Or year? Or five years?

*main
point* ———— Many experts believe the answer is "probably not." To see why, let's look at two prominent types of stock forecasting:

blueprint ————
- Technical analysis
- Fundamental analysis

*heading
identical to
blueprint
item* ———— ### Technical analysis

Technical analysis means looking at stock charts. Suppose a stock has gone up every day for the past 30 days. Can we assume it *will* go up again tomorrow? The answer is "no." Well, can we assume it's *likely* to go up tomorrow? The answer is "probably not."

Or suppose that every time Techronics has dropped from 45 to 30, it has bottomed out and begun climbing again. Can we assume that when it drops to 30 again, it will rise? No.

Lots of research shows that past performance is not a reliable indicator of future performance. According to Burton Malkiel in *A Random Walk through Wall Street*, "The stock market has little, if any, memory."

*heading
identical to
blueprint
item* ———— ### Fundamental analysis

Fundamental analysis means looking at a company's value—and trying to determine its future earnings. To do that, analysts consider the management of a company, the future demand for its product, the possible risks involved, the dividends it's paying, etc.

For example, suppose an analyst spends time at Techronics and believes the company has a great product, great financing, a great management team, and tremendous growth potential. He also believes the market has undervalued the Techronics stock. Does that mean the stock is likely to go up? Some experts would say, "Buy!" Others would say, "Hmmmm … I think I'll just put my money in index funds."

In other words, experts are more inclined to accept fundamental analysis than technical analysis; however, there's still lots of controversy and disagreement about its practical effectiveness.

FIGURE 5.2   Memo with Blueprint and Headings to Match

You don't have to use bullets for a blueprint, but you'll probably want to use them most of the time. A bulleted list gains emphasis, and a blueprint is usually something you want to emphasize.

There's one important caution with blueprints, though: Don't write a blueprint that your reader will probably skip. Many manuals begin with a lengthy list of everything they're going to cover. Has anybody ever read one of those lists all the way through?

What causes readers to skip blueprints?

- *Long blueprints.* After reading three or four items in a lengthy blueprint, most readers would rather skip the book and see the movie. Instead of listing the 20 issues your report covers, just say that you'll be covering 20 issues (without listing them). That way, your reader understands what the structure will be (one issue after another until you've covered 20 of them).
- *Complex blueprints.* If your blueprint has unfamiliar jargon, then your reader simply isn't understanding your words. Either rewrite the jargon into familiar words or skip the blueprint.

Most chapters in this book begin with blueprints. You'll find you can use blueprints often in your writing, too.

CREATE "TO DO" LISTS FOR YOUR READERS

A "to do" list is simply a list of things you need to do. That leads to an important writing tip.

Suppose you receive a *very* important letter—let's say two pages long—that asks you to do four things. However, those four things are scattered throughout the letter and mostly buried in the middle of paragraphs. That's an all-too-common way writers ask their readers to do several things, but it's not very effective, is it?

So as you read through the important letter, what will you do? At least mentally, you'll create a "to do" list—listing the four things you have to do. Perhaps you'll even highlight those four things in the letter or write out a separate list.

Now let's turn things around: Suppose you're the writer of that two-page letter and *really, really* want everyone who receives it to do those four things. Well, you can't depend on every reader to go over your letter carefully and create "to do" lists, can you?

But what if you revise your letter drastically so it has a list of those four things— perhaps as a blueprint with four parts following (one part for each thing you want your readers to do)? In other words, what if you create the "to do" list for them? You'll surely get better responses.

PREPARE GOOD EXECUTIVE SUMMARIES

Most people don't like to start reading a report with the introduction. They want to start *before* the introduction! In other words, they want to start with the executive summary.

An executive summary is usually one page long. It can certainly be less, but it is seldom more, except in special circumstances. And it's usually the first thing all readers—not just executives—read. In fact, far more people read executive summaries than read the report itself.

An executive summary normally answers these four questions for your readers:

1. What does this report look into? (Be brief—say this part in a few sentences, not a few paragraphs.)
2. What does it find? (Give your bottom line here—as close to the beginning of the executive summary as you can.)
3. What are the most important things in the report? (Assume your readers read only the executive summary—what do they *absolutely* need to know? Often these will be your report's key recommendations.)
4. What's the structure of the report? (Don't go into great detail, but do list the main sections of the report, perhaps with a sentence or two of explanation for each item.)

Figure 5.3 is a sample executive summary. Notice how it answers those four questions.

FIGURE 5.3 Sample Executive Summary

Executive Summary

main point of report

what report looks into

We looked at the performance of your middle managers. We found they're not performing nearly as well as they should be.

headings

What we recommend

example

bulleted paragraphs with italicized headings

- *Allow good middle managers to fail occasionally.* Your middle managers are afraid to innovate because they know there will be a big penalty for failure. For example, one said to us, "Why should I try anything when I'll just get my head chopped off if I'm wrong?" That was a common complaint.

- *Clarify the important responsibilities for each middle manager.* We found too many middle managers thought their most important responsibilities were administrative, such as getting their weekly status reports done and supervising their people. They didn't understand they needed to think strategically, too.

- *Reward good performers.* You have no bonus system now. We recommend you create such a system and make sure it rewards the most important responsibilities of your middle managers. For example, you could award large bonuses for innovative ideas.

first person

What we cover

report's structure

- Chapter 1, Clarifying the problem. We explain the problem you asked us to solve and explain the reason it exists.

- Chapter 2, Our approach. This chapter tells you our methodology for looking into the problems and coming up with our recommendations.

- Chapter 3, Our data gathering. This chapter gives you the detailed results of our surveys and other data we looked at.

- Chapter 4, Interviews with your staff. In this chapter, we give you the detailed results of our interviews with your vice presidents, middle managers, and other selected staff.

- Chapter 5, Recommendations. We give you the recommendations for your company as a whole and for each division.

Keep in mind the following tips when you're preparing your executive summary:

- *Avoid unnecessary jargon.* What if you explain a lot of special terminology in the report itself? Can you assume the readers of your executive summary will know those terms? No. You have to write your executive summary as though it's the very first thing your readers look at. It usually is.
- *Use Plain English.* Especially be sure to use first person (usually *we*). If you avoid first person, you'll probably end up writing the executive summary—and the entire report—in passive voice.
- *Use good layout.* Some writers feel so constrained by keeping an executive summary to one page that they forget the importance of good layout. Your readers will appreciate headings (if appropriate) and bullets. Bulleted paragraphs with italicized headings are especially useful (that's what this list is). An illustration is fine, too. Notice the good layout techniques in the sample executive summary (Fig. 5.3).
- *Use examples.* Some writers also feel so constrained by keeping an executive summary to one page that they make it entirely abstract. Abstract writing usually fails. An example or two in your executive summary may be the most memorable part of it. Notice the examples in the sample executive summary (Fig. 5.3).

EXERCISES

A. Look at the first page of the *Wall Street Journal*. Where do you find the bottom line for the day?

B. Look at a journal or professional magazine from your field of study to see if it uses any techniques for getting the bottom line up front. Are the techniques effective? Is the writing Plain English?

C. Rewrite this entire memo so that it has a better subject line and begins with the main point. Be sure to use a clear style and good layout, too.

> To: Department Heads
> From: [you]
> Subject: Policy change
> Date: May 26
>
> Reorganizations, space changes, and house cleaning frequently result in identification of property that is no longer needed. This property includes such excess items as wooden or metal file boxes; wooden, plastic, or metal letter trays; hanging file frames with folders; and unused office supplies such as bond paper, copier paper, and boxes of pens and pencils. Excess property must be sent to the Property Management Section. However, only reusable items should be sent—not those that have been damaged. This new policy can help our office save money and be kind to the environment.

D. For this exercise, choose an article from a journal or professional magazine in your field. Then analyze the *first two or three pages* in terms of Plain English. The format is a memo to the class. Your paper should be two or three pages long (single-spaced with double spacing between paragraphs—just as in most business writing).

Specifically:

- Choose an article from the past 12 months (so you're looking at fairly recent writing). Attach a copy of it to your paper.
- Craft your subject line.
- Have your bottom line up front. This is an important part of this exercise.
- Use a blueprint.
- Use convincing details in your analysis: not just that the sentence length is good or bad, but how long the average sentence length is, and how you would shorten some of the long sentences. And not just that there are too many passive verbs, but what they are and how you would change them to active voice. Don't be too sketchy in your analysis.
- If you find any bad things about the writing in the article, do a little rewriting to show that it actually could have been better.
- Consider using something other than just words—a diagram, table, whatever. This is not a requirement.
- Use a grammar checker for your own writing (i.e., temporarily delete all excerpts from the source you're analyzing), and attach the results to the end of your paper. Consider using a grammar checker for the writing you're analyzing.

  Finally, be sure to guide your readers through your analysis so they don't have to study either your analysis or the article. Think of "walking your reader through" your paper.

E. Do you know how to make a Web site? A Web site can also serve as a nonlinear report: Want the executive summary? Click here. Want the sources we consulted? Click here.

For this exercise, create a "Web site report" for Exercise D. That is, instead of using a memo to present your analysis of a journal or professional magazine, use a Web site. Construct it so users can click on various hyperlinks and get all the information.

CHAPTER 6

Illustrating Your Ideas

Readers are likely to notice—and remember!—your illustrations.

Norm Betaque, then senior vice president at a successful company in Washington, D.C., often dealt with complex concepts he had to express clearly to his clients. He once told me he tries to use illustrations to communicate those concepts: "Whenever I write something complicated," he told me, "I think, 'Can I draw a picture of this?'"

Great advice for all of us! Think about yourself as a reader. If there's an illustration on a page, don't you look at it first? And aren't you more likely to remember an illustration longer than some paragraphs full of words?

The nice thing is that computers today have taken illustrations out of the graphics shop and onto our desks. Many illustrations today are simple to do—yet writers often don't think about doing them, even though illustrations are immensely valuable for communicating complex ideas.

I remember a story another friend told me. He took a 10-page report, expertly researched and carefully written, to the top person of a large (actually, huge) organization. At the end of the 10 pages, he used a diagram to summarize the content of the report. My friend recalled that the top person skimmed the 10 pages, pulled off the diagram, and with his elbow shoved the other 10 pages out of the way, making room for just the diagram. Then the person held up the diagram and said to my friend, "Tell me about this."

My friend recalled this incident months later—and could still picture that elbow shoving the 10 pages full of words out of the way. Imagine how hard his office had worked to prepare those 10 pages!

Shoving the pages of words is a metaphor for the way many of us feel: Show us the picture! That's not because readers don't want to read the words; that's because pictures often tell the story quickly and memorably.

The story tells us something else important, too: The top person didn't want to study the diagram and try to figure it out for himself. He said, "Tell me about this." Too often, business writers put an illustration in their documents with little or no explanation before or after it. Apparently, they expect the readers to stop reading, study every item on the illustration, ponder it, and then start reading again.

From my experience, few readers have the patience to behave that way. Instead, you have to help your reader.

A Note on Type

The standard type design for illustrations is:

- a sans serif font (such as Arial)
- 2 points smaller type size than your body text

So if your body text is 12-point Times New Roman, try using 10-point Arial for the text for your illustrations.

This is a good standard because sans serif type is readable in smaller sizes and contrasts nicely with your body text (which probably has serifs).

 For a quick lesson on this topic, go to http://www.professorbailey.com.

Think of it this way. Suppose that instead of writing, you're talking to someone right next to you. As you're talking, you reach on your desk and pick up a graph to help make your point. You wouldn't simply hand it to your listener and wait while he tried to figure it out for himself, would you? Instead, you'd tell him why you're giving it to him: "This bar chart shows you that our sales are starting to decline." Then you'd hand it to him to look at for a few seconds. And then you'd add, "Notice that last year we leveled off . . . [and so on]."

You need to do the same kind of explaining when you write:

- Lead into your illustration by telling your readers why you're showing it to them—just as you'd tell a listener.
- Show it to them by placing it appropriately in your text.
- Then tell your readers anything else you want them to be sure to notice.

Not all illustrations require a lot of help for the reader. Sometimes a simple table or diagram can almost stand on its own. Just be sure to follow this principle: Don't expect your readers to spend a lot of time studying your illustration. Most of them will be impatient to move on if your illustration doesn't make immediate sense to them.

This chapter shows you illustrations you can easily do on a personal computer:

- tables
- flowcharts
- decision trees
- clip art
- simple drawings
- graphs

You'll see an example of each one. You'll also see different ways to weave illustrations into your document.

TABLES

A table shows rows and columns of data. It isn't a "graphical" illustration, but it does look different from normal text, and it can summarize information effectively. Whenever you're presenting a lot of numbers, think about using a table.

Here's an example that uses a table to restate the numbers—notice that the writer uses it to *reinforce* her explanation:

> A stock option lets option holders buy a specified number of shares of their company's stock at a predetermined price. The options always have a limited life—usually 5 or 10 years—for which they are valid. You usually receive options from your employer.
>
> Let me give you an example. Let's suppose Joe has worked for ABC Corporation for 20 years. To show appreciation, ABC's management awards Joe 2000 stock options at $10 with a life span of 10 years. Joe now has the right to buy 2000 shares of ABC anytime during the next 10 years at a price of $10 per share.
>
> The theory behind stock options is that the price of the stock will increase during the life of the options. If this happens, the holder can buy the stock at the original (lower) price from the market and make a nice profit. (The company makes up the difference in price.)
>
> Let's take our ABC example one step farther. Nine years have passed. The price of ABC is now $45 a share, and Joe still has his options for 2000 shares at $10. He decides it is time to cash in his option. As you can see in the summary below, Joe's options are now worth quite a bit—$90,000 in today's market:

Stock options	2,000
Option price	$10
Price when Joe exercises option	$45
What Joe pays	2,000 shares $\times$ $10 = $20,000
Market value at exercise	2,000 shares $\times$ $45 = $90,000

The table puts the whole story together, doesn't it? And the paragraph before it tells the reader exactly what to concentrate on ("$90,000 in today's market").

By the way, notice how effectively the writer uses an example (Joe's stock options) to explain the term *stock option*. Chapter 3, you'll recall, emphasized the importance of examples.

FLOWCHARTS

A flowchart shows the order things occur in. Perhaps you want to tell somebody the steps in a process—for instance, the steps an operations research analyst might typically use to solve a problem. Figure 6.1 shows how one person used a flowchart to help readers see those steps.

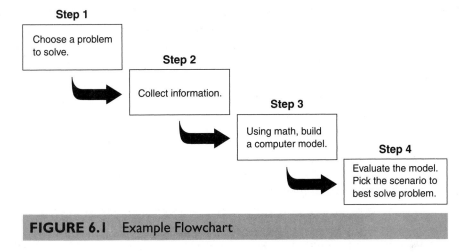

Step 1

Choose a problem to solve.

Step 2

Collect information.

Step 3

Using math, build a computer model.

Step 4

Evaluate the model. Pick the scenario to best solve problem.

FIGURE 6.1 Example Flowchart

The first thought of most writers would probably be to present the same information using bullets or a numbered list. But the flowchart helps us see the relationship better, doesn't it?

The writer doesn't simply show the readers the flowchart, though, hoping they will understand it. He then presents an example and asks the readers to follow along.

> Follow the diagram as we go through an example. Let's pretend you're in charge of a multimillion-dollar manufacturing plant. It produces motorcycles. You've read many articles about the use of robots in the automotive industry. Could robots help your company?
>
> *Step 1.* Should you replace some—or all—of your workforce with robots to produce motorcycles?
>
> *Step 2.* You ask an operations research analyst to research this idea. Here are a few of the many questions that your research analyst should research:
>
> - How much do these robots cost?
> - How much is their daily output?
> - What is the probability they will break down?
> - How much are the average repair and maintenance costs?
> - Is a warranty available?
>
> *Step 3.* Your operations research analyst writes a computer program that lets you look at different scenarios. It lets you type in the number of robots and whether you'd like a warranty. It then gives you a report with the expected daily output and a list of all costs.
>
> *Step 4.* You compare the results of the model with your current workforce numbers, remembering to use common sense. For example, the model can't answer all of your questions, such as the impact on employee morale for those still left.

The explanation and example help us understand the flowchart. The writer has done an excellent job of weaving the illustration into his document.

Do You Have to Use Form 8615 to
Figure Your Child's Tax?

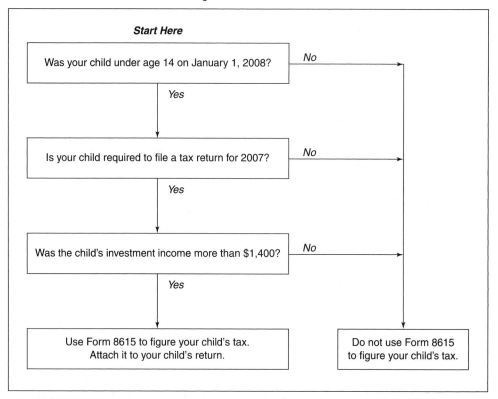

FIGURE 6.2   Example Decision Tree

DECISION TREES

A decision tree shows the flow of logic, usually with yes or no responses. It helps readers step through complex logic to reach a decision. What's more complex than federal tax law? In Figure 6.2, the IRS uses a decision tree to help you decide if you need to use a particular tax form (I've simplified the decision tree slightly).

Can you imagine trying to explain all that in wordy paragraph form? If you have complex logic, try a decision tree. It can make all the difference!

CLIP ART

When personal computers first gained access to rudimentary clip art, clip art quickly got a bad reputation. Many people saw it as empty illustration, often irrelevant to the topic at hand. The complaints had some merit, partly because there simply wasn't enough good clip art available and partly because overeager users wanted to show off. After all, if your computer can do a neat trick, it's often hard to resist doing it.

Today, lots of excellent clip art is available. It's everywhere, and it's cheap. I personally enjoy watching the creative ways people use the same clip art items to make different points.

This next example uses standard clip art to help us understand the concept of hoteling (which means reserving *office space* when you're on business travel, just as you reserve a hotel room):

> Imagine this: Your company sends you to a sister office in Sacramento. You have a tough job to do. You don't have time to worry about whether or not the Sacramento office will have a desk and accessories available. What if you get there and nothing is ready: no desk, no computer, not even a telephone for making or receiving calls? A waste of time, wasn't it? Well, that's what certain executives thought. They looked into this problem and developed what we now call "hoteling."
>
> Simply put, all branch offices in a company reserve vacant office space for visitors from other branches. All offices in a company subscribe. Managers confirm the visit and set everything up, just as in Figure 6.3.

You've probably seen these clip art figures before because they're so versatile. The writer doesn't use them to explain a complex point. She uses them to reinforce a

FIGURE 6.3 Example Clip Art

Step 1: I plan my trip and let my manager know.

Step 2: Managers at both offices get in touch.

Step 3: The manager where I'll visit agrees to arrange for "hoteling."

Step 4: I travel to an office already set up for me.

point—to let you see it rather than just read it. That's a valuable reason for illustrations. Use them for important points you don't want your readers to miss.

Titles for Illustrations

Sometimes titles aren't necessary for your illustrations. If you do give your illustration a title, try to make it explanatory rather than brief: "How to arrange for hoteling" instead of "Hoteling."

Why won't readers miss a point you illustrate? Well, they may skip your text, but they usually won't skip your pictures.

Notice also that the writer does a good job preparing the reader to read the illustration: "Managers confirm the visit and set everything up, just like this:"—using a colon to lead into it. You usually want to use a colon to end the sentence just before an illustration. A colon says, "Keep on reading—here comes something more about what I just said." That "something" is your illustration!

SIMPLE DRAWINGS

You don't need commercial clip art to make simple illustrations. You can draw your own with lines and simple geometric shapes, which are available on most office computers. Figure 6.4 is a simple drawing showing how ships at sea receive satellite signals:

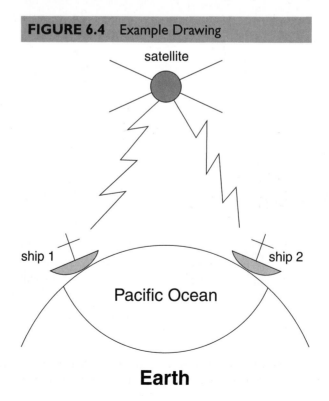

FIGURE 6.4 Example Drawing

A simple drawing is sometimes better than a photograph or sophisticated clip art. A simple drawing has no extra lines, nothing except what you want to show to make your point. Photographs and clip art, on the other hand, can have extraneous detail of no interest to you or your reader.

Figure 6.5, for example, is a simple drawing showing the parts of an airport's runway.

touchdown point   midpoint   rollout

FIGURE 6.5 A Second Example Drawing

Lots more effective than a photograph! You can also do quite a bit just with dots and arrows. In Figure 6.6, the writer shows that commercial aircraft will no longer have to fly specific "highways in the sky." Instead, with the program called "free flight," they can go directly to their destination.

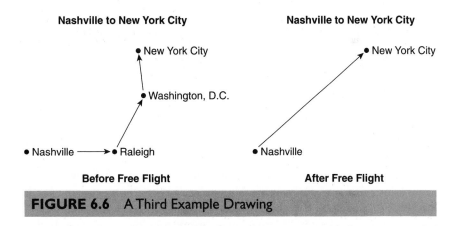

FIGURE 6.6 A Third Example Drawing

GRAPHS

Most office computers have the ability to make graphs. Anytime you want to compare numbers, think graphs!

This next example is a pair of simple pie charts, but they have far more impact than a wordy paragraph:

There's no doubt about who is in charge when it comes to government contracting—the government. Why do contractors want government business?

In one word: revenue. It is not easy to find a contract that generates hundreds of millions, perhaps even billions, of dollars of revenue in the commercial market.

If you were a contractor, which scenario would *you* choose?

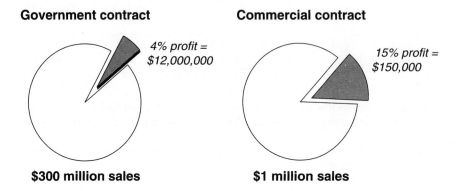

Most of us would prefer the scenario on the first pie chart. Profits as a percent of sales are lower (only 4%), but look at the dollar value of profit— $12,000,000!

The writer does a good job of leading into the graphs—and of telling us, afterward, what we were supposed to learn. That's the way to weave an illustration into a document!

Here are some general tips for graphs:

- Avoid three-dimensional bar charts—it's hard to tell the value of each bar. Either 2-D or 3-D for pie charts is all right because the 3-D effect doesn't cause a problem with reading the value of each slice of the pie.
- Generally, don't use grid lines for bar charts. They add clutter. Instead, put the numbers (the value of your data) on the bars. The *Wall Street Journal* often does this.
- Use an exploded pie chart if you want to emphasize a particular slice (the previous example has two exploded pie charts).
- Use snazzy graphics—as in the newsmagazines—only if you want to be eye-catching and the tone permits. Many effective brochures use eye-catching graphics as part of their illustrations.
- Avoid snazzy graphics if you want a serious tone or if you want the focus to be on your data rather than on capturing the reader's attention.

EXERCISES

A. Find a good or bad illustration from a journal or professional magazine in your field, bring it to class, and be prepared to explain its strengths and weaknesses.

B. Newsmagazines typically use illustrations to get your attention. Find a good or bad illustration from a newsmagazine, bring it to class, and be prepared to explain its strengths and weaknesses.

C. Find an example of some writing that does a good job weaving an illustration into the document. Bring that example to class, and be prepared to explain why you think it does a good job.

D. Choose an illustration (from any source) that particularly catches your attention, and write a one- to two-page memo to the class analyzing its strengths and weaknesses. Remember to use a Plain English style and good layout. Craft your subject line, and put your main point up front. Be sure to include a copy of the illustration you're analyzing.

E. Choose any special term from your field of work or study; then, in two to four pages, define it so everybody in your class can understand it clearly. Be sure to choose a term most people in the class aren't already familiar with—the challenge is to communicate something you know to an audience that doesn't know it.

- Use at least one illustration in your letter. If you take an illustration from another source, be sure to document it. Then include another illustration that you think of yourself.
- Weave your illustration into your text. That is, be sure to introduce and explain it.
- Use a grammar checker and attach the results.
- Make the format a memo to the class.

Remember to use a Plain English style and good layout. Be sure to put your main point up front.

You probably also want to look at Appendix D before you write your memo. It shows you a good sample response to this exercise.

CHAPTER 7

Getting Beyond Periods and Commas

You need to learn to use all the marks of punctuation.

In seventh grade, you probably thought (as I did) that punctuation was simply a way to go wrong—a way to make mistakes your teacher would catch. But punctuation isn't just a hurdle. It's an important tool, the next step to becoming good at expressing yourself on paper.

So don't think of punctuation as a way to go wrong; think of it as a way to go right! Here are two key roles for punctuation:

- *Helping your readers understand how to read your sentences.* Periods, commas, and other punctuation marks help people make their way through your sentences. Used correctly, these marks are like signposts—"slow down," "stop," "keep going"; used incorrectly, they take readers into dead ends and cause unnecessary detours and U-turns.

- *Emphasizing important ideas.* A second key role for punctuation is to help readers notice your important ideas. A question mark gives emphasis, doesn't it? And so do dashes, colons, and ellipses. Good punctuation lets you do in writing what your voice inflection and pauses do when you're talking.

This chapter won't cover all the marks of punctuation, but it covers the most important ones. They may have seemed hard to learn in seventh grade, when they didn't mean much; as adults, though, you can learn them rather quickly.

Before getting into specifics, let's take a look at good punctuation in the hands of a great writer. Charles Ellis is making the point that too many investors don't understand market history. So when there's a big loss in the market, they are shocked—when they should have expected a big loss at sometime or another.

Here's how Ellis puts it—look at all the different (and effective) uses of punctuation:

> Only knowing history and understanding its lessons can insulate us from being surprised. Just as a teenage driver is genuinely amazed by his or her all too predictable accidents—"Dad, the guy came out of *nowhere!*"—investment managers are surprised by adverse performance caused by "anomalies" and "six sigma events." Actually, those surprises are all within life's bell curve of

the normal distribution of experience. They are not truly "surprises": They are actuarial *expectations*.[1]

So get ready to take the next step in becoming a good writer. Here are the marks this chapter covers:

- question mark
- dash
- colon
- semicolon
- ellipsis
- comma

QUESTION MARK

The question mark is the easiest mark to use. You don't have to know any grammar! Too often, though, writers avoid this important mark. Here are three good rules for using it.

Rule 1: Use a Question Mark When You're Seeking Information

Often, people in business are seeking information from each other. In talking, they'd simply say something like this:

How many people in your department will be taking annual leave in June?

In writing, though, people sometimes unnecessarily avoid the question mark. Instead, they bury the spoken question and turn it into a deadly declarative sentence, like this:

Request this office be informed of the number of people in your department who will be taking annual leave in June.

The declarative sentence doesn't have nearly the emphasis of the question, does it?

Rule 2: Use a Question Mark as a Tag at the End of a Sentence

Another good use of a question is to add it to the end of a sentence:

June is a good time for a vacation, isn't it?

You're not seeking information and surely don't expect an answer. You just want more emphasis than the period would give. Think of this type of question as a quick "wake-up" call to your reader.

---

[1]Charles D. Ellis, *Winning the Loser's Game* (New York: McGraw-Hill, 2002), p. 25. (Note: I almost used this quotation in the chapter on comparisons—but it's so good with punctuation that I kept it for here. But do note, once again, the value of a good comparison in making your point!)

Rule 3: Ask a Question You're Going to Answer

A third good use of the question is when you—the writer—are going to give the answer:

> Why is June a good time for people in our company to take annual leave? The main reason is that our workload will be lower then but will pick up its normal pace in July and August.

The question draws your readers in and gets them to pay attention to the answer.

One good use of this type of question is to hook your reader at the beginning of a report or article. For example, look at effectiveness of the question mark in an article from *Contract Management,* a professional journal. This is how the article starts:

Uncle Sam:	Want to know a secret?
J. Public:	Sure! What is it?
Uncle Sam:	I've got millions of dollars to give people who come up with worthy ideas.
J. Public:	Really? How do I get some of this money?
Uncle Sam:	Send me a USP.[2]

USP, it turns out, means "unsolicited proposal." The questions help draw the reader in.

Another good place for a question you'll answer is in headings. When you make your heading a question, your reader normally stays tuned in to get the answer. Think of the question in a heading as a hook that catches readers and draws them into the narrative that follows.

Here's the heading (and following two sentences) from a Coca-Cola annual report:

> **Doesn't there come a point when you simply can't expand any further?** No. As long as people continue to consume approximately 64 ounces of fluid every day, our growth opportunities will be virtually unlimited.

And here's another heading and following sentence from one of Prudential's annual reports:

> **Are we prepared for the future?**
> Yes.

See how the headings draw us into the text that follows? And notice that the first sentence after each heading immediately answers the question—another good practice.

By the way, the technique of using a question for a heading is useful not only for business writing but also for your college papers. Try it!

---

[2]Kenneth Askew, "Do You Want to Know a Secret?" *Contract Management,* December 1996, p. 20.

DASH

The dash is a terrific mark of punctuation, often replacing a comma and adding emphasis. Here are two good uses for it.

Rule 1: Use a Dash at the End of a Sentence to Emphasize What Comes Next

You can put the dash at the end of a sentence to emphasize whatever comes next. For example, you can have a dash followed by a word, a list, or even another sentence:

Sentence—word.

Sentence—list.

Sentence—sentence.

Let's look at an example of each:

There's one month that's better than any other for a vacation—June.

These are the best months for a vacation—June, July, and August.

June is a great month for a vacation—the weather is perfect.

Look at the first example again. What if the writer had said this?

One month that is better than any other for a vacation is June.

That's not a bad sentence, but it loses some emphasis. Sometimes you want more emphasis, other times less. Better writers can write both types of sentence.

Rule 2: Use Dashes to Emphasize an Idea in the Middle of a Sentence

Normally the ideas at the beginning and end of a sentence get the most emphasis. What if you want to emphasize something in the middle?

The reviewers looked at everything in the files—including last month's payroll records—and found everything correct.

Could you use other marks instead of dashes? Yes—commas and parentheses:

The reviewers looked at everything in the files, including last month's payroll records, and found everything correct.

The reviewers looked at everything in the files (including last month's payroll records) and found everything correct.

The difference is the amount of emphasis:

- Dashes emphasize the most.
- Commas are standard.
- Parentheses are like a whispered aside.

What Are the Types of Dashes?

There are three dashes:

     em dash: —

     en dash: –

     half en dash: -

Here are their uses:

- Use the em dash for most punctuation.
- Use the en dash to mean "to" (example: 2–4 p.m.).
- Use the half en dash for hyphenated words and breaks in words at the ends of lines. Another name for the half en dash is the hyphen.

Newspapers sometimes use the en dash instead of an em dash. That's because the en dash is a spacesaver for the narrow columns of text.

You can find all of these marks at Insert > Symbol in Microsoft Word.

You can use punctuation to control emphasis just as you can use typography (bold, italic, upright).

 For a quick lesson on this topic, go to http://www.professorbailey.com.

Let's look at some examples of dashes from annual reports:

> We are expanding and investing in our most important asset—IBM people. (IBM)

> The magic of Coca-Cola—and our ability to enhance that magic and expand our brand portfolio—gives us tremendous growth potential. (Coca-Cola)

> By collaborating with us, one of our suppliers helped identify cost savings totaling 40 percent—12 percent will come from the supplier, 7 percent will come from a sub-supplier, and Ford will contribute savings of 21 percent. (Ford)

COLON

A colon is similar to the dash, but it's not as versatile and has a slightly more formal tone.

Rule 1: Use a Colon at the End of a Sentence to Emphasize What Comes Next

This is the same as rule 1 for the dash:

     Sentence: word.

     Sentence: list.

     Sentence: sentence.

Here are the same examples you saw for the dash, this time using the colon:

> There's one month that's better than any other for a vacation: June.
>
> These are the best months for a vacation: June, July, and August.
>
> June is a great month for a vacation: the weather is perfect.

The emphasis is the same as for the dash; the tone is more formal.

You may wonder if you should use a capital letter for the first word after the colon. Only if it's a proper name. But many people do use a capital letter if there's a full sentence after the colon:

> June is a great month for a vacation: <u>T</u>he weather is perfect.
>
> June is a great month for a vacation: <u>t</u>he weather is perfect.

Both are correct. The first version (with the capital letter) is more common.

You may also wonder if you always need a full sentence before the colon. No. As long as the reader won't be confused, you can have a sentence fragment as a lead-in. Here's a good example from an annual report by PepsiCo (which owns Pepsi-Cola):

> The result: a 19% gain in ongoing profits.

Rule 2: Use a Colon to Point to a List or Indented Material

Using a colon to point to a list is, by far, the most common use for the colon. You can see it on almost every page in this book. You don't need more examples.

But there is more to say about this rule. There used to be a requirement that the colon had to follow a complete sentence when introducing an indented list. So, in the past, you wouldn't normally have seen a lead-in like this:

> The best months for a vacation are:
>
> - June
> - July
> - August

Instead, you'd have seen a complete sentence, like this:

> The best months for a vacation are <u>the following</u>:
>
> - June
> - July
> - August

That rule is starting to change. You'll often see the first version now (without "the following"). You'll also see simple, nonsentence lead-ins like "Specifically:" and "For example:" in reputable publications today.

What I've said applies to indented lists. But for lists that are not indented, the convention is different: For lists that are not indented, you shouldn't use a colon between a verb and a series of objects:

RIGHT: The best months for a vacation are:

- June
- July
- August

WRONG: The best months for a vacation are: June, July, and August.

Nor should you use a colon between a preposition and a series of objects when the list is not indented:

WRONG: The best months for a vacation are in: June, July, and August.

Just leave out the colon. Here are some good uses of colons from annual reports:

The boldness that comes from self-confidence, and the clarity that comes from simplicity, lead to one of the small company's greatest competitive advantages: speed. (General Electric)

In the search [for acquisitions], we adopt the same attitude one might find appropriate in looking for a spouse: It pays to be active, interested and open-minded, but it does not pay to be in a hurry. (Berkshire-Hathaway)

Charlie and I frequently get approached about acquisitions that don't come close to meeting our tests: We've found that if you advertise an interest in buying collies, a lot of people will call hoping to sell you their cocker spaniels. A line from a country song expresses our feeling about new ventures, turnarounds, or auction-like sales: "When the phone don't ring, you'll know it's me." (Berkshire-Hathaway)

SEMICOLON

The semicolon is, by far, the most misused mark of punctuation per time of use. Many writers avoid it; most writers unfamiliar with it probably should.

The main function of a semicolon is to separate *similar grammatical units*. Think of it as the point of balance between two ideas:

RIGHT: Sentence; sentence.

RIGHT: long phrase; long phrase

WRONG: Sentence; dependent clause.

WRONG: Sentence; phrase.

Rule 1: Use a Semicolon to Separate Two Related Sentences

This is the most common use of a semicolon. Here's an example:

June is a good time for a vacation; February usually isn't.

Notice there's a full sentence on each side of the semicolon. That's also what is happening in this slightly more complex sentence:

This is my advice for vacations: in summer, go north; in winter, go south.

"In summer, go north" could stand alone as a sentence. So could "In winter, go south." In our example, then, the semicolon is separating two related sentences.

Colons, Dashes, and Semicolons

Colons and dashes usually point to more information about what you just said—an example, an explanation, and so forth:

Go north for skiing: The mountains are awesome.

Semicolons usually separate ideas that balance or contrast:

Go north for skiing; go south for swimming.

Skiing in the north is great; however, you'd better be an expert.

The difference is subjective but real.

Sometimes there's a word or phrase that explicitly says what the relationship is between the two sentences—words like *however, for example,* and *therefore.* These are conjunctive adverbs, and you can find a list of the common ones at the end of the next chapter. Traditionally, these words have a period or semicolon before them (and a comma after) when they begin the second sentence:

June is a good time for a vacation; <u>however,</u> February usually isn't.

Be careful, though. Some people make errors by always putting a semicolon before a word like *however.* But the word *however* can move to different places in the second sentence:

June is a good time for a vacation; February, <u>however,</u> usually isn't.

June is a good time for a vacation; February usually isn't, <u>however.</u>

Notice that the semicolon stays put (at the boundary between the two sentences) even though the word *however* moved.

Rule 2: Use a Semicolon to Separate Certain Complicated Phrases

A less common use for the semicolon is to separate certain complicated phrases. Normally you put a comma after each item in a series. But what if one or more of the items has commas in it, like this?

WRONG: Three good months for a vacation are June, because the weather is good, July, because of the holiday, and August, because it gets you ready for the fall.

Now let's try again, this time with semicolons to separate the items:

> RIGHT: Three good months for a vacation are June, because the weather is good; July, because of the holiday; and August, because it gets you ready for the fall.

You'll sometimes see reputable publications put a comma (instead of a semicolon) before the last *and*. But that doesn't make much sense to me.

By the way, there's an even better way to do complicated lists than using semicolons. Use bullets:

> BETTER: Three good months for a vacation are:
> - June, because the weather is good
> - July, because of the holiday
> - August, because it gets you ready for the fall

Here are some good uses of semicolons from annual reports:

> [about acquiring a second insurance company] Hollywood has had good luck with sequels; I believe we, too, will. (Berkshire-Hathaway)

> After several failures of this type, I finally remembered some useful advice I once got from a golf pro (who, like all pros who had anything to do with my game, wishes to remain anonymous). Said the pro: "Practice doesn't make perfect; practice makes permanent." And thereafter I revised my strategy and tried to buy good businesses at fair prices rather than fair businesses at good prices." (Berkshire-Hathaway)

> The sweetest fruit of boundaryless behavior has been the demise of "Not-Invented-Here" and its utter disappearance from our company. We quickly began to learn from each other: productivity solutions from Lighting; "quick response" asset management from Appliances; transaction effectiveness from GE Capital; the application of "bullet train" cost-reduction techniques from Aircraft Engines; and global account management from Plastics—just to name a few. (General Electric)

ELLIPSIS

An older name for ellipsis is "ellipsis points." With a typewriter, you made an ellipsis with three spaced dots: space dot space dot space dot space (. . .). Today, for example, you choose Insert > Symbol in Microsoft Word to get the ellipsis as a single character (. . .). That's an advantage because those three dots stay together on the same line of type. The three spaced dots might have put part of the ellipsis at the end of one line and the rest at the beginning of the next line.

Have you ever seen four dots? The extra dot is the period at the end of a sentence. Put the period first and then add the ellipsis.

So what is the function of an ellipsis? It's a wonderful mark. It has such a strong impact, you want to use it sparingly (just as you don't overuse exclamation points). But "sparingly" doesn't mean or imply "never." The ellipsis should definitely be part of your arsenal.

Rule 1: Use an Ellipsis to Show a Reflective or Dramatic Pause

Think of the ellipsis as a dash with something extra. It adds emphasis by pausing for a beat or two:

> In the northern tier of states, January is cold . . . way too cold.
>
> Minnesota is beautiful in the summer . . . a wonderland of lakes and forests.
>
> Minnesota is beautiful in the summer . . . don't you think?

Rule 2: Use an Ellipsis to Show That a List Could Be Much Longer

The ellipsis also serves as a pause in this usage, a pause for the reader to understand that the list could go on . . . and on:

> The best months for a vacation are January and February and March and . . . it's always a good month for a vacation!

Rule 3: Use an Ellipsis to Show You've Left Out Words in a Quotation

When you're quoting someone else, you don't always need to include every word. To show your reader you've left out something, just replace the missing words with an ellipsis.

Suppose this is your quotation, and you want to leave out the part I've italicized:

> One of the fascinating things about Charles Darwin is that he really does seem to have been one of those men whose careers quite unexpectedly and fortuitously are decided for them by a single stroke of fortune. For twenty-two years nothing much happens, no exceptional abilities are revealed; then suddenly a chance is offered, *things can go either this way or that, but luck steps in, or rather a chain of lucky events,* and away he soars into the blue never to return.[3]

The ellipsis just adds clutter in these cases and doesn't give substantial help to your reader. Just leave the ellipsis out.

You wouldn't be changing the meaning by leaving out those words, but you need to show your reader that you're not giving a complete quote. Just substitute an ellipsis for the missing words:

> One of the fascinating things about Charles Darwin is that he really does seem to have been one of those men whose careers quite unexpectedly and fortuitously are decided for them by a single stroke of fortune. For twenty-two years nothing much happens, no exceptional abilities are revealed; then suddenly a chance is offered . . . and away he soars into the blue never to return.[4]

---

[3]Alan Moorehead, *Darwin and the Beagle* (New York: Harper and Row, 1969), p. 19.

[4]Ibid., p. 19.

A Note on Ellipsis

You don't need to use an ellipsis to show you've left out words from the beginning or end of a quotation, just the middle. For example, you don't have to do either of these:

> ". . . he really does seem to have been one of those men whose careers quite unexpectedly and fortuitously are decided for them by a single stroke of fortune."

> "One of the fascinating things about Charles Darwin is that he really does seem to have been one of those men whose careers quite unexpectedly and fortuitously are decided for them. . . . "

The ellipsis just adds clutter in these cases and doesn't give substantial help to your reader. Just leave the ellipsis out.

The result is a quotation that's simpler to read and has more impact.

Here are some good uses of ellipses from annual reports:

> In a single word, our appreciation for your growing support could be described as nothing other than . . . well, *infinite.* (Coca-Cola)

> For Anheuser-Busch, we're out to be our own toughest competitor . . . and to get to the future first. (Anheuser-Busch)

COMMA

Everybody uses commas, but not everybody uses them correctly. The end of the next chapter covers a common error with commas: the comma splice. This section covers four rules for commas you need to know.

Rule 1: Use a Comma after Introductory Material

Before a sentence (or "independent clause"), you can have several constructions: a word, a phrase, or a dependent clause. Normally, put a comma between that construction and the independent clause that follows:

> word, independent clause
> phrase, independent clause
> dependent clause, independent clause

Here are examples:

> However, February is a good time for a skiing vacation.
> For many people, February is a good time for a skiing vacation.
> If you like the outdoors, February is a good time for a skiing vacation.

Punctuation and Journalism

Journalists often leave out optional punctuation. That's because many journalists write for newspapers and magazines that have two or more columns of text across the page. Leaving out punctuation makes fitting words into those narrow columns easier to do. However, I believe that can cause confusion. I put in all optional punctuation.

The comma is optional in the second example because the introductory construction passes both of these tests:

- It's short.
- It's a phrase (that is, there's no verb in it).

Rule 2: Use a Comma to Separate Two Sentences Joined by a Coordinating Conjunction

This is an important rule because it applies to a common construction:

Sentence, <u>coordinating conjunction</u> sentence.

These are the coordinating conjunctions:

and   *but*   *or*   *nor*   *for*   *so*   *yet*

Here's an example:

June is a good month to go to the beach, and February is a good month to go to a ski area.

Be sure there's a full sentence on both sides of the coordinating conjunction. The comma in this example is an error:

WRONG: I like swimming in the ocean, and skiing in the mountains.

The words after the coordinating conjunction aren't a full sentence. To correct the error, just leave out the comma.

Rule 3: Use a Comma to Set Off Parenthetical Material

You've already learned this rule. Remember this rule for using a dash?

The reviewers looked at everything in the files—including last month's payroll records—and found everything correct.

The dashes set off a parenthetical element. You could also use commas (or parentheses):

The reviewers looked at everything in the files, including last month's payroll records, and found everything correct.

Rule 4: Use a Comma to Separate Items in a Series

In the 1970s, there was a movement to do away with most optional punctuation, most notoriously doing away with the "serial comma." The serial comma is the comma just before the word *and* in this example:

> June, July, and August are good months for a vacation.

Leaving out that comma is still optional for a simple series involving only single words or short phrases, but the emphasis today is on putting in that mark. I agree. What's the harm? And putting it in may prevent misreading.

Throughout this chapter, I've emphasized the need for a variety of punctuation. True. But a good writer can still do wonders with only the comma. Here's an excerpt from an annual report:

> In the 10 seconds it takes to read this sentence, some 126,000 people will reach for one of our products at work, on the corner, at home, as they eat, study, dance, get dressed, get gas, get going. (Coca-Cola)

EXERCISES

A. Punctuate these sentences correctly (avoid periods—use other marks like dashes, etc.).
   1. You should diversify your portfolio and rebalance it periodically.
   2. You should diversify your portfolio and you should rebalance it periodically.
   3. Your portfolio which definitely should be diversified needs periodic rebalancing.
   4. Mutual funds can specialize in large-caps, mid-caps, and small caps.
   5. If you want to diversify a great deal you should consider index funds.
   6. Mutual funds can specialize in growth funds they can also specialize in value funds.
   7. Online brokers have some big advantages reduced fees and easy access.
   8. Consider before investing the expenses of a particular mutual fund.
   9. Before investing in a particular mutual fund, you should consider its expenses.
   10. On the one hand mutual funds have expenses on the other they have potential profits.

B. Look in any published writing and find examples you really like of sentences with one or more of these marks:
   - question mark
   - dash
   - colon (other than to introduce a list)
   - semicolon
   - ellipsis

   Copy down those sentences, and be prepared to share them with the class.

C. Find some good professional writing (magazines, journals, newspapers, books, etc.). Copy down five sentences (or brief passages) with punctuation you especially like, and be prepared to share them with the class.

D. Write a two-page memo to the class analyzing the punctuation in one of these sources:
   - a journal or professional magazine from your field
   - a news or business magazine
   - a newspaper

- an annual report
- a Web site

Does the source use a wide variety of punctuation? Does it use the journalistic technique of leaving out optional punctuation? Is the punctuation effective? Point out especially effective punctuation; identify several places punctuation could be better, and show how.

In your memo, be sure to use each of these marks of punctuation correctly:

- question mark
- dash
- colon (other than to introduce a list)
- semicolon
- ellipsis

Identify your favorite sentence (from your own writing—not from the source you're analyzing) by writing [favorite sentence] in square brackets right after that sentence.

Be sure to apply all the other lessons from this course, including a clear style, an effective layout, and a main point that's easy to find.

CHAPTER 8

Learning Commonsense Rules

Too many writers try to follow rules that don't exist.

Most rules for grammar and punctuation make sense. They help readers make their way through sentences and help writers express themselves clearly. How good the rules are is surprising, because no all-knowing benevolence designed them and gave them to us in divine perfection.

No—instead, the rules evolved, and they evolved quite well. But in any complex and dynamic situation, there are bound to be contradictions, misunderstandings, and murky areas. The purpose of this chapter is to help you learn some rules and unlearn some pretenders (that is, to unlearn some rules that aren't).

We'll start with the unlearning and then move to the learning part. The learning part will help you avoid three key errors.

OVERCOMING MYTHICAL RULES

To decide if a rule is mythical, let's first decide what makes a rule a rule. Linguists today generally agree that a rule is something that most educated people accept as a rule. Simple enough, so far. But that simple statement has serious implications:

- One implication is that rules change, or evolve, as educated people change their standards. Some rules your teacher learned as a child years ago—and then taught you—may no longer apply.
- Another implication is that some rules have greater acceptance than others. For example, almost everybody agrees that sentences should begin with capital letters. But how many agree that split infinitives are all right? Or even know what a split infinitive is?

To decide whether something is a rule to follow, I consider these questions:

- What do the grammar handbooks say? They try to describe what most educated people think.
- What do most professionally edited publications do?
- What makes sense?

There is rarely any conflict among those test questions.

But there is occasionally conflict between those tests and what most people learned in school. That is, many people try to follow rules that aren't even in the grammar handbooks! I call those myths, and here are the three biggest ones:

Myth 1: Never end a sentence with a preposition.
Myth 2: Never begin a sentence with *and* or *but*.
Myth 3: Never split an infinitive.

Yes, believe it or not, they are all myths! You can violate them all and be perfectly correct.

Myth 1: Never End a Sentence with a Preposition

I'm sure all of us have had a teacher or boss or parent or other authority figure insist that ending a sentence with a preposition is a serious error.

A common example of the error is this one:

Where's the book *at?*

That's not a good sentence, but the problem isn't that there's a preposition at the end. The problem is the word *at* is unnecessary. A better way to write it is this:

Where's the book?

Now let's look at examples where prepositions at the end make good sentences, not bad ones:

Here is the report we agree with.
Where is this information *from?*

Both of those sentences end with prepositions and sound natural, spoken. What if the writer had believed that prepositions shouldn't end sentences? This is probably what would have happened:

Here is the report with which we agree.
From where is this information?

Stiff, awkward, archaic.

Winston Churchill, the English statesman, agreed decades ago. He had a reputation as an excellent stylist. He once caught someone creating an awkward sentence by not ending a sentence with a preposition. According to *The Concise Oxford Dictionary of Quotations*, this was his tongue-in-cheek comment:

This is the sort of English up with which I will not put.

Churchill wasn't alone in disagreeing with the old myth. What may be surprising to you is that most standard and respected grammar books have *encouraged* writers to put prepositions at the ends of sentences when doing so would sound natural. They have said that for decades and decades. And they say that today.

In fact, if there were a scale—from "never end a sentence with a preposition" to "perfectly all right"—where along that scale would today's rule books fall? Here's my conclusion from looking at many recent books:

And here's what I believe many people *think* the rule books say:

Quite a difference!

Let's look at excerpts from the rule books, starting nearly a century ago. These excerpts are from some of the most famous books on grammar and usage from the twentieth century, and they all agree that prepositions at the end are okay:

> A preposition may stand at the end of a sentence or clause.[1]

> It is a cherished superstition that prepositions must . . . be kept true to their name & placed before the word they govern. . . .

> Those who lay down the universal principle that final prepositions are "inelegant" are unconsciously trying to deprive the English language of a valuable idiomatic resource, which has been used freely by all our greatest writers except those whose instinct for English idiom has been overpowered by notions of correctness derived from Latin standards.[2]

> Etymologically, the word *preposition* means "placed before." But to argue from this that a preposition must be placed before its object is like arguing that a butterfly must be a fly.[3]

---

[1]George Kittredge and Frank Farley. *Advanced English Grammar* (Boston: Ginn, 1913), p. 149.

[2]H. W. A. Fowler, *Dictionary of Modern English Usage* (New York: Greenwich House, 1926), p. 458. This was perhaps the most popular and standard book on usage during the early part of the 20th century.

[3]Bergen Evans and Cornelia Evans, *A Dictionary of Contemporary American Usage* (New York: Random House, 1957), p. 387. This is a standard book on usage.

> Years ago, students were warned not to end a sentence with a preposition; time, of course, has softened that rigid decree. Not only is the preposition acceptable at the end, sometimes it is more effective in that spot than anywhere else.[4]

> The preposition may follow rather than precede its object, and it may be placed at the end of a sentence.[5]

> Recent commentators—at least since Fowler 1926—are unanimous in their rejection of the notion that ending a sentence with a preposition is an error or an offense against propriety.[6]

These excerpts aren't exceptions to the advice the rule books gave in the twentieth century: They're the best-known and best-selling books on the subject. And they're *typical* of all the other books!

In other words, you'd have to work hard to find a professionally published rule book—for decades in the past—that says you shouldn't put a preposition at the end of a sentence.

What about today's professionally edited publications, such as books, newspapers, and magazines? Do they put prepositions at the end? Almost all of them do. You'll rarely see, "From where is this information" or "Here is the report with which we agree." That awkward hypercorrection would draw attention to itself and probably distract the reader.

So if people tell you that ending a sentence with a preposition is an error, ask for their rationale. Your rationale is that almost all rule books encourage it, professional writers do it, it sounds natural, and it makes sense. I believe those are tough arguments to counter.

Myth 2: Never Begin a Sentence with *and* or *but*

This is another edict I'm sure we've all heard. Again, most rule books don't consider it an error. In fact, the first two books I quoted in the previous section—the ones from 1913 and 1926—say nothing at all about beginning sentences with *and* or *but*. It wasn't even a mythical rule then!

The issue arises by midcentury, though. *Harbrace College Handbook* (as early as the first edition in 1941) says that *and* and *but* are good ways to begin sentences:

> Begin with a co-ordinating conjunction such as *but, and, or, nor,* or *yet.*

Webster's Dictionary of English Usage, a good source for today's rules, agrees with *Harbrace:*

> Everybody agrees that it's all right to begin a sentence with *and,* and nearly everybody admits to having been taught at some time that the practice was wrong.

---

[4]William Strunk and E. B. White, *Elements of Style* (New York: Macmillan, 1979), pp. 77–78. This was probably the most popular book on writing during the 20th century.

[5]John C. Hodges and Mary E. Whitten, *Harbrace College Handbook* (San Diego: Harcourt Brace Jovanovich, 1986), p. 13. This has been one of the most popular college handbooks ever.

[6]*Webster's Dictionary of English Usage* (Springfield, Mass.: Merriam-Webster, 1989), p. 763.

It then continues:

> Few commentators have actually put the prohibition in print.

In summary, here's an illustration showing what today's rule books say about beginning sentences with *and* or *but:*

And here's what many people think the rule books say:

Beginning sentences with *and* or *but* makes sense, too. Those words, at the beginning of a sentence, emphasize the relationship the next sentence is going to have with the one you just read. That's why you can almost always find sentences beginning with one of those words in the editorial pages of your newspaper. Editorials often start with an argument, then use the word *but,* and then give the counterargument.

Try an experiment. Look at the editorial page of your newspaper every day for the next week. Almost certainly you'll find sentences beginning with *and* or *but* every day there. If not in your newspaper, you'll surely find them in the *Wall Street Journal* editorial page, which aims directly at people in business, the people who read business writing every day.

Some people say, "Newspapers! So what!" From my experience, newspapers do a good job writing clearly. Otherwise, people wouldn't buy them. But my real point is that people read newspapers—day after day—complete with prepositions at the end, sentences beginning with *and* or *but,* and split infinitives, and never notice! Most people who adamantly believe in the myths have reads those so-called errors thousands of times without noticing them.

Your readers won't notice, either. They would more likely notice if you awkwardly shifted a preposition from the end of a sentence to the middle. Or they might get momentarily confused if you make a weak transition by not beginning a sentence with *but.*

So, again, if people tell you that beginning a sentence with *and* or *but* is an error, ask for their rationale. Your rationale is that the rule books encourage it, professional writers do it, it has rhetorical value, and it makes sense. Again, tough arguments to counter.

Myth 3: Never Split an Infinitive

The issue of split infinitives gets murkier than the other two myths. First, though, what is an infinitive? It's the word *to* followed by a verb form:

Infinitives: *to be, to find*

A split infinitive puts a modifier between the word *to* and the verb form:

Split infinitives: *to <u>always</u> be, to <u>never</u> find*

What Errors Do Readers Notice?

From my experience, readers notice typos and other errors that create readability problems. But they seldom notice such supposed "errors" as sentences beginning with *and* or *but*.

They may notice such "errors" when they're *editing* writing or *approving* it but not when they're the intended reader—the person someone's actually writing to. Readers are usually just trying to quickly understand what they're reading.

(By the way, did you notice that this sidebar has a sentence beginning with *but*, a sentence ending with a preposition, and a split infinitive?)

Those sound pretty good, don't they? In fact, English often puts the modifier just before what it modifies. Moving the modifier earlier or later slightly changes the emphasis:

*Un*split infinitives: *<u>always</u> to be, <u>never</u> to find*

Linguists tell us that the source of the myth is the grammarians in the 1700s. The language they learned in school was Latin. So they tried, in codifying English grammar, to impose the structure of Latin onto English—a different language with different origins! In Latin, infinitives are a single word (not the word *to* plus a verb form). So the Latin grammarians tried, with some success, to change English from what it had been (using split infinitives) to something else (not using split infinitives).

This is where the murkiness comes in. Grammar books that are certain prepositions can come at the ends of sentences are mixed about split infinitives. Here's what our 1913 grammar book said:

No modifier should be inserted between *to* and the infinitive.

But Fowler, our standard setter in 1926, didn't agree with that early book. He has a memorable tongue-in-cheek beginning to his discussion:

The English-speaking world may be divided into: (1) those who neither know nor care what a split infinitive is; (2) those who do not know, but care very much; (3) those who know & condemn; (4) those who know & approve; & (5) those who know & distinguish.

Lots of people are in categories 1 and 2 today. The right place, according to Fowler, is category 5: Don't put a lengthy, awkward modifier between *to* and the verb form. In other words, most split infinitives are just fine.

Evans and Evans, who wrote in 1957, agree with Fowler that many split infinitives are all right:

> The notion that it is a grammatical mistake to place a word between *to* and the simple form of a verb, as in *to quietly walk away,* is responsible for a great deal of bad writing by people who are trying to write well. Actually the rule against "splitting an infinitive" contradicts the principles of English grammar and the practice of our best writers.

The best-selling *Elements of Style,* the classic from 1959 by Strunk and White, is interesting on this point. It has a split personality. Strunk was White's professor and taught him in the early 1900s. Even then, about 100 years ago, Strunk grudgingly allowed an occasional split infinitive:

> There is a precedent from the fourteenth century down for interposing an adverb between to and the infinitive it governs, but the construction should be avoided unless the writer wishes to place unusual stress on the adverb.

Now here's the interesting part—and the source of that "split personality": White disagreed with his former teacher. In Strunk's part of the book, White added this note:

> For another side to the split infinitive, see Chapter V, Reminder 14.

Here is what White said there:

> The split infinitive is another trick of rhetoric in which the ear must be quicker than the handbook. Some infinitives seem to improve on being split.

White takes the "grudging" out of Strunk's advice. That's what we would expect from White. He was a writer, and one of the best ever to sit (oops! I mean, "to ever sit") in front of a typewriter.

Harbrace started in the Strunk camp and slowly came around to the White camp. In 1962, it cautioned against the "awkward splitting of infinitives" but didn't give examples of good split infinitives. In 1977, though, it added this comment, supporting split infinitives:

> Splitting an infinitive is often not only natural but desirable:
>> For her to *never* complain seems unreal.
>> I wished to *properly* understand programming.

Again, *Harbrace* is typical of the college grammar books.

What about a little more recent resource on usage, *Webster's Dictionary of English Usage?* As you might expect, it agrees that splitting infinitives isn't an error. It has this great comment on the early usage books:

> Critical opinion as expressed in usage books appears to have settled on a wary compromise. The commentators recognize that there is nothing grammatically wrong with the split infinitive, but they are loath to abandon a subject that is so dear to the public at large. Therefore, they tell us to avoid splitting infinitives except when splitting one improves clarity. Since improved clarity is very often the purpose and result of using a split infinitive, the advice does not amount to much. The upshot is that you can split them when you need to.

Here's the scale again, showing my impression of what today's rule books say about using split infinitives:

And here's what a lot of people think the rule books say:

Off the scale into "Never, never do it!"

So, once again, if people tell you that splitting an infinitive is an error, ask for their rationale. Your rationale is that today's rule books encourage it, professional writers do it, it sounds natural, and it makes sense. Once again, tough arguments to counter.

AVOIDING COMMON GRAMMAR ERRORS

You may think this book has a wildly liberated view of the rules. By no means. My standards are quite conservative: Do what the rule books say and what the professionals do. I've just pointed out that many people haven't read the rule books, and many people haven't noticed what the professionals are actually doing.

This section of the chapter covers three uncontroversial rules. I cover these rules because many people don't know them but need to:

- Keep your lists parallel.
- Make your pronouns agree.
- Avoid comma splices and fused sentences.

Many of your readers in business are aware of these rules, follow them, and will notice if you violate them. That's because, unlike with the myths, violating these rules can cause occasional misreading and confusion.

Is "Between You and I" Correct?

No. Say "between you and me."

The object of a preposition must be in the objective case. The word *me* is the objective form of the pronoun *I*.

Keep Your Lists Parallel

Chapter 4 talked about the value of lists, particularly indented ones, because they show you have more than one of something. When you make a list, you want to be sure each item in it has basically the same structure. The term for having a similar structure is "parallelism."

Is this list parallel?

A typical business report has these preliminary elements:

- a cover page
- a table of contents
- it also has an executive summary

No. The first two bullets are phrases. The last bullet is a complete sentence. Obviously, there are two ways to make the lists parallel: Make them all phrases or make them all sentences. The better, less wordy way is to make them all phrases:

A typical business report has these preliminary elements:

- a cover page
- a table of contents
- an executive summary

  For a quick lesson on this topic, go to http://www.professorbailey.com.

Now the list is parallel. What if the list isn't indented? Does parallelism still matter? Yes—here's an unindented list that lacks parallelism:

A typical business report has these preliminary elements: a cover page, a table of contents, and it also has an executive summary.

There are other ways to have parallelism errors. What if the list has all phrases, but the phrases are different types?

When you put together a table of contents for a business report, allow yourself time for:

- cover page preparation
- organizing a table of contents
- writing an executive summary

Not parallel. Each item in the list is a phrase but there are two different kinds of phrases. The first phrase ("cover page preparation") is a noun phrase; the other two are verb phrases. Normally, verb phrases have a more Plain English tone:

When you put together a table of contents for a business report, allow yourself time for:

- preparing a cover page
- organizing a table of contents
- writing an executive summary

Now the list is parallel with three verb phrases.

You can also violate parallelism if you have different kinds of full sentences:

In putting together a business report, you need to consider these elements:

- Do you need graphics on your cover page?
- Should the table of contents include a brief summary of each section of the report?
- An executive summary will be important to all your readers.

The problem is that two of the items in the list are questions and the last item isn't.

One other consideration is that lists can be parallel and still not be effective. They must follow the lead-in (the sentence before the list). For example, this list is parallel, but it doesn't follow the lead-in:

When you put together a table of contents for a business report, allow yourself time for:

- prepare a cover page
- organize a table of contents
- write an executive summary

You wouldn't say, "Allow yourself time for *prepare* a cover page." You'd say, "Allow yourself time for *preparing* a cover page." So be sure each item in your lists grammatically follows the lead-in, as this list does:

When you put together a table of contents for a business report, allow yourself time for:

- preparing a cover page
- organizing a table of contents
- writing an executive summary

Make Your Pronouns Agree

First, what is a pronoun? It's a word that takes the place of a noun:

antecedent   *pronoun*

Michael is the CEO.   He runs the company.

The noun that the pronoun replaces is its "antecedent." In this case, the pronoun *he* replaces the noun *Michael.* So far, no problem.

The problem occurs when the noun is singular and the pronoun is plural. Suppose, for example, you have 50 investment counselors working for you and want to explain what they do. This sentence has a pronoun agreement error:

antecedent   *pronoun*

An investment counselor works long hours. They
usually leave the company after a few months.

Now the noun (*investment counselor*) is singular, and the pronoun (*They*) is plural. The noun and pronoun don't agree in number.

How can you fix the error? Years ago, people simply used the word *he* in all cases to replace *they*—even though some of those 50 investment counselors were probably female. That solution doesn't work. Instead of changing the *pronoun,* try changing the *noun,* like this:

antecedent   *pronoun*

Investment counselors work long hours. They
usually leave the company after a few months.

Now both the noun (*investment counselors*) and the pronoun (*They*) are plural. They agree.

Sometimes changing the noun to plural doesn't work. You may need to be creative, but try to avoid "he/she" as your solution. It draws attention to itself and distracts the reader.

Avoid Comma Splices and Fused Sentences

This section describes two serious punctuation errors: *comma splices* and *fused sentences.* In fact, probably more students—over the years—have failed freshman composition because of these two errors than for any other reason.

I'm not sure why people consider these errors serious, but few people in business, and few professional writers, ever make them. So let's start with some definitions.

Comma Splice

A comma splice happens when you join two sentences with *only* a comma:

We hiked for two days, we were very tired.
The television is broken, the picture is fuzzy.

You can fix comma splices by changing the comma to almost any other mark of punctuation. In other words, you can change the comma to:

- a colon
- a semicolon
- a dash
- a period

These marks are "terminal" marks of punctuation because they can mark the ends of independent clauses—or "sentences." For instance, the following examples have terminal marks of punctuation between the sentences, so they're correct. They are *not* comma splices:

> We hiked for two days: we were very tired.
>
> We hiked for two days; we were very tired.
>
> We hiked for two days—we were very tired.
>
> We hiked for two days. We were very tired.

There's one other fix you need to know. Instead of changing the faulty comma to another mark of punctuation, you can simply add a word like *and* after it. Here, then, is a correct sentence—not a comma splice:

> We hiked for two days, *and* we were very tired.

Remove the word *and,* and you're back to a comma splice.

Words like *and* are "coordinating conjunctions." You'll simplify punctuation for the rest of your life if you take about two minutes to memorize the following complete list. I don't make this suggestion lightly—you simply cannot learn punctuation without knowing the coordinating conjunctions:

> *and   but   or   nor   for   so   yet*

Here are some tips to help you memorize them: Notice that there are only seven coordinating conjunctions, that none is longer than three letters, and that three of them rhyme (*or, nor, for*).

Fused Sentence

A fused sentence is simply a comma splice without the comma:

> We hiked for two days we were very tired.
>
> The television is broken the picture is fuzzy.

You fix fused sentences the same way you fix comma splices—by putting in some terminal punctuation (colon, semicolon, dash, period) or by adding a comma and a coordinating conjunction (like *and* or *but*).

A Little Complexity . . .

Let me explain the problem—the added complexity—involving comma splices and fused sentences. As I mentioned previously, this sentence is correct because it has a word like *and* after the comma separating the two sentences:

> We hiked for two days, so we were very tired.

Unfortunately, the next sentence is *not* correct because it has a different kind of conjunction after the comma:

> We hiked for two days, *therefore* we were very tired.

The word *therefore* is not a coordinating conjunction; instead, it's a "conjunctive adverb" (stay with me now).

When a conjunctive adverb (like *therefore*) begins a sentence, it needs some sort of terminal punctuation before it (colon, semicolon, dash, etc.). Commonly, you would find a semicolon or a period there. So both of these sentences are correct:

> We hiked for two days; therefore, we were very tired.
> We hiked for two days. Therefore, we were very tired.

But just a comma before the word *therefore* would be incorrect—a comma splice.

One word of caution: Sometimes these conjunctive adverbs can slip to the *middle* or *end* of a sentence; in those cases, the terminal mark of punctuation still comes between the two sentences—not immediately in front of the conjunctive adverb. Here are two correct sentences with the conjunctive adverb later in the second sentence:

> We hiked for two days; we were, *therefore,* very tired.
> We hiked for two days. We were, *therefore,* very tired.

Now for a little test. Does this sentence have correct punctuation?

> We hiked for two days, we were, therefore, very tired.

No. It's a comma splice. You can make the sentence correct by simply changing the first comma to a period or a semicolon.

You already have the complete list of *coordinating conjunctions* (remember: "*and, but, or, . . .*")? The complete list of *conjunctive adverbs* would be too long. But here's a list of the most common ones. I suggest you memorize the three really common ones (in italic type):

accordingly	*however*	nevertheless
as a result	indeed	next
consequently	in fact	otherwise
first	instead	still
for example	likewise	*therefore*
furthermore	moreover	unfortunately

These are the words that most often lure people into comma splices.

The only way you can solve the problem of comma splices and fused sentences is with a little bit of work. Half an hour? Maybe even an hour? But the result will be the end of a problem that, all too often, brands people as uneducated. In school or in business, that's not how you want people to know you.

EXERCISES

A. Look for sentences beginning with *and* or *but* in these sources and report to the class what you find:
   - the editorial page of a newspaper
   - the cover article in a business magazine
   - a journal or professional magazine from your field
   - the top 10 books on the nonfiction best-seller list

B. Look up the three myths this chapter covers in a grammar handbook. Report to the class what you find. Bring your grammar handbook to class. If everybody in class uses the same handbook, bring another one, too. You might bring your handbook from high school or work. Or bring a friend's handbook. Or find one in the library that this chapter refers to, such as H. W. Fowler's *A Dictionary of Modern English Usage,* William Strunk and E. B. White's *Elements of Style,* or *Webster's Dictionary of English Usage* (newer title: *Merriam-Webster's Dictionary of English Usage*).

C. How would you fix the pronoun agreement errors in these sentences?
   1. I know everyone has some interest in how much money they are receiving.
   2. I have to send my plans to the customer for their approval.
   3. A customer calls to report one of their computer systems is down.
   4. The Smithsonian wanted an interactive exhibit. They had the artifacts, but they didn't know how to display them.

D. Which sentences are comma splices and fused sentences? Identify each sentence that is wrong—and then fix the punctuation.
   1. The book was good, I was sleepy.
   2. The book was good, but I was sleepy.
   3. The book was good, unfortunately, I was sleepy.
   4. Even though the story was supposed to be a thriller, I couldn't stay awake.
   5. The waves lapped at the hull of the boat, and the fishing line dangled over the water.
   6. The decorations are up Halloween must be getting close.
   7. The decorations are up; Halloween must be getting close.
   8. The decorations are up, Halloween must be getting close.
   9. The decorations are up. Halloween must be getting close.
   10. The decorations are up: Halloween must be getting close.
   11. The rattlesnake frightened most people, nevertheless, it was only a baby snake.
   12. When we looked for the anchovies on our pizza, we discovered the cat had eaten them.
   13. We looked for the anchovies on our pizza, but we discovered the cat had eaten them.
   14. We looked for the anchovies on our pizza, we discovered the cat had eaten them.
   15. The copying machine will produce 30 copies a minute, moreover, it will enlarge or reduce the copies.

CHAPTER 9

Making the Most of E-mail

*Craft your e-mail with your readers in mind. Once you press "send,"
the world has a record of what you sent!*

Though e-mail sometimes comes across as light and breezy, it's serious business for most organizations. I interviewed a number of experienced professionals in business and asked what tips they have for people sending e-mail. The answers were very consistent. Here's what they suggested:

- Be brief.
- Be careful with your tone.
- Remember you're creating a public document.
- Watch your spelling and grammar.

BE BRIEF

One person I interviewed told me, "I shudder every time I get new e-mail messages from a certain person. They go on and on. . . ." Too many offices have people who get on that keyboard and pour out everything on their mind (in the order they think it!).

One of the biggest problems we all face today is information overload. When I speak to business audiences, I often ask, "How many e-mail messages do you get every day? A lot, right?" And I see heads nodding up and down. So just because e-mail is easy to send, don't become your office's problem e-mailer.

Being brief doesn't mean being blunt, of course. Nor does it mean omitting important information. But you don't want to get the reputation as a primary cause of information overload. Here are some things you can do:

- *Use Plain English.* Almost everybody today using e-mail writes in Plain English—even if they wouldn't consider using it for something on paper. Pronouns, contractions, ordinary words—everything from Chapter 2—are fully appropriate in e-mail (and on paper, too, of course). I've been in some of the biggest bureaucracies in the world. Even there, most bureaucrats are writing their e-mail in Plain English. Don't hesitate to use Plain English in the e-mail you write.

- *Use an informative subject line.* As I showed in Chapter 5, you should try to get your message across in the subject line whenever possible: "Meeting for security representatives" is better than "Outdated directives" if your goal is to get someone to attend a meeting.

From: Fred Brown   Sent: Thu 7/27/2008 7:50 AM
To: Janice Robinson
Cc:
Subject: May I come early?

Janice,

I'd like to show up a little early in order to get my computer
presentation set up. How about 8:30? Can you meet me
then?

See you Wednesday!

Fred

FIGURE 9.1 Brief, Efficient E-mail

- *Start with your main point.* More people probably read the first sentence in any document than any other. So think as you write, "If there were only one sentence I could send, what would it be?" Then start your e-mail with that sentence. I guarantee that your readers will be appreciative. Figure 9.1 does a good job of getting to the point in the first sentence.

Use Normal Typography

I'M NOT SURE WHY SOME WRITERS USE ALL UPPERCASE LETTERS IN THEIR E-MAIL. PEOPLE I INTERVIEWED HATE THAT—THEY SAY IT SEEMS AS THOUGH THE WRITER IS SHOUTING AT THEM.

other writers use all lowercase letters when they write. again, the people i interviewed said that comes across to them as unprofessional and sloppy.

- *Use bullets.* If bullets are helpful on paper, they're doubly so for e-mail. You can't always be sure that the bullet symbols and spacing will translate perfectly to your reader's system, but even if the bullets look like they were done on a 1950s typewriter, they'll be better than lengthy paragraphs.

- *Send more than one e-mail for unrelated points.* If you have several unrelated points, consider sending an e-mail for each one. Readers may not get all the way through a longer e-mail before they hit that delete key, so if your points are important, separate e-mails will stay within your reader's attention span. Be reasonable with this approach, of course—find the proper balance between a long e-mail and too many e-mail messages.

- *Consider numbering paragraphs for related points.* Sometimes you have more than one related point to make in your e-mail. Readers of e-mail, often prone to skim and perhaps unable to see your whole document at once on the screen, may

```
From:    Fred Brown              Sent: Thu 7/27/2008 7:50 AM
To:      Janice Robinson
Cc:
Subject: Thoughts on Fred Robinson's visit

Janice,

I have two thoughts about our meeting with Fred:

1. I recommend we invite the president and the entire HR
staff. The issue Fred will be covering is going to hit us for
sure, maybe not this week but certainly during the next few
months.

2. We should let Fred know we want his help for the next few
weeks at least. Can we get on his calendar right away? Can
you arrange the contracting?

Thanks!

John
```

FIGURE 9.2 Multipurpose E-mail with Numbered Paragraphs

miss your later points. One way to handle that situation is to open the e-mail by telling your reader how many points you have—and then numbering the points within the e-mail (see Fig. 9.2).

- *Also consider using headings for related points.* Readers appreciate seeing the labels for the parts of a document, so even for a moderately short e-mail, headings will show your readers that you have several related points to cover (see Fig. 9.3).

- *Use attachments for longer documents.* If you're sending out something that's long, your readers may print it out first. By making it an attachment, you can use all the nice layout features of your word processing program (bold, italic, variety of type-faces) that your reader's e-mail system may not have. But readers don't routinely like to click on attachments, so use this technique mainly for longer documents.

- *Disseminate lengthy documents online.* If you or your company have a Web site, consider sending people there for lengthy documents or for documents that re-quire frequent updating. That way, a simple link—rather than an e-mail with an attachment—gets the document for them.

BE CAREFUL WITH YOUR TONE

I first used e-mail in the mid-1980s—well before most people had heard of it. I was cor-responding from Washington, D.C., to some computer experts in England. I'd never met them in person. I'd always make my messages perfectly efficient: right to the point, no extra words, good-bye!

From: Fred Brown   Sent: Thu 7/27/2008 7:50 AM
To: Janice Robinson
Cc:
Subject: Thoughts on Fred Robinson s visit

Janice,

I have two thoughts about our meeting with Fred:

Who to invite
I recommend we invite the president and the entire HR staff.
The issue Fred will be covering is going to hit us for sure,
maybe not this week but certainly during the next few
months.

Future help from Fred
We should let Fred know we want his help for the next few
weeks at least. Can we get on his calendar right away? Can
you arrange the contracting?

Thanks!

John

FIGURE 9.3 Multipurpose E-mail with Headings

The people in England, however, always began with something personal: "How was your weekend, Ed? Did you go to the game?" Then they'd get to business. I realized they were right. By setting a friendly tone, they made me more willing to work with them on whatever our business was at the time.

Use a Businesslike E-mail Address

An e-mail address that may be cute or creative to an undergraduate may seem odd or worse in a business situation. So if you have a need to use your personal e-mail address to correspond with someone in business, you might want to avoid such addresses as "skullkid," "occultwizard," and "foxybabe," . . . or worse!

P.S. I didn't make those up.

You don't need to talk about weekends in every e-mail, of course. We don't have the time. But getting the atmosphere right in e-mail is as important as the friendly chatter that often takes place before important business meetings.

There's a second reason that tone is important in e-mail. Often we think of e-mail as a replacement for written documents, like memos and letters. It certainly does that. But it has also replaced many phone calls. With phone calls, your voice helps set the tone. Your voice, of course, has inflections and pauses that may be a crucial part of your message. That's one reason why e-mail has adopted not just conventions of writing but also conventions of speaking—such as exclamation points and a little friendly chatter. So when you set the tone for your e-mail, you have to decide not just what looks like good writing but also what sounds like you—when talking to that person.

S. I. Hayakawa, a well-known linguist in the middle of the twentieth century, had a term for language that isn't intended to carry substantive meaning: "polite noise." When we greet someone by saying, for example, "How are you doing?" we don't expect all the details. By asking, we're simply expressing a friendly attitude toward that person. That person normally expresses a friendly attitude back by saying something like, "Not bad—how about you?"

Polite noise doesn't have a place in all conversations, but it does have a place in some of them. Similarly, polite noise has a place in some but not all e-mail messages. Most of us can figure out when.

Another point on tone involves the salutation. Should you always have a salutation (such as "Fred" or "Dear Jennifer") before the body of your e-mail? The people I interviewed said you usually should. It's all too easy to reply to an e-mail with only the body of the response: "Thanks—see you then." We see that all the time. But some of the people I interviewed felt that leaving off the salutation gives an unnecessary brusqueness and impersonal nature to the message. My recommendation is to use a salutation all the time.

I also recommend you put your name at the end of your e-mail. That helps set a good tone—rather then ending brusquely. And if your e-mail address isn't informative, readers may not know who sent it. How often have you received an e-mail from something like greatgolfer@fairways.com and wondered who in the world that was?

Can Your Tone Be Too Familiar?

You bet! The test is whether or not you would say something face-to-face (or on the phone) with someone. Don't make your e-mail more familiar in tone than your talking would be.

One way we're seeing people vary their tone is by varying the salutation. A half-century ago, letters all started with "Dear Sir." E-mail can quite correctly begin with "Hi, Brent" or "Good morning, Paige." Each of those sets a different tone: "Hi, Brent" shows familiarity with the reader—consider it for people you're familiar with and like. "Good morning, Paige" is more friendly than "Dear Paige." But if you're not on a first-name basis, "Dear Ms. Bundon" or "Good morning, Ms. Bundon" would be more appropriate.

REMEMBER YOU'RE CREATING A PUBLIC DOCUMENT

So far, I've mainly talked about avoiding an unintentionally blunt or unfriendly tone. But a bigger problem, according to the people I interviewed, is coming across, probably intentionally, as angry or sarcastic in e-mail.

Sometimes it's legitimate to express anger in writing. But here's a test that angry e-mail should pass before you send it in a business situation:

- Would you say it to your reader's face?
- Would you say it to that person with the person's boss standing next to you? With your boss standing next to you? With the company president and human resource director standing next to you?

If not, you'd probably better not send it—because all those people may very well see it.

So here's good advice: Write as though your entire company is reading your e-mail.

That nasty e-mail you just sent can be useful evidence against you. It's a public document that's now completely out of your control. Your reader can forward it to anybody—and probably will. You don't want your e-mail to be the cause of a lost reputation, a special counseling session, or even legal troubles. Nor do you want it to be the cause of legal troubles for your company.

WATCH YOUR SPELLING AND GRAMMAR

As a professor of business communication, I'm pleased by the writing most of my students hand in and disappointed by the illiterate e-mail a handful of them send me. Their grammatical errors, misspelled words, typos, and general incoherence are part of their message as far as I'm concerned.

This isn't just a problem with students. The business people I interviewed about e-mail all share my concern that too many e-mail messages come across as illiterate or sloppy.

  For a quick lesson on this topic, go to http://www.professorbailey.com.

Remember that people reading your products—e-mail, letters, reports—are constantly developing opinions about your capability. So don't be like Billy Irving in Figure 9.4.

FIGURE 9.4 Too Common—Lots of Errors!

```
From:    Billy Irving              Sent: Thu 7/27/2008 3:25 PM
To:      Sally Lawrence
Cc:
Subject: My job applicatoin

Ms. Lawreance
I sent my resumme to your last week did you recieve it?
Thank you for your atention, I hope to be hearing form you
soon.
Billy
```

Do you think Billy's going to get the job?

You can solve most of these problems by proofreading everything you send. I always proofread my drafts. If you haven't been doing that, you'll probably be surprised by what you've been sending!

EXERCISES

A. Find an e-mail you like because it has a good tone. Attach that e-mail to one you write to your instructor explaining what you like about the one you found.

B. Find an e-mail you like because it's well written. Attach that e-mail to one you write to your instructor explaining what you like about the one you found.

C. Write an e-mail to your instructor that tells what you especially like and don't like about the e-mail you receive. Your e-mail should be the equivalent of a one- to two-page paper. Be sure to use good layout.

CHAPTER 10

Writing for the Web

Web surfers want information fast!

The most important advice for writing for the Web, of course, is to use Plain English—to use all the things you've read about so far in the book. In fact, if you don't use Plain English, who wants to look at your site?

However, Web pages, because of their special nature, have special requirements as well. There's no absolute standard for what Web pages should look like or how you should write for them—the Web is too varied. That's one of the main reasons for its appeal.

But there are some things you should consider whenever you're writing for the Web. Not all of them apply all of the time. But they do apply most of the time.

Here's what this chapter covers:

- Understand how viewers look at Web pages.
- Don't write what viewers won't read.
- Write in chunks.
- Make your home page user-friendly.
- Make your content pages efficient.
- Make good design choices.

UNDERSTAND HOW VIEWERS LOOK AT WEB PAGES

Have you ever watched people surf the Web? Click! Click! Click! Even the gentlest soul seems to turn into an impatient, mouse-clicking speed demon when looking at that monitor!

But do you think that's what viewers do all the time? I don't think so.

Let's consider an example. Suppose you want to buy a new car, and you're pretty sure of the model you want. So you go to the Web to look for a review.

When you get to an appropriate site, you'll probably look quickly for a link that takes you to new cars. You don't care about anything else on that page—the words, the color, the images are a blur. You just want to find that link! Right?

Once you find a link that might work, you'll probably click on it. What then? You're looking for another link, aren't you? You'll keep speeding through the site until you find a page reviewing the model car you want.

When you find the page with the review, will you still be hurrying? Probably not. If you're like me, you'll slow down and read that page carefully—maybe every sentence, maybe every table, fact, and illustration.

So what does all that mean for writing for the Web? Well, there are two kinds of pages:

- *Navigation pages.* Navigation pages take you to the place you want to go. They don't usually have a lot of content. For example, home pages are usually navigation pages. When viewers visit home pages, they're usually looking for a link to go someplace else on the site. So home pages—like all navigation pages—should be as brief, as efficient, and as uncluttered as possible.
- *Content pages.* A content page is your destination. It can have a lot of information—including paragraph after paragraph of text—and still be efficient.

When you write for the Web:

- You want your navigation pages to be as brief as possible.
- You want the *structure* of your content pages to be absolutely clear to your viewers. Structure is particularly important because content pages may have a lot on them. You don't want your viewers to get lost or confused as they scroll down them.

DON'T WRITE WHAT VIEWERS WON'T READ

Steve Krug, in an excellent book on Web usability, uses the term *happy talk*. Happy talk is the writing on a site that people don't read. Krug says it "must die."

Here's how he says you can identify happy talk:

> If you're not sure whether something is happy talk, there's one sure-fire test: if you listen very closely while you're reading it, you can hear a tiny voice in the back of your head saying, "Blah blah blah blah blah. . . . "[1]

We've all seen happy talk, haven't we? *Seen* it but not read it. Look especially for happy talk on your navigation pages, the pages viewers are speeding through. For example, how likely is it that viewers are going to study the corporate vision statement on a home page? Delete it!

Ruthlessly edit *all* text.

WRITE IN CHUNKS

If you're about to write a book about the Civil War, you'd organize it so your readers would start on page 1 and then read page 2 and so on to the end. In fact, you'd expect most of your readers to go through it that way.

But if you created a Web site covering the same material, you'd organize it differently, wouldn't you? You'd plan for much smaller chunks (who'd go though Chapter 1 on the

---

[1]Steve Krug, *Don't Make Me Think* (Indianapolis: New Riders, 2000), p. 46.

Web if it's 20 pages long?); you'd have links for some of the people's names (click on Stonewall Jackson and get a brief bio); you'd have places to pull up maps, such as the Battle of Gettysburg.

Let's suppose instead of a book on the Civil War you're writing a long business report on paper. Once again, you'd want to organize it as logically as possible—so your readers could go through it, page after page, in order. But if you were writing that same report for viewing on the Web, would it have the same structure?

Of course not. You'd want to have a home page for your Web report with links to the chapters and various other parts. For example, you'd have a link to your executive summary, a link to your recommendations and conclusions, a link to your methodology, and so forth.

You'd want to organize your chapters within that report differently, too. You'd probably begin each chapter with a summary and then have links to the chapter's various parts. That way, you wouldn't have any part of your Web report that was excessively long. And you'd probably want to have links for any unfamiliar terminology (click on electronic data interchange and find out what it means).

MAKE YOUR HOME PAGE USER-FRIENDLY

The home page is usually the first one your viewers see. It's typically a navigation page, so it should be as brief and efficient as possible.

 For a quick lesson on this topic, go to http://www.professorbailey.com.

Several things go on home pages that I won't cover yet—site name, buttons, and so forth. As far as the writing goes, though, here are my suggestions:

- *Don't have anything unnecessary on your home page.* Most viewers will never even see the non-essential stuff. So why add clutter? For example, a home page should rarely have a company's vision statement, biographies of the company's officers, or a letter from the chairman to the shareholders. If those need to be on the site at all, put them elsewhere!

- *Start with your site's purpose.* Let your viewers know why your site exists—and be brief. For example, what could the purpose statement be for a site that helps people learn about cars? Here's the purpose statement from Edmunds.com:

    Edmunds.com provides True Market Value® pricing, unbiased car reviews, ratings, and expert advice to help you get a fair deal.

    Clear and to the point, isn't it?

- *Include a prominent table of contents.* Your buttons and other links, of course, serve as your table of contents. Sometimes, though, home pages have a lot of various buttons and links. The trick is to be sure that the main sections of your site are the most prominent ones. Let's consider an example. Figure 10.1 is a simplified home page on a topic you're already familiar with (layout)—notice the purpose statement in the first sentence and the table of contents in the links near the top of the page.

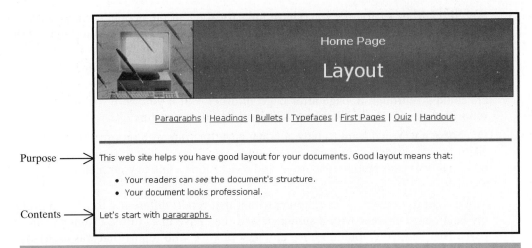

Purpose —→

Contents —→

FIGURE 10.1 Example of a Good Simplified Home Page

MAKE YOUR CONTENT PAGES EFFICIENT

Your viewers may need to step down through a series of navigation pages before they get to the content page they're after. All of those navigation pages need to be efficient, keeping in mind the principle of "less is more."

Once your viewers get to the content page they're after, what should it look like? Well, the amount of material on content pages can vary hugely. Let's suppose you'll have a fair amount of text for your viewers to go through. How should you write a content page like that? Here are my suggestions:

- *Start with the page's purpose or bottom line.* Look at Figure 10.2 — a sample good content page.
- *Give a blueprint for the page.* It's a good idea to have a blueprint on your content page, especially if the page is long. A blueprint, you'll remember from an earlier chapter, simply lists the main sections coming up in a document — serving as a "table of contents." If a blueprint is useful for a printed document, it's especially useful for long Web pages. That's because viewers can see only a part of a long Web page at a time — they have to scroll to see more. So if a Web page starts with a blueprint, viewers can have the page's structure in mind as they scroll down it. That can help keep them from getting lost. Figure 10.2 includes a blueprint.
- *Use headings that match that list exactly.* When you have a blueprint, you want to have a heading for each blueprint item. It's important that the words in the blueprint are identical to the words in the headings. In other words, don't have a *blueprint item* that says "Interior design" and a *heading* that says "What's inside." Figure 10.2 shows headings that match the blueprint exactly.

If you use this structure, your content pages will be "skimmable." Then when viewers are in a hurry, they can skim to find the information they want. Notice in particular how "skimmable" Figure 10.2 is.

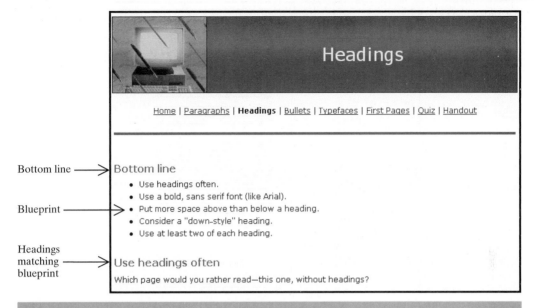

Bottom line ⟶

Blueprint ⟶

Headings
matching ⟶
blueprint

FIGURE 10.2 Beginning of a Good Content Page

If you scroll down on that Web page (see Fig. 10.3 for the next part of Fig. 10.2), you'll see that it does another good thing: It uses illustrations rather than just text to make its point!

Content pages usually benefit from illustrations.

MAKE GOOD DESIGN CHOICES

Standards are evolving on the Web. However, here are some pretty standard choices:

- *Font.* The most common fonts for the Web are Verdana and Georgia:

This is Verdana   This is Georgia

  They're common because they were specifically designed to be readable on Web pages. Notice that Verdana is sans serif; Georgia has serifs. In the chapter on lay-out, I recommended a serifed font (Times New Roman) for body text. Does that mean you should use the serifed font (Georgia) for body text on Web pages? No. Actually, the sans serif font (Verdana) is probably more common for body text. That's because we usually look at Web pages on monitors—which don't have the same resolution as printed type. So the serifs for a font like Georgia tend to add clutter. That said, both fonts are okay. You'll see many professional sites using Verdana and many others using Georgia. Can you use Times New Roman and Arial—common fonts for printed material? Sure, they're good, too.

- *Type size.* There's no standard type size because there's no standard way to view a Web page: What size is your viewer's monitor? What's the setting for the

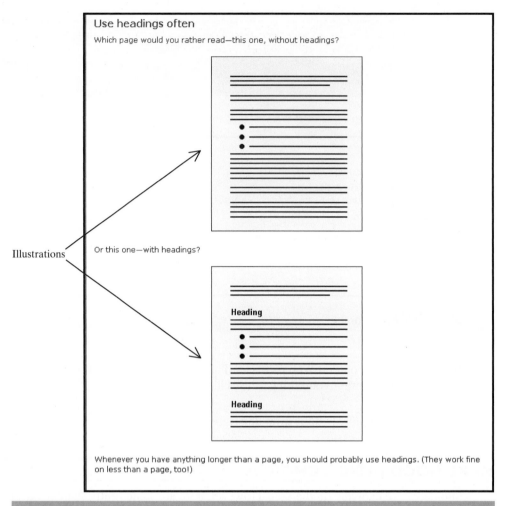

FIGURE 10.3   Example of Content Page with Illustrations

monitor's resolution? You get the idea. However, the convention is to use a relatively small type size. A large size means fewer words per line, causing unnecessary scrolling. Try 10-point Verdana or 12-point Georgia for body text. They have about the same apparent size.

Note: Web designers don't always use point size to designate type size on Web pages. However, my recommendations give you an idea of what works.

- *Colors.* There are lots of wonderful ways to use colors. Amateurs run into problems by using too many colors and by using color combinations that don't work together. By far the most common background color for a Web page is white. The most common type color is black. Reserve blue type for links. If you follow those conventions, you still have lots of elbow room for using the colors of your choice elsewhere on the page.

- *Naming.* Suppose the name on a link is "New Cars"—but the page it takes you to has the title "This year's automobiles." We know they mean the same thing, but most viewers will pause, won't they? So be sure the name of your link matches the name on the page. If the link is "New Cars," the page title should also be "New Cars."
- *Links.* Here are some conventions:
  - Use a consistent design. Keep the same relative design on all of your pages, including color scheme, font choices, and placement. You want your viewers to feel they're still on your site when they go to a new page.
  - Don't put a home page link on the home page. This is a very strong convention (though I'm not sure it's entirely "user-friendly"). Suppose your site has a home page and two content pages. Here's what the links would look like on your home page:

    <u>New Cars</u> | <u>Used Cars</u>

    The design of your home page should make it clear to your viewers that that's the page they're on.
  - Do put a home page link on all of your content pages. So the links for your first content page ("New Cars") would look like this:

    <u>Home</u> | New Cars | <u>Used Cars</u>

    And the links for the other content page ("Used Cars") would look like this:

    <u>Home</u> | <u>New Cars</u> | Used Cars
  - Differentiate the link for the content page we're on. See the link for the "Used Cars" page? There's no underline for the words "Used Cars." That differentiates it from the other links and serves as a "you are here" sign to the viewers. It tells them that they're already on the "Used Cars" page.
  - Keep your links in the same order on all of your pages. In other words, don't put "New Cars" as the first link on the "New Cars" page and "Used Cars" as the first link on the "Used Cars" page. You'll just confuse your viewers.

EXERCISE

Create a simple Web site (a home page and two content pages is fine) that tells the class about two things you like. Do you like cats and soccer? Have a home page and then a page about cats and a page about soccer.

If you know how to publish your site, do so. If you don't, then simply create a "paper" site—a page or so for each of your site's pages.

Be sure to follow *all* of the advice in this chapter. And keep your content pages relatively brief (two or three screens is fine). Be sure to illustrate your content pages.

Note: Think of this as a *business* Web site. So don't go crazy with clip art, fonts, colors, and such. Think of a business person looking at a printout of your site. Then be sure that printout would look businesslike. That doesn't mean your site can't be interesting, fascinating, informative. It should be. But it shouldn't look amateurish.

CHAPTER 11

Preparing a Résumé and Cover Letter

Use Plain English for your résumé, too.

ow do you get a job? There are many ways, but—as you might suspect—the best way is to know someone in the company you're applying to!

In fact, Dr. Heidi Golding has done some interesting research in this area. After looking at a relatively small sample of companies, she found that people who know someone in the company ("networking") have a far greater chance of getting hired than people who go through the help wanted ads:

> Whereas applicants recruited through advertising comprise the largest share of applications, only 5.7% of [them] . . . receive job offers. Networks are much more effective with 22.1% of applicants . . . offered a job.[1]

But whatever route you take, you're almost certainly going to have to prepare a résumé and a cover letter. If they're unimpressive, you'll probably be in the 94.3% of unsuccessful applicants using the help wanted ads or in the 77.9% of unsuccessful applicants who knew someone in the company!

So for many students, the first piece of business writing they do is also among the most important—a résumé with a cover letter when applying for a job:

- A *résumé* is simply a page or two summarizing your qualifications for a job. Most résumés today are about a page and a half. Few meet the old convention of a single page.
- A *cover letter* is the letter that you send with your résumé. It explains what job you're applying for and highlights your key qualifications. It should set a professional tone without sounding stiff.

Everything you've learned so far in this book will help you. As you write these important documents, you'll want them to have:

- a style that's easy to read
- a serious tone

---

[1]Heidi Lynn Wiedenman Golding, "Employer Search and the Quest for Information: An Analysis of the Consequences of Employer Search Techniques," Ph.D. diss., University of Maryland at College Park, 1996.

- an inviting layout
- examples that show how good you are
- key information up front
- punctuation and grammar that are correct and help highlight your most important information

In other words, they should use Plain English!

Although a résumé and cover letter don't usually get you the job all by themselves, they're important for getting you an interview—getting you past the initial reviewer, through the door, and face-to-face with the decision makers. This chapter shows you how to give yourself your best chance to get through that door—and then what to do!

We'll look at:

- preparing a résumé
- preparing a cover letter

PREPARING A RÉSUMÉ

Figure 11.1 is a sample résumé—notice that it's in Plain English.

This example is a *chronological* résumé, one of two main types (the other type is *functional*).

To tell if a résumé is chronological or not, look at the Employment section. If it lists people's jobs by job title and dates, then it's a chronological résumé. Just to keep life from being too simple, a chronological résumé is almost always in *reverse chronological order*. That is, the most recent job comes first, then the next most recent, and so on. Notice that in our sample, the internship ended in 2007 but the computer lab assistant job didn't end until a year later. That's why the computer lab assistant job comes first on the résumé—it's more recent.

Next look at Figure 11.2. It's an example of a functional résumé.

Notice that the functional résumé doesn't show what jobs the person held—only what functions (or skills) the person can perform (database development, other computer experience). Theoretically, a functional résumé lets reviewers quickly see if you have the necessary skills to do the job. That is, if reviewers need somebody to do certain functions, a functional résumé highlights them.

In practice, the great majority of résumé are chronological rather than functional. That's because reviewers are often suspicious that a functional résumé is hiding something. Because there's no chronology, reviewers can't tell exactly what you've been doing.

For example:

- Been in jail doing 5–10 for breaking and entering? Choose a functional résumé. You can hide the jail time because there's no chronology showing where you were when.
- Gotten fired twice? A functional résumé doesn't give chronology, so reviewers won't be able to tell from it where you worked.

FIGURE 11.1 Chronological Résumé

- Never held a job longer than a month? The functional résumé is for you. It doesn't show how long you held each job. Reviewers have to wait for your job application to get all the details you tried so hard to hide.

See the problem? Even if you have an unblemished record with outstanding jobs, the functional résumé doesn't easily show that. Because it doesn't, reviewers are often naturally suspicious.

Jerome K. Pinon

222 Tumbleweed Road
Sandstone, CO 33333
jerome@sandstone.edu
(719) 444-4444

Objective   Database developer (working with Microsoft Access)

Education   *Student, University of Sandstone*
I expect to graduate at the end of May with a B.S. in Information
Technology. I have 36 credit hours in my major, including courses in:

- Database Design
- Database Administration
- Systems Design

I received a grade of A in each of those courses.
Overall GPA: 3.46/4.00 Major GPA: 3.78/4.00

Database   Databases: Excellent knowledge of Microsoft Access
Development   Languages: Good knowledge of Visual Basic and C++

I have experience with the entire development process. During a
summer internship I worked as part of a development team building
forms and reports to support the new marketing division. I learned
how a development team functions in the corporate world while
handling a complex project.

I also have experience working individually. During the same
internship, I programmed a prototype database showing sales
information. I was the only intern out of six allowed to have my own
project. As a result of my internship and courses at the university,
I have an excellent command of Microsoft Access.

Other   I also have good experience with computers. I gained practical
Computer   knowledge of computers by working 20 hours a week setting up
Experience   computers, updating them, and handling questions from students
and faculty. I learned the value of patience in getting everything just
right. As a result, the lab director chose me to train new assistants.

Strengths   I think of myself as a problem solver—which is why database
development appeals to me. I enjoy discovering a creative approach
and working on it until I succeed.

*headings reflect
job functions or
skills you have*

FIGURE 11.2   Functional Résumé

There is a solution, though: the combination functional and chronological résumé. Simply use a functional résumé and then include another section — Employment — giving brief information about where you worked and what dates. Here's a sample entry:

Employment   Computer Lab Assistant, University of Sandstone (2007–2008)

Internship: Assistant Database Programmer, Data Resources, Inc. (Summer 2007)

So is there a good reason to use a purely functional résumé? Perhaps (occasionally) for an entry level job if skills are particularly important. How about a combination functional and chronological résumé? More often — but still probably sparingly.

In other words, choose a chronological résumé, like the great majority of applicants, unless you have a strong reason not to. Most reviewers prefer it. That's why the rest of this chapter concentrates on the chronological résumé.

Complete Sentences Versus Action Verbs

For many years, the standard for résumés was to begin with verbs, leaving out the subjects. For example, instead of saying, "I expect to graduate at the end of May," the old standard was to say, "Graduate at the end of May."

The idea was that beginning with verbs — especially action verbs like *earned* and *selected* — made the writer sound more achievement oriented. Leaving out the subjects also cut down on the number of words. I recommend skipping the action verbs and writing full sentences — just the way we talk. That way, your writing won't sound unnatural and occasionally cause misreading.

Information Almost Every Résumé Should Have

There are many options for what to put in a résumé, but there are some requirements, too.

Information to identify you

Obviously, you want reviewers to know your name and how to get hold of you to arrange for that interview. Your identifying information almost always goes at the top of the page.

Hints:

- Put your name in the largest, boldest type on the page.
- Be sure to separate your identifying information from the rest of the résumé, either with white space (as in Fig. 11.3) or a line across the page (as in Figs. 11.1 and 11.2).
- Make your identifying information symmetrical with the rest of the information on the page — normally by centering it beneath your name. In Figure 11.3, there are two addresses, so one goes on each side of the page.
- Normally give your e-mail address and phone number as part of your identifying information.

Jerome K. Pinon

until May 31
222 Tumbleweed Road
Sandstone, CO 33333
jerome@sandstone.edu
(719) 444-4444

after May 31
55 Gila Bend St.
Dry Mesa, CO 66666
jerome@drymesa.com
(719) 777-7777

Objective

Database developer (working with Microsoft Access)

Education

Student, University of Sandstone
I expect to graduate at the end of May with a B.S. in Information Technology. I have 36 credit hours in my major, including courses in:

- Database Design
- Database Administration
- Systems Design

I received a grade of A in each of those courses.
Overall GPA: 3.46/4.00 Major GPA: 3.78/4.00

Computer

Databases: Excellent knowledge of Microsoft Access
Languages: Good knowledge of Visual Basic and C++

Employment

Computer Lab Assistant, University of Sandstone (2007–08)
I gained practical knowledge of computers by working 20 hours a week setting up computers, updating them, and handling questions from students and faculty. I learned the value of patience in getting everything just right. As a result, the lab director chose me to train new assistants.

FIGURE 11.3   Another Attractive Format (First Page)

Objective

An objective isn't really required information, but it's so common it's almost standard. It should come right after your identifying information.

Notice the objective in Figure 11.1: "Database developer (working with Microsoft Access)." If Jerome has his heart set on being a database developer, then he has a good objective: It's clear, specific, believable.

But he'd better not be looking for any other position, because companies will probably exclude her.

What about a more general objective: "A responsible position using my background in information technology"? That's all right. It alerts reviewers to the category of work you're interested in.

What if your real objective is "Any job, please, any job—I need the money" and you don't want an objective to be specific at all? Just leave the objective off. Several reviewers tell me they skip reading objectives entirely because they're usually generic or artificial.

So don't be too generic. And don't set an artificial tone by saying something like this: "A position that will take advantage of my talent as a quick learner." That gets the résumé off to a poor start.

Education

This normally comes right after your objective, if you have one. Sometimes your education is key: If you don't have the right degree, reviewers have no need to read further. They're simply not going to offer you an interview.

Other times, education isn't nearly as important as your experience. Even in that case, you normally want to have your education before your experience. The reason? Education usually takes only a little space to dispose of, and it's almost always of some interest to the reviewer.

No Typos!

Reviewers time and again tell me they're shocked at how often résumés have typos, obvious misspellings, and grammatical errors. Those résumés are going to end up in the wrong pile!

Figure 11.1 shows how to handle the Education section for people who are students. But what if you have a degree or two? Then start with your highest degree. Here's an example:

Education M.B.A., Accounting and Finance (2008)

B.B.A., Accounting (2005)

Sometimes a simple list of your degrees is all you need. But be sure to elaborate on anything that might help your cause.

Hints:

- Give your overall grade point average if it's good; give the GPA for your major if it's good. Otherwise, leave both out. The major GPA may be especially important for some jobs. If, for example, a job requires certain skills (as with a computer programmer), your education in other areas (writing and speaking excepted, of course!) may be less important.

- If you have any academic honors, include them. Be sure to explain what they mean. For example, the Dawson Prize may not mean much, but if you add that it's for the best student in your major—and there were 25 other students in your major—you've made a good point.

- Consider listing key courses that show you have the qualifications to do the job you're seeking.

Employment

This is normally the most important section of a résumé for reviewers. Start with your most recent job, and list all your jobs in *reverse* chronological order.

Hints:

- *Use white space.* Too often, the Employment section has big paragraphs and looks forbidding—just the part of your résumé that you want to look inviting!
- *Avoid unfamiliar terms.* Use terminology everybody in your field knows, of course, but too often this section might as well be in Greek. Work hard to use your reader's vocabulary, not yours.
- *Give examples.* The sample résumé in Figure 11.1 uses examples in the Employment section. What if they weren't there? The résumé would sound pretty generic, wouldn't it? Examples are often the most important communication in any résumé.
- *Show your quality.* Don't just tell what you did—tell how well you did it! Reviewers are looking for your positive traits. Be careful with your tone because you don't want to come across as egotistical. Notice how Figure 11.1 handles the matter of quality: "As a result, the lab director chose me to train new assistants." And "I was the only intern out of six allowed to have my own project."
- *Be honest.* For example, don't take credit for running a large project if you played only a small part in it.

The Biggest Mistake on Résumés!

The biggest mistake is leaving out how well you did something. Let your quality come through wherever possible.

Too often, résumés read like job descriptions—dry and objective. Reviewers do want to know *what* you did, but they also want to know *how well* you did it. Look for ways to bring out your accomplishments without having an overbearing tone.

Notice in the sample résumés the many ways the writers bring out what they've learned, how well they did things, and what their strengths are. Reviewers should feel a sense of good quality throughout those résumés—and throughout yours, too!

What if you have no full-time employment in your field—not even an internship? Most employers understand that we all had to start somewhere. Just make the most of what you put on the résumé. For example, I've had students put a positive spin on these jobs:

 For a quick lesson on this topic, go to http://www.professorbailey.com.

I painted the exterior parts of houses—and received good recommendations from customers for the careful job I did.

I was responsible for checking guests in and out of the hotel and for training all new employees. This position required a pleasant personality for dealing with the public, excellent phone skills, and the ability to think quickly in difficult situations.

I promoted our product by designing eye-catching advertisements and creative displays.

As a sales clerk, I worked 40 hours a week. I maintained good customer relations, which resulted in higher sales. The store gave me added responsibility—including the authority to make deposits and authorize financial reports.

I was responsible for delivering the paper each morning. I delivered it regardless of the weather—rain, sleet, or snow.

Other Sections You Might Want to Use

You've just read about the sections almost all résumés have. Now let's consider other sections of a résumé that help show you at your best. Here are some possibilities:

- *Summary.* Instead of starting with "Objective," consider starting with "Summary." Essentially, this is an "executive summary" of your résumé—a couple of sentences a busy reviewer will probably look at first. This works especially well for résumés with lots of information in them.

- *Strengths.* New graduates applying for their first full-time job usually don't have much to put in the Employment section. As a result, there's little way to show how well they've done something (there aren't any "accomplishments"!). A section on strengths, such as the one in Figure 11.1, can help show your good qualities. By the way, many businesses are looking for people who can communicate well. If you're good at writing or speaking, say so!

- *Skills.* Figure 11.1 has a section giving the person's computer skills. If the job you're applying for requires skills that you have, list them here. If you're good at them, say so ("excellent knowledge of Microsoft Access").

- *Training.* Had any training courses the Education section wouldn't show? List them here.

- *Honors or awards.* If you have any honors or awards that are relevant to the job you're applying for or that show you're good at something, put them in a separate section. Be sure to explain what they mean. Otherwise, cynical reviewers will assume they don't mean much.

- *Scholarships.* Normally you'll want to include this information.

- *Affiliations.* Membership in a professional group doesn't usually mean anything. But if you're an active member and the affiliation is relevant to the job you're applying for, consider listing it in a separate section near the end of your résumé.

- *Personal matters.* Some personal matters are inappropriate for résumés (race, religion, age, national origin, sex)—by law, reviewers can't consider them. Occasionally, some other personal matters are worth highlighting. Suppose, for example, you're a rugby star, and you're applying to be the assistant manager of a sporting goods store. Your rugby experience could be an extremely important qualification. Such mentions are the exception rather than the rule, though.

- *References.* In the past, many résumés ended with something like this: "References available on request." That's unnecessary information. If they're not available, you won't get very far in the hiring process! If you're an inexperienced person looking for anything to put on your résumé just to make it look like you've done something, consider using this section and adding an adjective: "Excellent references available." Be sure you really do have such references!

PREPARING A COVER LETTER

You'll want to send a cover letter with your résumé. Take a look at the example (Fig. 11.4).

The main purpose of a cover letter is to tell why you're sending a résumé. Reviewers often tell me that cover letters need to be specific—a company might have advertisements for several different positions. So the first thing reviewers want to do is match the cover letter and résumé with the right position.

FIGURE 11.4 Sample Cover Letter

222 Tumbleweed Road
Sandstone, CO 66666
May 8, 2008

Software Engineering Corporation
777 Rocky Point Drive
Colorado Springs, CO 33333

Dear Director of Human Resources:

identifies job right away — Please accept my application for the position of database developer (entry level). I saw your advertisement on Sunday, May 6, in the *Colorado Springs Gazette.*

shows enthusiasm — I'm graduating from the University of Sandstone in two weeks and would love to come by for an interview. As you can see from my résumé, I have:

highlights qualifications —
- just the academic background you're seeking (B.S., Information Technology)
- courses in database development
- an internship doing just what you want—developing databases using Microsoft Access

gives contact information — My phone number is (719) 444-4444. My e-mail address is jerome@sandstone.edu.

Thank you for considering me.

Sincerely,

Jerome Pinon

Jerome K. Pinon

But . . . as long as you have the reviewer's attention, why not make the most of it? That's why you should use your cover letter to highlight your most important qualifications. Your goal is to get the reviewer to put your résumé in the right pile—the one the reviewer wants to look at more closely. The wrong pile is in the trash can.

Hints:

- *Keep your cover letter short.* For many hiring situations, you'll probably have the reviewer's attention only briefly. If you make your letter look inviting, the reviewer will probably read it. Normally keep it to less than page.

- *Use the cover letter to tailor your application.* Note, for example, how you meet the exact qualifications in the advertisement. That's what Figure 11.4 (the example you just read) does.

- *Don't be afraid to repeat important information from your résumé.* Sometimes résumés circulate within a company, but cover letters don't. So you shouldn't put important information only in the cover letter (put it in the résumé, too). But the cover letter can—and should—repeat your key qualifications. That's purposeful redundancy!

- *Don't be afraid to let your personality come through a little.* For example, a cover letter can show your enthusiasm for the job you're applying for.

- *Use your spelling checker.* A typo can be fatal!

- *Close your letter carefully.* You may just want to set a polite tone. That's what Figure 11.4 does ("Thank you for considering me."). But you may want to have a call for action: "I would welcome the opportunity to discuss the position and my qualifications in person."

EXERCISES

Find an advertisement for a job you'd like to apply for, one that matches up well with your qualifications. Then prepare a résumé and cover letter for that job. When you hand in your résumé and cover letter, attach the advertisement so your instructor can see how well you've tailored both documents.

CHAPTER 12

Documenting Your Sources

Let your readers know which words and ideas you've taken from other sources.

Y ou might go your entire business career without ever having to formally document a source. Many times, though, you'll need to informally document one. This chapter will discuss both types.

What is informal documentation? Here, for example, is a brief quotation from a chairman of the board at Coca-Cola:

> Not long ago, I shared with our management team these insightful words of the German poet and playwright Goethe, which have definite relevance for us today: "Whatever you do or dream you can, begin it. Boldness has genius, power and magic in it. Begin it now."

> When you look at the Coca-Cola Company . . . , we *are* just beginning. Our most recent actions and our entire history as a Company have brought us to this point, equipped as never before to tap the myriad opportunities ahead of us.

The chairman makes it clear, by using quotation marks, which are Goethe's words and which are his own. That's good informal documentation.

So what is the difference between informal and formal documentation?

- *Informal documentation.* This includes a brief mention of the source (such as the mention of Goethe) and then something to identify where the borrowed words begin and end—such as quotation marks. No footnotes. No endnotes. No parenthetical documentation. If you need to document anything in business writing, you'll almost always use informal documentation. Readers in business usually don't need the added information that footnotes give.
- *Formal documentation.* You guessed it: Formal documentation adds footnotes or endnotes or parenthetical documentation—something to tell your readers enough to track down your exact source. You'll rarely use formal documentation in business, perhaps only for research reports or other writing when reviewers may want to be able to read the material you've referred to.

Let's look at another good example of informal documentation, this time from Warren Buffet, the famed billionaire. He's making the point in his inimitable way that some accounting procedures don't make sense:

> Managers thinking about accounting issues should never forget one of Abraham Lincoln's favorite riddles: "How many legs does a dog have if you

call his tail a leg?" The answer: "Four, because calling a tail a leg doesn't make it a leg." It behooves managers to remember that Abe's right even if an auditor is willing to certify that the tail is a leg.

Square Brackets

Use square brackets to put *your* words in the middle of a quotation:

> "The printer worked for 14 years [a long time!] without needing any repairs."

> "The book by Alan Morehead [*sic*] is terrific!"

The word *sic* is Latin for "thus." It's a way of telling your readers that the quotation has an error—in this case, the name should be "Moorehead."

Notice that Buffet uses the borrowed material fairly by attributing it to his source (Lincoln) and by using quotation marks.

So "informal" documentation doesn't mean sloppy or haphazard. Writers still must clearly show when they're using someone else's words or ideas. But with informal documentation, writers don't need to identify their sources as comprehensively as with formal documentation.

This chapter gives you a brief look at the basics of documentation. It doesn't replace detailed books on the subject, but it does look at these two topics:

- *How can you identify borrowed material?* You'll need to learn this whether you're using informal or formal documentation.
- *How can you formally document a source?* The most common method to formally document your sources is parenthetical documentation. It has replaced the more cumbersome methods of footnoting and endnoting. The second part of this chapter shows you how to use parenthetical documentation.

IDENTIFYING BORROWED MATERIAL

Identifying borrowed material means letting your readers know where it starts and stops. One way to understand how to identify that material is to think of it as having a "frame" around it.

The term *frame* is a metaphor for letting your readers know:

- when you *start* using someone else's words or ideas (that's the opening part of your frame)
- when you *stop* using someone else's words or ideas (that's the closing part of your frame)

Let's look at how to frame a short quotation, a long quotation, a paraphrase, and a mixed quotation and paraphrase.

Framing a Short Quotation

One of the most common types of borrowed material is the short quotation. Suppose you want to quote this sentence in your document:

> One of the fascinating things about Charles Darwin is that he really does seem to have been one of those men whose careers quite unexpectedly and fortuitously are decided for them by a single stroke of fortune.

Ellipsis

Use ellipsis to show you've left out words in the middle of a quotation:

> "The day . . . seemed to never end."

The ellipsis shows there were other words between *day* and *seemed* in the original quotation.

You can read more about ellipsis in Chapter 7.

Framing a quotation is simple: You let your readers know where the quotation begins by using an opening quotation mark; you let your readers know where the quotation ends by using a closing quotation mark. Your readers will then have no doubt where your words stop and someone else's begin. Using quotation marks as a frame is obvious.

But that's not the whole story. There's one other requirement: You need to briefly identify the source of the quotation before your readers read it. That way they'll have some idea of where those words came from.

Here's a good example of using a short quotation in a document—notice that the sentence before the quotation gives the source:

> According to the book *Darwin and the Beagle,* Darwin owed part of his success to luck: "One of the fascinating things about Charles Darwin is that he really does seem to have been one of those men whose careers quite unexpectedly and fortuitously are decided for them by a single stroke of fortune." I agree. But in addition to luck, Darwin had a large dose of genius.

This example tells your readers which words are yours and which are from *Darwin and the Beagle.* That's enough for informal documentation. It's fair to your source and fair to your readers. That's all the documenting that most business writing needs to do.

Framing a Long Quotation

What if you want to quote something longer than a sentence? Then you need to use a block quotation. Here's an example (the block quotation is the indented part in the middle):

> Alan Moorehead wrote a fascinating book about Darwin's genius in discovering and documenting the theory of evolution. This is the way Moorehead begins the book:

> One of the fascinating things about Charles Darwin is that he really does seem to have been one of those men whose careers quite unexpectedly and fortuitously are decided for them by a single stroke of fortune. For twenty-two years nothing much happens, no exceptional abilities are revealed; then suddenly a chance is offered, things can go either this way or that, but luck steps in, or rather a chain of lucky events, and away he soars into the blue never to return.

What a beginning! Moorehead captures us with his enthusiasm and poetic words and, like Darwin, we are off on a voyage of discovery.

Notice that this example *doesn't use quotation marks.* Instead, it identifies the quoted words by indenting them.

Quotation marks aren't necessary for a long quotation because of two reasons:

- The sentence leading into the quotation makes it clear to your readers that they're about to read someone else's words.
- Indenting clearly shows where the quoted material starts and stops.

When is a quotation long enough to make it a block quotation? Unfortunately, the documentation books vary on defining "long." Here's what the most prominent ones say:

> If a quotation runs to more than four typed lines, set it off from your text by beginning a new line, indenting one inch (or ten spaces if you are using a typewriter) from the left margin, and typing it double-spaced, without adding quotation marks. (*MLA Handbook for Writers of Research Papers*)

> In general a prose quotation of two or more sentences that runs to eight or more lines of text in a paper should be set off from the text in single-spacing and indented in its entirety four spaces from the left margin, with no quotation marks at the beginning or end. (*A Manual for Writers of Term Papers, Theses, and Dissertations*)

> Display a quotation of 40 or more words in a free-standing block of typewritten lines, and omit the quotation marks. (*Publication Manual of the American Psychological Association*)

Identifying Titles

In general, use italic to identify the title of something you can physically "pick up"—a book, magazine, newspaper, CD-ROM, and so forth:

> *Eight Modern Essayists, Business Week, Wilmington Morning Star*

Use quotation marks to identify something within those works—a chapter, an article, an editorial:

> "Once More to the Lake," "A Cyberspace Safe-Deposit Box," "Potential Jurors Face Probing Questions"

 For a quick lesson on this topic, go to http://www.professorbailey.com.

Not much consistency. I recommend defining a long quotation as anything over four lines.

I also recommend:

- single-spacing your block quotations (most business writing never uses double spacing)
- indenting them from the left the same distance as you indent your bullets (I use half an inch)

Then your document will have a consistent look. The box tells you how to handle titles.

Framing a Paraphrase

Quotations are easy to frame: Quotation marks or indenting clearly shows where someone else's words begin and end. But what if you don't want to use someone else's exact words? What if, instead, you want to rephrase them into your own words?

Rephrasing someone else's words into your own is a paraphrase. You still need to apply the "frame," but this time without quotation marks. To frame a paraphrase:

- Introduce it by naming your source (such as "According to . . . "). That shows your readers where a paraphrase begins.
- Immediately after the paraphrase, show by the content of your text that you're now back to your own words.

Here's an example of a paraphrase (note: I've underlined it to identify it for you, but you wouldn't normally underline a paraphrase):

> According to Alan Moorehead, <u>Darwin owed much of his success to an amazing bit of luck</u>. I agree. But in addition to luck, Darwin had a large dose of genius.

Notice the frame:

- We can tell the *beginning* of the paraphrase because the author's name immediately precedes it.
- We can tell the *end* of the paraphrase by the sentence afterward ("I agree."). That sentence makes it clear that the writer is now back to his own words and is paraphrasing no more.

Framing a Mixed Paraphrase and Quotation

Sometimes you want to paraphrase but can't resist including a few good words from the original. In that case, you're paraphrasing *and* quoting. Frame the material as you would a paraphrase, but put quotation marks around the quoted material:

> According to Alan Moorehead, Darwin owed much of his success to "a single stroke of fortune." I agree. But in addition to luck, Darwin had a large dose of genius.

Now you've accurately told your reader which words belong to you and which to your original source.

USING PARENTHETICAL DOCUMENTATION

If you decide to formally document your sources, you probably want to use parenthetical documentation. It's more common than footnotes.

Parenthetical documentation has two parts:

- parenthetical information within your document
- a "Works Cited" list on a separate page (or pages) at the end of your document

Parenthetical Information Within Your Text

Remember looking at this example of framing a short quotation?

> According to the book *Darwin and the Beagle,* Darwin owed part of his success to luck: "One of the fascinating things about Charles Darwin is that he really does seem to have been one of those men whose careers quite unexpectedly and fortuitously are decided for them by a single stroke of fortune." I agree. But in addition to luck, Darwin had a large dose of genius.

That's informal documentation. For *formal* documentation, though, you need to tell your readers more. You need to identify your source more specifically *so your readers can find it.* For the example we're working with, you'd need to add this information about the book:

- author
- place of publication
- publisher
- date of publication
- page number

You can tell your readers where you've listed that information by using a superscript number, like this:

> According to the book *Darwin and the Beagle,* Darwin owed part of his success to luck: "One of the fascinating things about Charles Darwin is that he really does seem to have been one of those men whose careers quite unexpectedly and fortuitously are decided for them by a single stroke of fortune."[1]
> I agree. But in addition to luck, Darwin had a large dose of genius.

The superscript number 1 means there's extra information about the quotation in footnote 1 at the bottom of your page. Or that information could be in endnote 1 at the back of your document.

More common today, though, is parenthetical documentation. One type of parenthetical documentation, which *The MLA Handbook for Writers of Research Papers* prescribes, looks like this:

> According to the book *Darwin and the Beagle,* Darwin owed part of his success to luck: "One of the fascinating things about Charles Darwin is that he

really does seem to have been one of those men whose careers quite unexpectedly and fortuitously are decided for them by a single stroke of fortune" (Moorehead 19). I agree. But in addition to luck, Darwin had a large dose of genius.

The information in parentheses tells your reader that the source is by someone with the last name of Moorehead and that the quotation came from page 19. At the end of your document, you'd have a complete list of your sources—a page or more called "Works Cited." There you'd list all your sources and all the information about them. The entry about Moorehead on the Works Cited page would look like this:

Moorehead, Alan. *Darwin and the Beagle.* New York: Harper and Row, 1969.

What If You Cite More Than One Publication by an Author?

Writing (Moorehead 19) doesn't help enough if you have two or more publications in your Works Cited list by that author. In such cases, MLA format calls for giving the author's name, a short title, and the page number: (Moorehead, *Darwin* 19).

What if you'd introduced the quotation by using the author's name instead of the book's title? Then your parenthetical documentation would have needed less information in it:

According to Alan Moorehead, Darwin owed part of his success to luck: "One of the fascinating things about Charles Darwin is that he really does seem to have been one of those men whose careers quite unexpectedly and fortuitously are decided for them by a single stroke of fortune" (19). I agree. But in addition to luck, Darwin had a large dose of genius.

Only the page number is in parentheses because your readers already know who the author is—your introduction to the quotation told them.

You can use parenthetical documentation with any type of borrowed material, not just with short quotations. Here's the long quotation with parenthetical documentation:

Alan Moorehead wrote a fascinating book about Darwin's genius in discovering and documenting the theory of evolution. This is the way Moorehead begins the book:

One of the fascinating things about Charles Darwin is that he really does seem to have been one of those men whose careers quite unexpectedly and fortuitously are decided for them by a single stroke of fortune. For twenty-two years nothing much happens, no exceptional abilities are revealed; then suddenly a chance is offered, things can go either this way or that, but luck steps in, or rather a chain of lucky events, and away he soars into the blue never to return. (19)

What a beginning! Moorehead captures us with his enthusiasm and poetic words and, like Darwin, we are off on a voyage of discovery.

You can also use parenthetical documentation with paraphrases. It's especially helpful then because it clearly marks the *end* of the paraphrase:

According to Alan Moorehead, Darwin owed much of his success to an amazing bit of luck (19). I agree. But in addition to luck, Darwin had a large dose of genius.

The parenthetical information leaves no doubt where the paraphrase ends.

A "Works Cited" List

Information in parentheses gives your readers only brief information: author and page number. But it also tells your readers there's more information at the end of your document—a list of all the works you've cited. That list gives the same detailed information that footnotes and endnotes used to give. Figure 12.1 is an example of such a list.

You can use the entries in this Works Cited list as examples for your documentation. It's in alphabetical order and uses a standard format (from the *MLA Handbook*).

FIGURE 12.1 Works Cited Page

Works Cited

magazine — Barr, Stephen, and Roy Harris. "Incomplete Education." *CFO* April 1997: 30–39.

e-mail — Hiller, Janet. "Suggestions for Horseback Riding Vacation." E-mail to Elizabeth Melton. 26 May 2008.

letter — --- Letter to Elizabeth Melton. 2 June 2008.

CD-ROM — "Surfing in the Atlantic." CD-ROM. Wrightsville Beach, NC: Waveriders. 2007

memo — Melton, Elizabeth. Memo to Janet Hiller. 5 January 2008.

editorial — "Mexico's Moment." Editorial. *Wall Street Journal* 5 July 2000:A1.

book — Moorehead, Alan. *Darwin and the Beagle.* New York: Harper and Row, 1969.

Web site — "Summertime Safety for Pets." *Wrightsville Beach Magazine.* http://www.wrightsvillebeachmagazine.com/coverpage.htm (9 July 2003).

journal — Wansink, Brian, and Michael L. Ray. "Advertising Strategies To Increase Usage Frequency." *Journal of Marketing* 60.1 (1996): 31–47.

Let's look at the entries in more detail:

- The first entry ("Barr") shows how to list more than one author. The information for a typical magazine entry is in this order: authors' names, title of the article, title of the magazine, date, page numbers.
- The second entry shows how to handle e-mail. List the author's name, author's e-mail address in angle brackets, subject line, type of e-mail (personal e-mail, office communication), and date of access. Note: Be careful! Some people really don't want their e-mail address publicized. If there's any doubt, leave it off.
- The third entry (---) shows how to repeat an entry for the same author. Use three hyphens and alphabetize the entries.
- The fourth entry ("Surfing in the Atlantic") shows how to do electronic media and an entry without an author. The information for electronic media is in this order: author (if any), title, publication medium (CD-ROM, in this case), place of publication, publisher, date. In this entry, for example, "Waveriders" is the publisher.
- The fifth entry, a memo, is self-explanatory.
- The sixth entry ("Mexico's Moment") is a standard entry for a newspaper editorial or article. The last item ("A1") is the page number.
- The seventh entry ("Moorehead") is a standard entry for a book.
- The eighth entry is for a Web site. The date at the end of the entry is the date of access.
- The final entry is a standard entry for a journal. The information after the journal's title is in this order: volume number, issue, year, page numbers.

The examples should take care of most situations. Improvise as necessary, keeping in mind that your goal is to precisely identify your sources. Or better yet, look up a format in a documentation guide.

EXERCISES

A. Show that you know how to identify borrowed material in a document. Write a very short paragraph that includes a brief quotation from this passage:

> The careful study of investing history can be very useful to investors, but which history or which period of history should we study? After a long and favorable market in America, there is a natural temptation to think the past 20 years are representative of history. They're not—any more than the beautiful days of summer define the climate in New England.[1]

Include parenthetical documentation after the quotation (which is from page 155 of *Winning the Loser's Game* by Charles Ellis).

B. Write a paragraph or so that includes a *long quotation* from the excerpt from *Winning the Loser's Game.* Include parenthetical documentation after the long quotation.

C. Write a paragraph that includes a paraphrase from that excerpt. Don't include parenthetical documentation. Be sure your readers would know where your paraphrasing begins and (especially) ends.

---

[1]Charles D. Ellis, *Winning the Loser's Game,* 4th ed. (New York: McGraw-Hill, 2002), p. 154.

D. Write a paragraph that includes a mixed quotation and paraphrase from that excerpt. Don't include parenthetical documentation.

E. If your class has access to a discussion board (such as on a program like Blackboard), have a discussion on this topic: "What are the ethical implications of good documentation?"

F. Choose a topic in the news and find at least two sources about it (perhaps an article in a news magazine and an editorial from your paper). Then write a memo to the class giving your opinion of the news event. Be sure to include in your memo all four of these:

- a short quotation
- a long quotation
- a paraphrase
- a mixed paraphrase and quotation

Use formal documentation and attach a Works Cited page to your memo. Your goal is not to write a wonderful essay but to show that you know how to:

- use borrowed material
- document it

That's where your emphasis should be.

PART II
Speaking

CHAPTER 13

What Is Business Speaking?

What you do to prepare your presentation makes all the difference!

At some point on the job, you're probably going to have to express your ideas verbally to several people at the same time. You'll know that in advance, and those people will expect you to be prepared. That's a business presentation!

For many people, especially newcomers, terror sets in early. It stays there, at various levels of the conscious and subconscious mind, until time has done its work and the fearsome event is finally over.

A business presentation isn't hazing or a rite of passage, though. It's an important way for communicating information. And you'll probably find that people in the audience, including your supervisors, make some of their most important judgments about you based on how well you can give a business presentation. That, of course, is one cause for the terror.

Is there anything you can do to prepare for that moment? To reduce—in fact, to *eliminate*—the terror? To look forward to a business presentation rather than to fear it? In other words . . . is there anything you can do to *succeed* rather than fail?

Of course! This part of the book is a thorough and practical approach to help you succeed. You'll get detailed advice for all phases of a presentation, from creating it to giving it. Knowledge is power, and understanding—really understanding—what goes on "under the hood" in a presentation will give you confidence.

The key advice about presentations is this: *Most presentations succeed or fail long before you stand up!* That's good. That means you can solve all sorts of problems, just you and your computer, before anybody else looks!

In fact, a good design for your presentation and effective rehearsal make all the difference.

And once you understand how to prepare a presentation and, as a result, once you give a few successful ones, the terror will disappear. It will move to someone else down the hall. The weight will be gone from your shoulders, and your ability to present will become an asset, not a liability.

What do you need to do before you stand up to give your presentation? This part of the book will tell you. A starting point is to design a presentation that's easy to deliver. If, for instance, you try to give a presentation with no visual aids, you're putting a lot of pressure on yourself to remember everything you need to say. And you're putting pressure on your audience to pay attention to *you* every single second.

But if you design a presentation with excellent visual aids—that help both you and your audience stay on track—you're well on your way to success. Your presentation will be easier to deliver, and your audience will more likely understand what you're saying. That's just one example of what preparing in advance can do to help.

The time to learn how to present is now, today, in this course. Becoming a successful speaker today will give you the confidence to succeed tomorrow, when all eyes in the conference room turn to you.

WHAT TYPES OF BUSINESS PRESENTATIONS ARE THERE?

The most common type of business presentation, by far, is one in front of only a few people, often in a conference room. You may be showing your boss and some associates your ideas on solving a problem. Or you could be talking to clients. Or to prospective clients. Or to just about anyone.

When people gather in a conference room to hear you and perhaps others give a presentation, they usually don't expect a certain type of presentation. Although visual aids are often appropriate, there are times to stay seated and use no visual aids. Some suggestions in this book can help you be effective with that approach as well. Other times, you'll want to be seated part of the time and use visual aids another part. Many times, you'll want to use a computer presentation. There can be any combination.

Some business presentations take place outside a conference room. You could be in an auditorium with hundreds of people listening—especially at annual meetings and other large conferences.

Or you could be in someone else's office, just you and that person, giving a desktop presentation. Good preparation for a one-on-one presentation is just as important as good preparation for an audience of thousands—if that one person is a decision maker about to make the most important decision in your career!

This part of the book emphasizes the conference room presentation, but you'll see that the principles work for just about every speaking situation, even that all-important job interview that your great résumé got you.

COMPUTER PRESENTATIONS

There has been a revolution in business speaking. Computer presentations are absolutely dominant, and other types of visual aids have almost disappeared. Most businesses expect their important presentations to be via computer.

   For a quick lesson on this topic, go to http://www.professorbailey.com.

That's why one key topic in this part is how to give computer presentations. They're not the future—they're the present. They're here, and they're terrific:

- They're surprisingly easy to prepare.
- They're easier to give than just about any other type of presentation.

I'm sure you've already given some of them. This part of the book should help you give them better!

WHAT DOES THIS PART OF THE BOOK COVER?

This part covers far more than how to give computer presentations. In fact, you'll see many important connections between the writing and speaking parts of this book. Remember reading about examples in Chapter 3? Still crucial! And remember the value of layout and illustrations? You'll see their value again in the form of visual aids. Throughout, then, you should feel a synergy between writing and speaking. After all, they're simply different forms of communication.

The first part of this book showed you there's no mystery to becoming a good writer. The same goes for business speaking. There's no mystery. You simply need to know how to prepare a good business presentation and then apply yourself to the task. Once you've had a couple of successes, you'll put the fear behind you and actually look forward to your next presentation.

EXERCISE

For this exercise, give a 3- to 5-minute presentation to the class. Your topic? Interview someone in the class, and help the class get to know that person.

The purpose of this presentation is to be an icebreaker, a presentation with interesting content and little pressure on you as the presenter. It also helps you get to know all the students in your class so they won't be a faceless monolith when you're giving presentations to them in the future. By getting to know something about them, you should be more comfortable with them.

During the interview:

- Get typical biographical material such as employment, family, education, and so on—whatever the person is comfortable telling you.
- But also ask the type of question that can bring forth other interesting material, too. For example, what's the most exciting thing that person has done? What is the person most proud of? What would that person like to be doing in five years? The class may want to brainstorm other interesting questions before the interviewing starts.

During the presentation:

- Use whatever notes or visual aids you need to help you give your presentation. Choose whatever will make you most comfortable when you present.
- Work especially on having a natural-sounding voice—with the pauses most of us have when talking.
- At the beginning of your speech, ask the person you interviewed to come to the front of the room and sit there during your presentation. That way, the class can more easily associate what you are saying with the person you interviewed.

Be sure you say nothing in your presentation that would embarrass the person you interviewed.

CHAPTER 14

Using Good Techniques of Delivery

Computer presentations are fine—but you still need to master the techniques of delivery.

Once you've designed a good presentation, you're well on your way to success. That is, the more confident you are of your material, the more sure you are of your structure, and the more helpful your visual aids are, the easier your presentation will be to deliver.

Before you learn how to design that good presentation, let's review some fundamentals of delivering one. The reason for reviewing those fundamentals now is that all the later chapters have exercises asking you to give presentations. You'll want to understand these fundamentals before standing up in front of your class.

Here are the suggestions this chapter gives:

- Move around the room.
- Use some noticeable gestures.
- Vary your voice's inflection and loudness.
- Make eye contact to all parts of the room.
- Be careful with humor.
- Involve your audience.
- Be creative with group presentations.

MOVE AROUND THE ROOM

Too many speakers are as stationary as a potted plant. And, partially as a result, they're just about as interesting!

Why move around the room? One reason is that moving can help *you*. What if someone asks you to stand with your feet in the same spot without moving for 5 to 10 minutes?

You can feel the stiffness just thinking about it, can't you? Yet that's what many speakers do. They stand in the same spot during their entire presentation!

Moving around, then, helps you stay more relaxed during your presentation. Your goal isn't jittery movement, repetitive pacing, or obtrusive stalking—just natural movement about the front of the room and occasionally to the sides and even to the back (if you're daring!).

Movement does more than help just you, though. It can also help the people in your audience. When you move, they're no longer looking at the same place and no longer hearing you from the same direction.

Break Those Patterns!

Too often speaker and audience get in a rut: "Here's a slide with some bullets. Let's talk about it." "Here's another slide with some bullets. Let's talk about it." And on . . . and on.

Look for opportunities to break those patterns—such as moving around the room and involving your audience. You'll see these suggestions throughout this chapter.

I think of presentations as too often having a "glass wall" between the speaker and the audience: Speakers stay on one side of the glass wall and do the talking; people in the audience stay on the other side and do the listening. That makes for a static, boring situation unless other good things are happening.

One way to break through that glass wall is with some movement! Here are some ways:

- *Begin your introduction on the side you will normally not be on.* Most speakers today using visual aids stay on the audience's left (with transparency presentations, speakers usually stayed on the other side—that audience's left because of the design of the overhead projector). So consider starting your introduction to the audience's right, saying a few words, and then taking your position to the audience's left. Then show your first visual aid—probably your cover slide (see Fig. 14.1).

- *Move toward your audience.* Later in this chapter you'll get suggestions on how to involve your audience. During the audience involvement, leave the front of the room and walk into the audience. Moving into the audience's space gets *everybody's* attention level up a notch or two.

- *Walk into the U.* If you're talking in a room with tables in a U arrangement, walk into the middle for key parts of your presentation (see Fig. 14.2).

- *Walk to one side of the audience.* If you're talking in a room with a rectangular table, move past the first chair or two of the audience and talk there for a minute or two. Then return to the normal area near the screen. This is an easy, nonthreatening way to get closer to the people in your audience and to raise their energy a little. The people in the chairs you're standing beside may have to turn their heads a little to see you, but your movement usually outweighs that temporary inconvenience (see Fig. 14.3).

I once saw a woman do a good job of moving during her presentation. She works for a company that publishes books, magazines, and journals for the scientific community. She was explaining part of her job: making sure her company has the copyright for whatever it publishes. To be sure we understood her clearly, she gave an example—how she got an author from another company to assign the copyright for his article to her company. He originally didn't want to, and her job was to persuade him.

To tell us this, the speaker paused after presenting a slide, *stepped forward past the first one or two chairs of the conference table,* and said, "Let me give you an example."

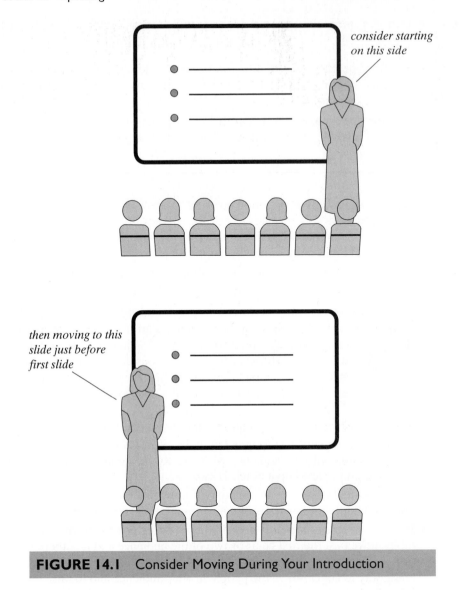

consider starting on this side

then moving to this slide just before first slide

FIGURE 14.1   Consider Moving During Your Introduction

The pause and her movement toward us broke the pattern of her presentation and got everybody's attention. She told the story and then stepped back and continued with her computer presentation. Opportunities like that—a story, a longer example, a discussion—should occur during most presentations (including *yours!*).

She had clearly planned this movement to take advantage of her opportunity—designed it into her presentation and then rehearsed it. Can't you design that kind of movement into your presentations, too? It's easy to do and appropriate no matter how formal your speaking situation. And it makes a nice moment during your presentation.

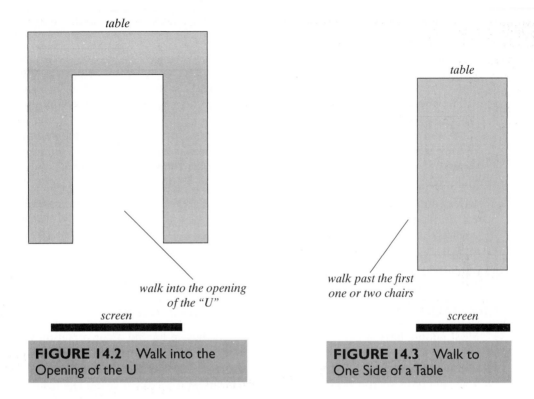

FIGURE 14.2 Walk into the Opening of the U

FIGURE 14.3 Walk to One Side of a Table

USE SOME NOTICEABLE GESTURES

Have you ever had someone say, "Don't gesture so much! That's just a poor substitute for finding the right words!" Bad advice! Gestures can *reinforce* your words. And they can help you come across as energetic and lifelike—rather than as dull and lifeless.

Most people who do gesture during a presentation are too confined, limiting themselves to a few hand gestures for emphasis. And their hands rarely get farther than a foot or so from their sides.

Talk the Way You Talk!

Remember the advice in the writing section of this book: Write the way you talk? You shouldn't get highfalutin when you're giving a business presentation, either. Talk naturally, no matter how large the audience, as though you're talking to a friend, neighbor, or co-worker.

Should you program all your gestures? No—not unless you want to come across as a robot. And you don't want to fall into repetitive patterns of gestures (such as constantly letting one hand flap off to one side) that may distract your audience. Just let your hands and body move naturally, as if you were talking to a close friend about something important.

During your rehearsal, you can plan a few key gestures—not just gestures for emphasis but gestures for description or pointing or showing a reaction. For example, you might plan to use gestures to show the size of something: "The new packaging we're ordering will be about this high [gesture] and this wide [gesture]." Or you might count on your fingers as you're naming the three steps you recommend for something. Or you might make a slight ducking movement to show how a bad thing just missed happening. Or you might hold your hands out to the side and give a "Who me?" look to humorously show you're guilty of an indiscretion but don't want to admit it ("Of course, *I* never felt that way!").

After you become an experienced speaker, these gestures will come automatically to you during your presentation. You won't even think of programming them—just as you wouldn't think of programming your voice inflection. But until gesturing comes naturally, it's a good idea to plan one or two important gestures. You'll find your audience will react favorably and likely remember the point you're making, too!

VARY YOUR VOICE'S INFLECTION AND LOUDNESS

Most people have a perfectly fine voice when they're having a conversation with a close friend; some people lose that voice when giving a presentation. In other words, just as inexperienced speakers lose their natural animation and gesturing when giving a presentation, so, too, do they often lose their natural speaking voice. The result is an apparent monotone.

During a presentation, the voice usually isn't really monotone—there's just a lack of pauses. Almost all of us have numerous pauses of varying lengths when we talk naturally to friends. In fact, punctuation often takes the place of these pauses in writing. Inexperienced, nervous speakers, however, sometimes have their words come out evenly spaced: "The . . . next . . . thing . . . we . . . need . . . to . . . cover . . . is . . . how . . . many . . . ." The metronome delivery removes all emphasis and makes the audience have to work too hard.

If people have accused you of having a monotone during presentations, listen to see if the problem is really a lack of pauses. Or have a friend listen when you rehearse. Or videotape yourself and listen.

Speaking with natural pauses gives your voice animation. Another way to animate your voice is to vary your loudness. You can emphasize by being a little louder—or by being a little softer. Either one is a pattern breaker. Both are important for keeping your audience listening. And both are perfectly commonplace during normal conversation, so you don't need to worry about sounding strange.

Some people are afraid of being louder or softer, feeling as though they'll come across like nineteenth-century actors on the stage. Well, most of us don't want to come across that way. Just try for a little louder, a little softer. Save dramatic changes in loudness for occasional dramatic moments.

Your goal shouldn't be to come across as an actor during your presentation or as something you aren't. Your goal should be to come across as *you*—at your very best! Speak

---

Quavery Voice?

When you get nervous, does your voice get quavery? What you need to do is take a deep breath. But you probably don't want to do that in front of everyone, do you?

So create a diversion! Pause for a sip of water and take that deep breath just before taking the sip. Or ask someone in the audience a question. During the answer, take your breath.

By the way, a bottle of water is good to keep handy for when your throat gets dry.

---

with your level of gesturing, your level of animation, your level of inflection, pauses, loudness, softness. Your level, that is, when you're at your best.

MAKE EYE CONTACT WITH ALL PARTS OF THE ROOM

Making eye contact is obvious. But even good speakers can forget to include everyone, looking instead at a few people close to the front or in the middle. Be sure to:

- Look to each side of the room. Include the outer edges. Hold your eye contact a few seconds there on a particular person.
- Look to the very back of the room.

You don't have to make eye contact with everyone in a large room, of course—just a few all over the room.

 For a quick lesson on this topic, go to http://www.professorbailey.com.

If you're in a small conference room aiming your presentation at one decision maker, should you keep eye contact exclusively on that person? No. The decision maker will feel uncomfortable (scratching becomes hard to do!). Focus your attention on the decision maker about a third of the time to get nonverbal feedback, but include everyone else in the room, too.

Also consider occasionally having prolonged eye contact with one person. Nightclub singers can sing an entire song to one person in the room (a singer picked me out 20 years ago—and I *still* remember!). Other people don't feel left out at all; in fact, they pay full attention to what's going on. You don't want to embarrass people, but 15–30 seconds looking at one person while making a point is very effective—and another way to have one of those pattern breakers I mentioned at the beginning of the chapter.

BE CAREFUL WITH HUMOR

You can usually feel the audience stiffen up as you begin telling a joke. People are afraid you're about to insult someone, if only unintentionally. In other words, set-piece jokes require extra caution and may create tension in the audience until you get to the punch line and people realize that you have, in fact, told a perfectly acceptable joke. Is that extra tension worth the humor? That's for you to judge. And if you do tell a joke, try putting yourself on the humorous end. And never make a joke about people in your audience.

Most business presentations should limit humor to occasional light moments, spontaneous reactions, and friendly asides that may not be funny in the cold light of day but become humorous in the charged situation of a presentation.

For example, the woman telling the story about copyrights did more than just step forward and tell us the story. In addition, she took out a pointer, waved it a couple times, and said, "So I put on my Xena, Warrior Princess, costume and did battle with this author!" Nice humor, completely inoffensive, and an effective light moment.

INVOLVE YOUR AUDIENCE

One of the best ways to break through that "glass wall" is to actually make the people in your audience part of your presentation. They're bound to pay attention!

There are different degrees of involvement, not all of them appropriate to all situations:

- *Ask a question that doesn't require an individual to answer.* For example, you might ask, "How many of you have been with the company for longer than 10 years?" People will raise their hands, and you've succeeded in getting a response from your audience. The result is a pattern breaker and some activity in the brain cells out there.

- *Ask a question that* does *require an individual to answer.* Try not to put people on the spot. Make the question easy: "Bill, I noticed that your hand was up. How long have you been with the company?" Or you might ask a question that isn't necessarily easy but without calling on anybody by name: "Does anybody know what our security procedures were before I got here?" Either type of question sends energy throughout the audience.

- *Ask for someone to come to the front of the room to demonstrate something.* If you're demonstrating how easy some technology is to use, have someone volunteer to come forward and follow your directions. You could have demonstrated it yourself, but having a volunteer adds interest. This type of activity is especially appropriate for training. Be sure you never embarrass your volunteer.

Involving your audience, especially the more active types of involvement, often becomes the highlight of your presentation. Use involvement to make key points.

BE CREATIVE WITH GROUP PRESENTATIONS

Often companies send small teams of presenters to conferences and to other companies, especially to do marketing. The usual scenario is for one person to speak and then sit down; then the next person speaks and sits down; and so on. That can be effective, but often it is better for the presenters to work back and forth.

FIGURE 14.4 Using More Than One Presenter

Figure 14.4, for example, could be the flow of a presentation using two presenters. The effect is that there's one presentation, not several. The benefits include the following:

- The audience can tell that the presenters are prepared.
- There's enough variety to keep the audience attentive.

EXERCISES

A. Be prepared to read (you don't have to memorize) these quotations with good eye contact, gestures, and voice (inflection, loudness, softness—and, especially, pauses):

- "My fellow Americans, ask not what your country can do for you—ask what you can do for your country." (John F. Kennedy)
- "He is one of those orators of whom it was well said, 'Before they get up, they do not know what they are going to say; when they are speaking, they do not know what they are saying; and when they have sat down, they do not know what they have said.'" (Sir Winston Churchill)
- "Read your own compositions, and when you meet with a passage which you think is particularly fine, strike it out." (Samuel Johnson)
- "The right word may be effective, but no word was ever as effective as a rightly timed pause." (Mark Twain)

B. Choose a term from your major (like *index fund* or *management by walking around*), and use some sort of audience participation to help define it. Be creative!

C. Give a 3- to 6-minute presentation to the class. Your topic? Tell us a brief story:

- about something that happened to you
- that taught you something important

The fact that the story illustrates something important should give your presentation focus, and the "story" itself should make your presentation interesting. Here are some special requirements:

- Read your speech (that's right—*read* it) from a complete text—not from notes. Reading lets you focus on the techniques of delivery this chapter discusses. In other words, you can focus on *how* you give your presentation rather than worry about remembering what to say.

- Work especially on having a natural-sounding voice—instead of the wooden voice most people have when reading text. Plan a few noticeable pauses for effect, and have at least one time when your voice gets softer for emphasis.
- Use a few hand gestures during your speech. Plan one or two key gestures.
- Break away from your reading for a short time and use some brief audience involvement. Do this within the tone you've been setting, and make it an integral, related part of your presentation.
- Try to have as much eye contact as possible (which will be hard because you're reading) with all parts of your audience.

When you write your presentation, be sure to use Plain English—you certainly want your writing to sound spoken.

CHAPTER 15

Developing a Clear Structure

A clear structure for your presentation helps your audience . . . and you!

In my mind, this is the key chapter on presentations. It shows you how to have a clear structure for your presentation. And a clear structure—that is, a clear organization—for most presentations is crucial.

Too often, poorly structured presentations are like books without chapters: There's a blur of words, and people in the audience just hope they're somewhere near the end.

A clear structure can help presenters, too. If, when you're giving your presentation, you know where you are in it, you're free to concentrate on other things—such as what you're saying!

So how can you have a structure for your presentation that's so clear that both you and your audience can't get lost? Here's a simple and obvious structure:

- Begin with an introduction.
- Have several parts to the body of your presentation.
- Give your conclusion or ending.
- And have unmistakable transitions throughout.

Business Presentations

A business presentation, as Chapter 13 says, can use just about any format. But many presentations today use visual aids—usually Microsoft PowerPoint slides projected from a computer onto a screen. Presentations usually consist of a number of slides.

This chapter assumes you're doing that kind of presentation. If not, what's in this chapter adapts nicely to other kinds of presentation.

Does that sound too obvious? Maybe it is. But I have to say it because, all too often, speakers don't follow that structure. Instead, they start with some sort of an introduction and then go on . . . and on . . . and on—no discernible parts, just one slide after another after another. The end of the presentation is usually a trailing off with a finish that seems an afterthought.

But there's much more to say about the structure of a presentation than the obvious. The obvious is just a starting point. This chapter looks closely at each of the components of a good presentation.

I'll do that by presenting a model you can follow for organizing most of your business presentations. You can see this model at the end of the chapter (Fig. 15.2). It will be helpful if you look at that model now.

 For a quick lesson on this topic, go to http://www.professorbailey.com.

From working with countless professionals in business, I've found (and so have they) that this simple model really does work. Once these professionals apply the model, their presentations become immensely clearer. And this model doesn't take the life out of a presentation, either. You can be funny, poignant, or deadly serious—setting whatever tone you want. Let's look at the parts of the model:

- the introduction
- the middle part of the presentation
- the end

I'll finish by showing you an example that puts it all together.

THE INTRODUCTION

Most presentations go wrong here, leaving audiences desperately trying to understand what the speakers are talking about or why they're talking in the first place.

Again, picture yourself as a member of the audience. Wouldn't you want to know these things early in someone's presentation?

- What is your topic? Explain it so I can understand it.
- Why are you telling me about it?
- Are you going to conclude anything or make a recommendation? Tell me now.
- What will the structure of the body of your presentation be?

You can accomplish these things by following the model. It calls for you to show these slides—in this order—in your introduction:

- a cover slide
- an explanation slide (clarifying unfamiliar terms in your cover slide)
- a purpose slide
- a bottom-line slide
- a blueprint slide (naming the parts of the body of your presentation)

Have a Cover Slide

Your cover slide should get you (and your audience) off to a good start.

Too often I see presenters flash their cover slide on the screen and then take it off a second or so later. That means the cover slide didn't have much purpose. But there are four good things a cover slide should do:

1. Give the title of your presentation (preferably in Plain English). The title should be in a larger font than the subtitle.
2. Include a subtitle alluding to your purpose or bottom line.

3. Have an image that helps explain your topic (if possible) and sets the proper tone. The image should normally be fairly large. Often, it's the first thing your audience notices on your cover slide.

4. Have your name on it (and possibly your job title). You generally don't need to have the name of the people or company you're talking to on the slide. They know who they are—they want to know who you are.

If you're making a paper copy of your presentation to distribute afterward to your audience, you might want to have extra information on the paper copy of your cover slide—like the company you're talking to, the date, your e-mail address, etc. Fine. But put that extra information only on the *paper* copy. Don't clutter the slide you're actually presenting with that information.

Let's look at a sample cover slide. Suppose you own a golf academy, teaching golf mainly to beginners. You've decided to put together a computer presentation explaining a few important terms about keeping score. Here's your cover slide:

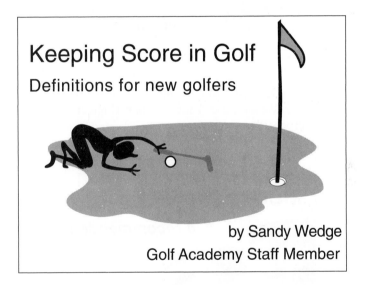

Notice how this slide meets the four requirements for a cover slide:

1. The title is in Plain English (it doesn't use terms like par and bogey, which beginners might not know).

2. The subtitle clearly establishes the purpose of your presentation: to inform beginners.

3. The image shows the presentation is about golf and sets a light, informal tone. This helps set beginners at ease. A photograph would have set a more formal tone.

4. Your name and title are on the slide.

You and your audience are now off to a good start.

What about a more typical business presentation? What would a cover slide look like for that? Here's one for a presentation on concurrent engineering:

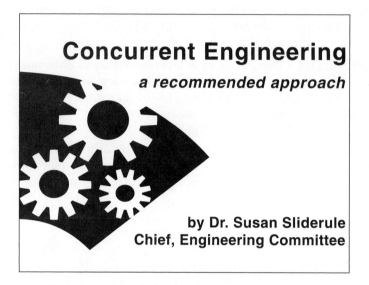

Is the title in Plain English? Maybe, maybe not. Audiences familiar with the term *concurrent engineering* would consider it Plain English. Others might prefer a cover slide with a different title:

What about the image on the slide? Does it help define concurrent engineering? Not really. But sometimes there isn't an image that works—especially for an abstract term. In that case, use an image that relates to your topic and sets the right tone.

Have an Explanation Slide

Your explanation slide should clarify anything unfamiliar to your audience on your cover slide.

I tell businesspeople that I often get lost on their cover slide. They think I'm joking, but I'm serious. The next step, then, in a presentation is to explain any unfamiliar terms on your cover slide. Why wait? If the terms were important enough to be on the cover slide, you only confuse and irritate your audience by waiting to define them.

The golf academy would probably want to give a quick overview of golf—since the presentation is aimed at beginners. Here's an explanation slide doing just that:

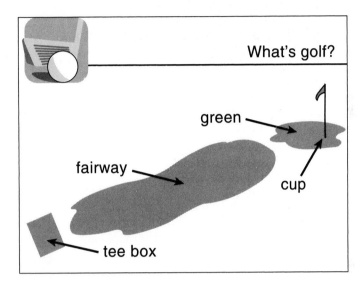

The speaker can now use this slide to explain what golf is. Notice that the slide doesn't have paragraphs full of words. The speaker will supply those—the slide is his visual aid.

Don't Define Everything

Be careful, on your explanation slide, not to explain every term your presentation will use—just enough to keep your audience from getting confused about your topic. You goal at this stage (right after the cover slide) is really very simple: letting people know what you're going to talk about.

What if there's nothing to clarify? Some topics are completely explanatory: "Quarterly Update." Then you don't need an explanation slide at all and can move along to the next part of your introduction.

What about the presentation on concurrent engineering? Whether the term *concurrent engineering* is actually on the cover slide or not doesn't really matter: The topic of the presentation is concurrent engineering. So if you're talking about concurrent engineering, take a couple of minutes right away, right after the cover slide, to explain it (unless you're positive everybody already knows what it means). If you're not positive, explain it. Those who already understand it will be interested in how you define it; those who don't will be glad you told them.

Here's what that explanation slide might look like:

What is concurrent engineering?

Designing — at the <u>same</u> time:
  * **a new product**
  * **<u>and</u> the process for producing it**
  * **<u>and</u> the process for maintaining it**

Does the explanation slide do the job? Does it sufficiently explain the term *concurrent engineering?* Probably not. Usually an explanation slide also needs an example. Perhaps that example could be verbal—in other words, the speaker could just tell the audience the example without using another visual aid. Or perhaps another visual aid would be helpful.

Suppose the company receiving the briefing makes automobiles. The speaker might want to give an example of concurrent engineering involving better headlights. She could say that it would be better to engineer not just the design of the headlights but also, at the same time, the design of the manufacturing process and the design of the maintenance process. This could be the visual aid she'd use:

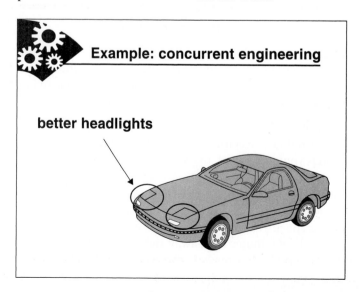

Example: concurrent engineering

better headlights

At this point in the presentation, your audience should definitely know *what* you're going to talk about. The next step is to tell your audience *why* you're going to talk about it.

Have a Purpose Slide

Your purpose slide should tell your audience *why* you're giving your presentation.

Once you're sure the people in your audience understand your topic, they probably want to know why you want to tell them about it. So . . . why are you giving this presentation? The purpose of a presentation is so important that it should be on a visual aid. That way, people in your audience can't miss it.

Here's the purpose slide for our sample presentation:

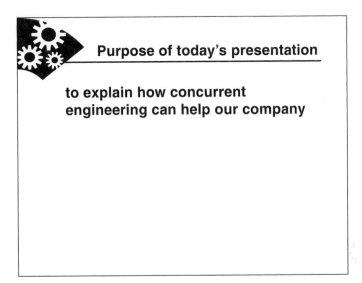

That may seem really simple and not worth a slide. But it is worth one. When I speak to business audiences, I usually begin by asking what makes for a bad presentation. Audiences always say one thing that really bothers them is they don't know why the speaker is talking to them.

One caution: Don't put a list on your purpose slide. If you do, your audience may think it's your blueprint slide. For example, if you tell your audience that you have three purposes, it's a natural assumption on their part that first you'll cover purpose 1 and then purpose 2 and then purpose 3.

So keep your purpose slide simple.

Have a Bottom-Line Slide—If You Have a Bottom Line

Not all presentations have a bottom line. Some simply inform. For example, if your purpose is simply to explain what concurrent engineering is, then you don't have a bottom line. But if your purpose is to convince your company to adopt it, then you do.

A bottom line is usually:

- a conclusion (example: concurrent engineering is a good approach)
- a recommendation (example: we need to adopt concurrent engineering)

If your presentation reaches a conclusion or gives a recommendation, then your presentation has a bottom line.

When do audience members want to know your bottom line? Up front—in the introduction. And that's where it should be. After all, if members of your audience were reading your presentation—rather than seeing you give it—they'd flip to the back to find your bottom line.

We can listen to a presentation much better when we know where it's going. And we can follow a speaker's logic better, too, if we know what the bottom line is up front:

- Are you going to ask someone in the audience to make a decision? Say so. Decision makers can listen a lot better (and certainly will) when they know up front they have to make a decision at the end.
- Are you announcing a new policy? Say so. People will pay attention if they know that what you're saying is actually going to have an impact on them.

Here's the bottom-line slide for our sample presentation on concurrent engineering:

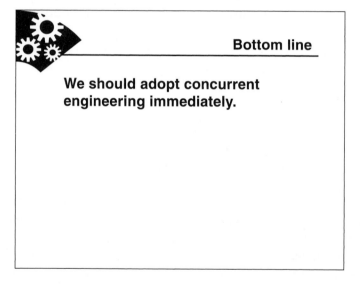

Have a Blueprint Slide

The blueprint slide comes at the end of your introduction.

Once you've clarified your topic and given your purpose, you'll want to tell your audience about the structure of the rest of your presentation. Remember the term *blueprint* from the writing section of the book? That's the name for this part of your introduction. Some people also call it a "road map" or "agenda." Either way, you're telling your audience what the middle parts of your presentation will be. Think of it as an outline of the *body* of your presentation.

For example, if the body of your presentation has three parts to it, a blueprint names those three parts at the end of your introduction—*before* you cover them. For our topic on concurrent engineering, this is the blueprint slide:

What we'll cover today

- **why we need to improve**
- **how concurrent engineering can help**
- **what you need to do to make it happen**

This slide shows that the body of your presentation will have three parts, and it names them. Now you're ready to begin the body of your presentation.

At this point (the end of your introduction), your audience knows this important information about your presentation:

- what your topic is (your cover slide and your explanation slide)
- why you're talking about it (your purpose slide)
- what your conclusion or recommendation is (your bottom-line slide)
- what the structure of the rest of your presentation will be (your blueprint slide)

That's an efficient beginning!

THE MIDDLE PART OF THE PRESENTATION

The middle of your presentation simply fulfills your blueprint. In our example on concurrent engineering, your blueprint has three topics. The middle—or body—of your presentation will now cover those three topics using more slides as visual aids.

Remember to use examples and comparisons throughout. They're at least as important for presentations as they are for writing. If you need a refresher, look over Chapter 3, "Using Examples and Comparisons."

Two other considerations for the middle part of your presentation are to use a moving blueprint slide and to decide how to handle questions.

Use a Moving Blueprint Slide

You may have an excellent structure for your presentation, complete with a blueprint up front telling your audience what that structure is. How can you be sure, once you're into the body of your presentation, that people in your audience know you've moved from the first part of the body of your presentation to the second part?

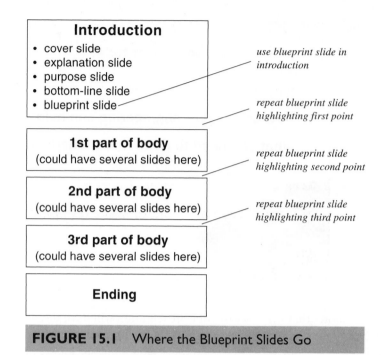

FIGURE 15.1   Where the Blueprint Slides Go

If you're using visual aids, the solution is simple: Repeat your blueprint slide. The name for that is a "moving blueprint slide." It's simply a repeat of your blueprint slide with some sort of highlighting for the part you're about to cover. Figure 15.1 is an illustration showing where to repeat the blueprint slide as a moving blueprint slide.

Here's an example of a moving blueprint slide you could use to move from the introduction to the first part of your presentation on concurrent engineering (notice the checkmark highlighting the subject you're about to cover):

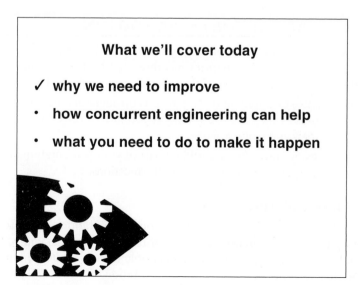

No mistaking that transition, is there? And when you're through talking about all the slides in the first part of the body and are ready to move to the second part, use the next moving blueprint slide:

Finally, when you're ready to move to the third part of your presentation, use another moving blueprint slide:

Members of your audience simply cannot get lost with this technique.

The check mark is one good way to highlight the point you're on. There are many, many other ways, too. You'll see another way in the sample presentation at the end of the chapter.

Is a Moving Blueprint Slide Necessary?

Usually! Most presentations take longer than just a few minutes. So if you have three parts of your presentation and spend 5 minutes on each part, showing the blueprint slide for each part is extremely helpful for keeping your audience (and you!) on track.

I've found the blueprint is helpful even for very short presentations. Remember: The moving blueprint slide is equivalent to headings in a written document. Headings are great even on a one-pager, aren't they?

What if you're not using visual aids? How can you signal you're moving from one part of your presentation to the next? Then you need to have really clear, strong words to make your transition. Simply saying "next" isn't enough. "Next" might refer to another subpoint or another example or another anything. Instead, you need to be absolutely explicit about what you're doing: "We've just finished the first part, so let's move on to the second one: how concurrent engineering can help you."

Even a strong transition like that doesn't work as well as a moving blueprint slide. Virtually everyone will notice the moving blueprint slide—every time a slide changes, the audience usually looks at it. But not everybody will be listening to every word you say. Even if you're terrific, people may be tuning you out momentarily, perhaps to ponder the great point you've just made! But if you had a moving blueprint slide, they could get back on track.

Decide How to Handle Questions

Something to consider during the body of your presentation is whether you want your audience to ask questions then or to save them for a question and answer session at the end. You should decide this before you start, so you can alert your audience to what you prefer.

Suppose, for example, you are speaking to a relatively small, friendly group about a complex matter. You want to be sure they are with you every step of the way. You'd want to encourage questions throughout. Otherwise, they might get lost early and have trouble catching up. To encourage questions in the middle parts of your presentation, stop at key points and ask for them. To show you're seriously offering to answer questions then, rather than just being polite, you might ask a question yourself: "Does everyone understand our timetable for converting to concurrent engineering? Jim— have I made sense so far?"

Building those cues into your presentation—even having visual aids saying "Questions?" pop up at the right times—makes sure you and your audience are on the same track.

In other situations, you may not want questions until the end of your presentation (or a section of it). For example, suppose you have a controversial topic and you've crafted your argument—if the audience will only sit still long enough to hear you without interrupting. Politely say early on that you'll have plenty of time at the end to handle any questions. You'd like to get through your presentation first. Most audiences will go along with you.

THE END

Many speakers carefully craft their introductions so they start with a good impression. Too often, those same speakers forget to craft their finish. But you want to end with a good impression, too.

Prepare for Q & A!

After you've prepared your presentation, prepare for the question-and-answer session. First, think of the questions you'd hate people to ask. Prepare the best answers you can and consider using visual aids to answer them. Using visual aids will help return control of the situation to you.

Also, think of questions people will likely ask. Consider moving that material into the body of your presentation. If that's not appropriate, prepare good answers, again possibly using visual aids.

One way to end is to simply sum up—briefly—what you've covered and to restate your bottom line. You may want to do that, especially for a complicated topic and a lengthy presentation, by repeating your blueprint slide. Or you could be creative and find a quotation or bit of humor that hits the mark.

A sure sign that you're through is to ask if anybody has any questions. When you do so, usually do these two things:

- Show a slide that says "Questions?" on it. That signals the formal part of your presentation is over.
- Move toward your audience. That shows a willingness to close the gap and be informal and honest.

And when you're handling questions, keep these points in mind:

- When you answer a question, look at the person who asked it. But don't look exclusively at that person. Remember you have an entire audience in the room, so look their way, too.
- Consider ending each question by asking the person who asked it, "Did I answer your question?" That shows your concern.
- Don't get hooked. Sometimes you know the questioner is trying to put you down. You'll naturally resent such a thing happening—especially in front of other people. But the worst thing you can do is show that resentment or get angry. Try some humor (not at the questioner's expense—tempting though that may be!). If that doesn't work—hmm . . . you're on your own! From my experience, though, I've never been glad later that I got angry in front of an audience, and I've never benefited from it.
- Don't let a questioner bore the rest of the audience. Some people just can't wait to hear themselves talk. Under the pretense of asking a question, they'll go on . . . and on. Usually the rest of the audience wants to move on as much as you do! I look for the tiniest space to jump in. Then I answer the question, and, as I finish,

turn to another part of the room and ask if anybody there has a question. In other words, I try to politely cut off the original questioner!

PUTTING IT ALL TOGETHER

Figure 15.2 shows the model this chapter describes. Notice that the first and last slides in the model are black (that is, opaque).

If you're giving a computer presentation, your first and last slides should be opaque: That is, make them completely black so that when you project them, the screen looks as though you aren't projecting anything. That way:

- You don't show your cover slide sooner than you want to. I like to have the room completely set up, the computer and projector running, when the audience comes into the room. But I don't like to show the cover slide until I stand up to begin. By projecting an opaque slide while the audience enters, all I have to do is click the mouse to move to my cover slide.

- You also don't have to finish your presentation by leaving your last slide on the screen or by showing the underlying computer program (like PowerPoint) you're using. Make your last slide opaque and you can finish the way you started—with the screen apparently blank.

In PowerPoint, you can turn the screen black—essentially creating an opaque slide— by pressing the B key. However, I like to actually have an opaque slide since I'm not always next to my computer when I present.

What would the slides for an actual presentation look like—following this model? You've seen a few slides by the golf academy. Figure 15.3 shows you what all of the

FIGURE 15.2   A Model: Good Structure for a Presentation

opaque slide (for computer presentation)

cover slide (title, subtitle, graphics, your name)

explanation slide (explaining anything unfamiliar on cover slide—usually with example)

purpose slide (avoid a list)

bottom line slide (optional—but often crucial!)

blueprint slide (different from body slides)

- title of 1st section
- title of 2nd section
- title of 3rd section

1st moving blueprint slide (highlight first point)

✓ title of 1st section
- title of 2nd section
- title of 3rd section

body slides for first section

2nd moving blueprint slide (highlight second point)

- title of 1st section
✓ title of 2nd section
- title of 3rd section

body slides for second section

3rd moving blueprint slide (highlight third point)

- title of 1st section
- title of 2nd section
✓ title of 3rd section

body slides for third section

ending slide (optional)

Questions?

opaque slide (for computer presentation)

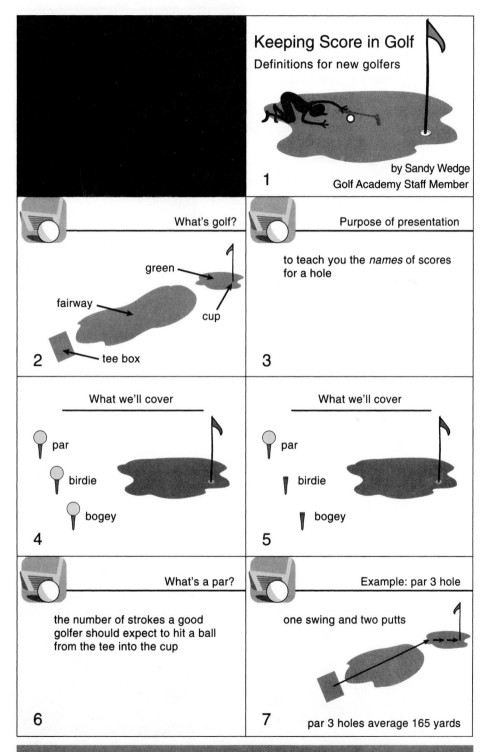

FIGURE 15.3 Presentation Following the Model (Note: The page numbers on the example wouldn't be on actual slides.)

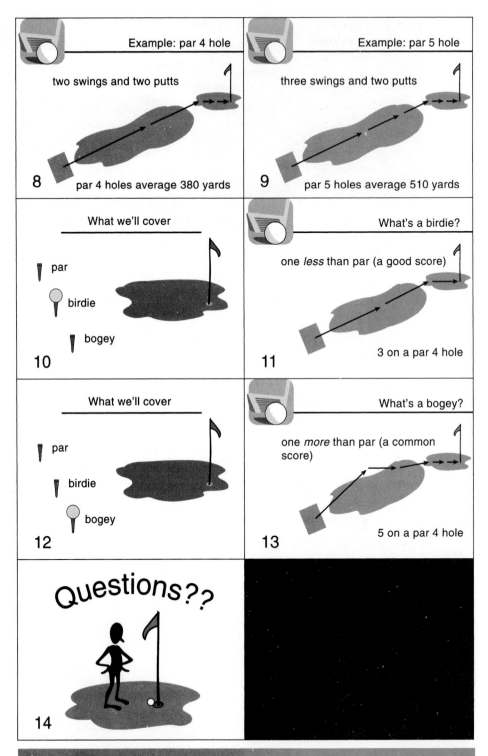

FIGURE 15.3   (Continued)

slides in the presentation look like. (Notice the presentation doesn't include the optional bottom-line slide. That's because the presentation doesn't have a bottom line—it simply informs.)

EXERCISE

Prepare and give a 4- to 6-minute presentation that encourages people in your class to participate in a hobby or sport you like. For example, if you like scuba diving, convince the class to become scuba divers. Follow the model in this chapter exactly. For now, don't worry too much about the design of your visual—you'll learn more about that later. But be sure to use the fundamentals of delivery you learned in Chapter 14.

Although this isn't a "business" topic, it lets you try all the techniques you've learned so far without having to do any research on the content of your presentation. The sample golf presentation could have been a response to this exercise.

CHAPTER 16

Designing Visual Aids

Your visual aids can be the difference between succeeding and failing.

Preparing visual aids has almost reached the point that if we can think of something, we can do it. Preparing visual aids is also fun. This chapter helps you design your visual aids effectively. I'll concentrate on designing slides for computer presentations.

Here are the suggestions I'll cover in more detail:

- Design your body slides using master slides.
- Make your blueprint slides distinguishable.
- Prefer a sans serif typeface.
- Place your content toward the top of the slide.
- Don't use too many words.
- Prefer images instead of words.

DESIGN YOUR BODY SLIDES USING MASTER SLIDES

I never use the templates that come with PowerPoint—I think they're often cluttered and draw attention to background elements too much. I don't know about you, but I want my audience looking at my *foreground* (my slide's content)—not my background. So I keep the design of my slides—font, background, title area—really simple. Therefore, I create my own "custom" template by using a great PowerPoint feature: master slides. I strongly recommend you use master slides, too.

What Is a Master Slide?

A master slide is, essentially, a template for your *body* slides.[1] Whatever you put on your master slide will appear on every body slide in your presentation. For example:

- If you put some clip art in the upper left corner of your master slide, that image will appear on the upper left corner of every slide you create (and be in exactly the same place—a good thing!).
- If you make the body text on your master slide 32-point bold Arial, that's what your body text will be on every slide you create (another good thing).

---

[1] I know—you can use master slides to do blueprint slides and so forth. But that can get awfully complicated. Most people use master slides solely to create their body slides.

In other words, the master slide is a template for your body slides. Let's look at a body slide for the presentation on golf:

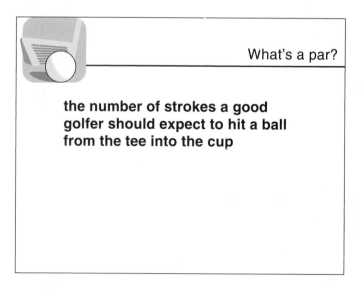

- See the clip art image of the golf club striking the ball? That image was on the master slide. Therefore, the same image appears automatically on this slide and every other slide. If you later decide you don't like that image, just change it on your master slide—and it will automatically change on all the rest of the slides in your presentation!
- See the text in the title area? The *formatting* for those words was done on the master slide—font, size, color, and location. If you later decide to change the font for the titles of your slides, just change it on your master slide. The font for your titles will then change throughout your presentation.
- See the body text? Again, the *formatting* for those words was done on the master slide—font, size, color, and location. Change your mind? Just change the font on the master slide!
- See the white background? The background was set on the master slide.

But . . . how do you keep those things off your opaque, cover, and blueprint slides? For example, you *don't* want a title area on your opaque slide. And you certainly *do* want a different design for your cover and blueprint slides. How can you get rid of the master elements for selected slides?

In PowerPoint, it's simple. First, insert a new slide. It will appear with the master elements on it. Then just go to Format > Background and put a check in the box "Omit background graphics from master." Voilà! The master elements disappear from that slide, and you can create whatever you like.

How Should You Design Your Master Slide?

A master slide lets you set up the design of your body slides. So what choices should you make? Here's a body slide from the last chapter:

Purpose of today's presentation

to explain how concurrent engineering can help our company

 For a quick lesson on this topic, go to http://www.professorbailey.com.

Let's look at the master elements on that slide (I recommend you use *all* these elements on your body slides):

- *A graphical image.* The first master element you probably noticed is the image in the upper left corner. That image isn't just decoration—it draws your audience's eyes to the title of your slide (the first place you want people to look). What image should you use? Something related to your topic, of course. Sometimes you can even use a smaller version of the graphical image from your cover slide. Notice the image on the cover slide and a body slide from the presentation on concurrent engineering:

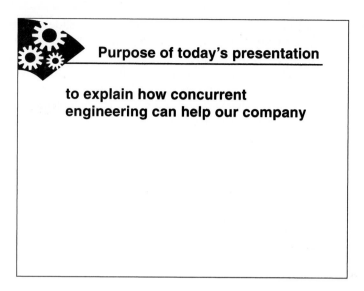

Nice trick, isn't it? You can use the same image again, too—on your blueprint slide. More about that later.

- *The slide's title.* Another master element is the *location* of the title area. I recommend putting the title area high on the slide (but not jammed at the top). The reason the title should be high is to leave a *lot* of room beneath the title area—in the content area. Images, especially, can fill up the content area quickly. Take a look at another slide from the golf presentation:

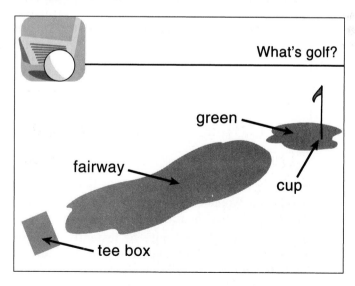

Good thing the title area is small, isn't it?

- *A separator.* Another master element is the line beneath the title. It appears on every slide beneath every title. It clearly separates the title area from the content area of the slide.

- *A white background.* Another master element is the slide's white background. It could have been any color. But white is a great background color—and by far the most common—because it allows for maximum contrast. Lots of colors contrast with white. So if you need, for example, an arrow on your slide, you have a choice of many colors for that arrow, and it will stand out well against a white background. Save colorful backgrounds for cover and blueprint slides—to differentiate them from your body slides. (By the way, if you think fancy backgrounds are good for slides, you might consider why most books have pages with a simple white background color.)
- *Font choices.* The final master element is the choice of fonts (in this case, Arial). A later section in this chapter goes into more detail on fonts.

MAKE YOUR BLUEPRINT SLIDE DISTINGUISHABLE

What if your blueprint slide looks just like your body slide? Here's a blueprint slide that looks like the body slides in the presentation:

What we'll cover today

- **why we need to improve**
- **how concurrent engineering can help**
- **what you need to do to make it happen**

That's always confusing to the audience, sort of like having headings in a written document look like body text. Would't it be better to have a different—but related—design for your blueprint slide? Notice the revised blueprint slide on the next page.

This blueprint slide will now stand out—be instantly recognizable—whenever it appears in your presentation. Your audience will now be sure to notice it—and not momentarily think they're seeing another body slide.

Here are some tips for designing a blueprint slide:

- *Change the title section so it doesn't resemble the title section in your body slide.* This is crucial in differentiating your blueprint slides from your body slides.
- *Consider keeping the same graphical image from your body slide but move it and make it bigger.* Keeping it relates the blueprint slide to the other slides in your

presentation. Changing its size and location distinguishes it from your other slides. You can't always do this, of course, but it's a handy technique.

- *Consider a colorful background.* If your cover slide uses a deep blue background color, consider using the same color for the background of your blueprint slide. That will make your blueprint slide seem part of your presentation yet different from your body slides. A colorful background is a surefire way to differentiate your blueprint slides from your body slides. Here's an example with a dark background:

> **What we'll cover today**
>
> • why we need to improve
>
> • how concurrent engineering can help
>
> • what you need to do to make it happen

Nobody would mistake that for a body slide, would they? And that's the reason to differentiate a blueprint slide from the body slides.

- *Use a check mark or some other indicator on your moving blueprint slide.* Be sure to put the check mark by the topic you're about to cover:

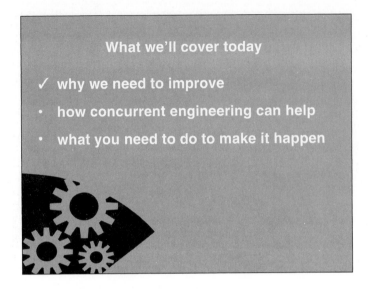

Some speakers make the mistake of putting check marks by the topics they've *already* covered. Don't do it—it gets confusing.

By the way, a check mark isn't the only way to show your audience which item you're about to cover. You could use a different color, a larger type size, an arrow, or any of a number of other possibilities.

• *Be creative.* Don't lock into these design tips as the only solution for blueprint slides. Just follow the principle of making your blueprint slide different from your body slides but clearly a member of the same family of slides. Here are some sample blueprint slides with different designs:

PREFER A SANS SERIF TYPEFACE

When you project a visual aid onto a screen, the image has much lower resolution than what you see on a printed page. For that reason, you normally want to use a sans serif typeface for presentations. That's because a typeface with serifs usually looks cluttered and busy, simply because the small serifs don't project well. Chapter 4, "Making Your Page Look Inviting," explains the difference between serif and sans serif typefaces.

Let's first look at a visual aid with a typeface I don't recommend for visual aids—Times New Roman (which has serifs):

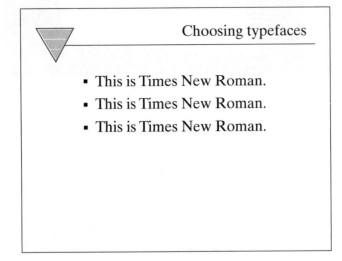

That looks reasonably good here, on the printed page, but imagine what happens to all those small serifs when you project it!

Now let's look at the two typefaces I do recommend—Arial and Comic Sans (both sans serif):

Arial is excellent for setting a formal tone; Comic Sans, an informal one. Both type-faces look cleaner than Times New Roman, don't they? That's because a serifed type (like Times New Roman) has thick and thin strokes making up each character; a sans serif typeface (like Arial and Comic Sans), though, has only thick strokes:

Times   Arial   Comic Sans

Thick strokes project better. That's one of the main reasons business presentations use Arial or Comic Sans most of the time.

Now let's consider type size. You might think bigger is better, but that's not really true. If the type is too big, then the slide seems to have too much text and not enough white space. Also, text that might fit on one line with a smaller size may take two lines with a larger size—again, cluttering the page.

There's no way to determine a standard type size because there are too many variables:

- How close is the projector to the screen?
- How large is the screen?
- How close is the audience to the screen?
- How bright is the projector?
- How bright is the light over the screen?

Despite those variables, my experience tells me these recommendations are usually safe:

- Use 32-point type for your basic text. For Arial, make everything bold or it will look washed out; for Comic Sans, don't normally use bold or it will look smudged and heavy.
- For slide titles, use 32 points and put the slide title in a dominant color (like red). For labels (such as for graphs), you may need to use as small as 20 points, but that's as small as you'll normally want to go.

PLACE YOUR CONTENT TOWARD THE TOP

Where should the words go? Let's say you have three bullets to put on a slide. Why is this spacing poor?

> ### Where should the words go?
>
> ▪ **This is a bulleted item.**
>
> ▪ **This is a bulleted item.**
>
> ▪ **This is a bulleted item.**

There are two problems:

- Often, not everybody in the audience can see the entire slide. The part they can't see is usually at the bottom. By putting words near the bottom of the slide, you risk having people not be able to read them. You've probably been in that situation many times yourself as a member of an audience.
- Another problem is that you want to have consistent spacing on all your slides. What if you have four bulleted items? Or five? Each slide would look a little different, and your presentation may look like a collection of random slides rather than something with a consistent design.

This spacing is better:

> ### Where should the words go?
>
> ▪ **This is a bulleted item.**
> ▪ **This is a bulleted item.**
> ▪ **This is a bulleted item.**

The bullets are now all near the top. You've avoided the area at the bottom and allowed yourself room to have the same spacing between bullets when your slides have more bullets on them.

You can't always avoid the bottom part of your slides. Graphs and photographs often take a lot of vertical space. In those cases, I'll sometimes omit the title section to make more room on the slide. Sometimes, though, I simply use the bottom of the slide.

DON'T USE TOO MANY WORDS

Inexperienced speakers are often afraid of forgetting something, so they put nearly everything they want to say on each slide. Bad things happen as a result:

- The speakers end up reading slides to the audience.
- They lose eye contact and face the screen (instead of the audience).
- Their voice inflection disappears because they're reading rather than simply talking.
- Audiences skim or ignore wordy slides, missing the message.
- Audiences finally stop paying attention altogether.

The saying that "less is more" certainly applies to creating slides. Here's a slide with too many words:

What is concurrent engineering?

Concurrent engineering is a systematic approach to the integrated, concurrent design of products and their related processes, including manufacture and support. This approach is intended to cause developers, from the outset, to consider all elements of the product life cycle from conception through disposal, including quality, cost, schedule, and user requirements.

Not very effective, is it? Yet that slide isn't an exaggeration. It's typical of what many poor presenters use. Compare that slide with the one you saw in the last chapter:

What is concurrent engineering?

Designing — at the <u>same</u> time:

- **a new product**
- **<u>and</u> the process for producing it**
- **<u>and</u> the process for maintaining it**

Doesn't the second one communicate better than the wordy one? Which would you rather read?

Here are some tips for reducing wordiness:

- *Use bullets.* Try to reduce your thoughts to bullets when you can. That way, you'll leave something for you to say to the audience. Audiences hate speakers to do nothing but read to them. Audiences are looking for "value added" from you, some reason to come to your presentation rather than just have you read your slides to them.

- *Use more than one slide.* If you have a lot to say, consider breaking it into parts and use several slides.

- *Use images.* If you can replace words with an image, you almost always have a better slide. And that's the next topic!

PREFER IMAGES INSTEAD OF WORDS

Sometimes you don't need words at all. You can use an image. Strive for images much of the time. Not only do they look more inviting, but also audiences are much more likely to remember them when your presentation is over.

The Best Images Carry Information!

Don't decorate your slides with useless clip art. Make sure your images carry information rather than simply distract.

For example, avoid putting a cute piece of clip art at the bottom of each slide simply as decoration. Your viewers will either ignore it entirely or, worse, tune you out while they look at it! (Exactly what part of what you're saying do you want your viewers to tune out?)

Many times I've asked audiences which slides they remembered the most from a series of presentations. The answer is seldom a bullet slide. That doesn't mean you should never use bullets. They're usually necessary. But with a little creative thought, you can sometimes get beyond them.

For example, let's return to electronic data interchange. Do you wonder what it means? Well, it's a way to have computers send complex data directly to each other rather than using paper and the post office. Even better, electronic data interchange has standards that let unlike computers—a mainframe and a PC, for example—send data back and forth. Suppose you want to give an example of electronic data interchange: a restaurant ordering food from a food vendor. You could use a bullet slide to describe the old-fashioned process:

> **Traditional Methods**
>
> 1. **Someone in the restaurant types an order.**
> 2. **The order is then printed.**
> 3. **The mailroom then mails the order to the food vendor.**
> 4. **After several days, someone at the food vendor receives the order.**
> 5. **Someone at the food vendor types a shipping request and an invoice.**

Or you could use clip art and replace almost all those words with several images. Here's the slide that the speaker, Lisa Janssen, actually used:

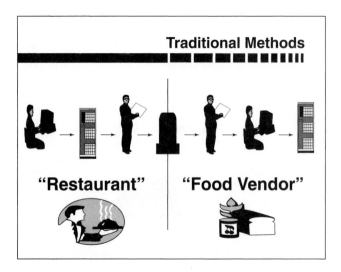

What a difference! As the presenter, Lisa then explained each step. Her slide is much more interesting than the word slide and gives the audience a process they can picture. They're now much more likely to listen, understand, and remember what Lisa says. And notice that Lisa uses clip art to *carry information* (a pictorial representation of each step)—not just as empty decoration.

You don't always need to have pictorial representations of what you're talking about to have excellent images. These next slides are some of my favorites. Gus Creedon is covering the same topic Lisa did (what is electronic data interchange?). Notice what a great job he does with just boxes circles, and arrows!

He begins by creating an analogy. For example, he says, suppose you have a German diplomat who wants to talk to a Chinese diplomat:

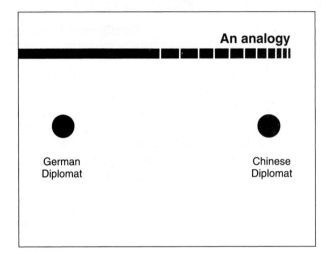

They can't speak directly to each other and be understood. For them to converse, they need interpreters:

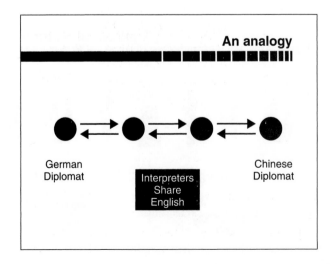

Now they can communicate—because the interpreters share a "common syntax and vocabulary":

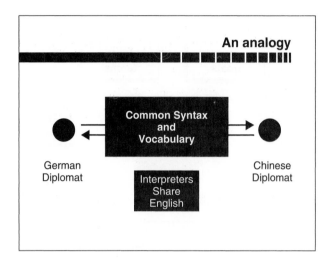

Electronic data interchange, he says, works the same way: It serves as the interpreter between computers, allowing them to share information even though the computers are different types with different software. Electronic data interchange, in other words, serves as the common syntax and vocabulary:

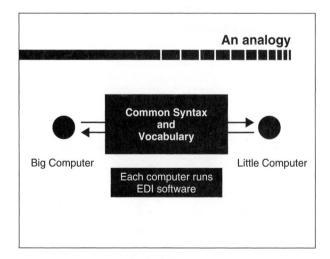

Gus's slides make excellent use of images, don't they? It's amazing what smart, creative people can do with just boxes, circles, and arrows.

What are some other good ways to use images? A common way is to show a process—so you may want to replace bullets with a flowchart. Here are a few suggestions:

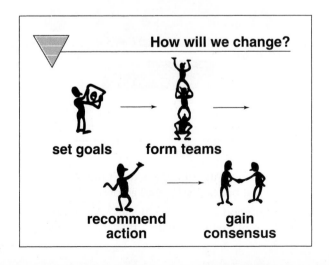

You can also use images for these:

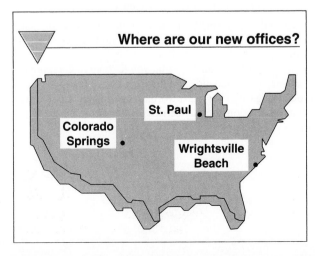

These sample slides look much better than text slides, don't they? Slides with images will look better to your audience, too!

EXERCISES

A. What's wrong with this slide?

> WHY YOUR COMPANY NEEDS AN EDUCATIONAL
> ASSISTANCE PROGRAM
>
> I. <u>PURPOSE:</u>
>   - HELP EMPLOYEES PAY FOR TUITION
>   - IT WILL REDUCE THE COMPANY'S COST
>
> II. <u>DESCRIPTION:</u>
>   - % OF TUITION MONEY ADVANCED TO
>   EMPLOYEE FOR DEGREE PROGRAMS
>   - EMPLOYEE RECEIVES REFUND
>
> III. <u>BENEFITS YOUR COMPANY BY:</u>
>   - INCREASING PRODUCTIVITY AND RETENTION
>   - REDUCED RECRUITMENT COSTS
>
> IV. <u>BENEFITS YOUR EMPLOYEES BY:</u>
>   - INCREASING THEIR OPPORTUNITIES
>   - SAVING THEM MONEY ON ADVANCED
> EDUCATION

B. This is an exercise in designing (not giving) a presentation. Prepare the visual aids for a presentation. You won't actually give it (yet). Your instructor will ask you either:

- to hand in paper copies of the visual aids you design, or
- to project them to the class without actually giving your presentation

Your topic is the same as the final exercise for Chapter 6: Choose a term from your field of work or study and then define it so everybody in the class understands everything you say. You can use the same term and content you used for that exercise. Plan for a presentation that would last 3–6 minutes if you actually gave it.

Here are some special requirements for your visual aids:

- Assume you'll be showing visual aids for much of your presentation. That is, you won't be talking without visual aids for 5 minutes, then flash one up, and then conclude.
- Follow the structure—exactly—that you learned in Chapter 15.
- Have *at least* one visual aid (not counting your cover and blueprint slides) that uses something other than just words: a drawing, picture, flowchart, whatever. Be sure your illustration actually carries useful information rather than simply decorates your slide.

CHAPTER 17

Giving a Presentation Using a Computer

Once you have a well-designed computer presentation, it's one of the easiest types to give.

Y ou've been reading bits and pieces about computer presentations throughout this section of the book. This is the chapter that tells you all about them!

Computer presentations require a lot of expensive equipment, but they're relatively easy to give. In fact, if you think of yourself as a nervous speaker, computer presentations can take much of the pressure off.

Here's what this chapter covers:

- What equipment do you need?
- How should you design your presentation?
- How should you give your presentation?

WHAT EQUIPMENT DO YOU NEED?

Today? Not much as an individual presenter! Just bring your presentation on some sort of portable media. Most places that host presentations will have a computer and projector for you.

That said, here are some things to think about:

- *Computer.* If you're using someone else's computer, try to get to the location of your presentation in advance. Load your presentation onto the computer and try it out. Be especially sure to try out any special characteristics of your presentation—such as hyperlinks. Most problems with computer presentations occur because something unexpected happens with the host computer.
- *A mouse.* Your best choice is a remote mouse—infrared or radio frequency. A remote mouse frees you from being near the computer. Most don't require any special software—just plug them in. And they're cheap.
- *The projector.* This is a crucial piece of equipment. As with the other equipment, be sure to test the projector before your presentation!
- *A screen.* Most conference rooms and other presentation rooms have permanent screens. If you don't have a screen and can't get a portable one, don't project onto

a whiteboard. The glossy finish will reflect the projector's light as a very bright image, destroying your audience's view. Try projecting onto a wall, instead. Also, you want the screen to be behind you when you face the audience, not way off to the side. That way, people in your audience can easily glance from you to the screen and back without turning their heads a lot.

HOW SHOULD YOU DESIGN YOUR PRESENTATION?

Once you've decided to give a computer presentation, you're probably going to put a lot of effort into designing it. After all, if you're not using a computer's good features, you might as well be giving a presentation using old-fashioned transparencies.

Should You Give Your Audience a Paper Copy of Your Visual Aids in Advance?

Rarely. A copy of your visual aids is almost always a great distraction. Pass out the paper copy afterward.

Also, what makes for a good handout and what makes for a good visual aid are different. A handout needs more information on it than a visual aid. Speakers who use their visual aids as handouts usually have cluttered ineffective visual aids.

If you want to prepare handouts, use an "annotated presentation." Chapter 19 tells you how.

Here's the advice I give:

- Build almost everything on your slides. (That is, bring the elements on one at a time.)
- Choose your transition effects carefully.
- Consider using special features such as sound and video.

Build Almost Everything on Your Slides

One of the most important benefits of a computer presentation is that you can show a part of a slide at a time. For example, you can show one bullet, then add the next bullet, then add the next . . . and so on. That way, your audience isn't distracted by reading the third bullet while you're still on the first one.

Also, computer presentations can show images—such as graphs—one part at a time. For example, you can show only the first bar in a bar chart, talk about it, then add the second bar, talk about it, etc.

This capability of using "builds" has these two advantages:

- It focuses your audience's attention on the proper part of the screen at the proper time.
- It lets you—the speaker—figure out the best way to present a slide before you stand up to give the presentation. For example, if you're presenting a line graph,

you can show only the graph's axes first and explain them. Then you can show one line on the graph and explain it; then you can show the next line, and explain it; and so on. This takes a great deal of pressure off you as the speaker because—before you ever stand up—you've solved the order you want to use for presenting the elements of every slide.

I build almost everything—except the title area—unless I have a good reason not to. Let's look at an example. Remember seeing this slide in Chapter 15?

What is concurrent engineering?

Designing—at the same time:

- **a new product**
- **and the process for producing it**
- **and the process for maintaining it**

If you project it all at once, you know that members of your audience will be reading the third bullet while you're still talking about the first one. That's not good for you or them. Instead, just project the slide an element at a time. So the first image might look like this:

What is concurrent engineering?

Just the title. As a presenter, I usually show my audience only the title of the slide at first. That way, I can introduce the slide before showing anything substantive.

Next, I just project the lead-in to the bullets, like this:

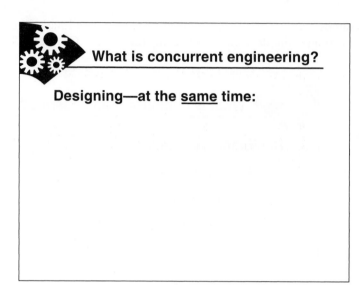

As the speaker, I'd probably pause here and ask the audience, "So what's another word for *same?*" If the audience needed help, I'd say "Concurrent!" Having defined *concurrent,* I'm ready to show the first bullet:

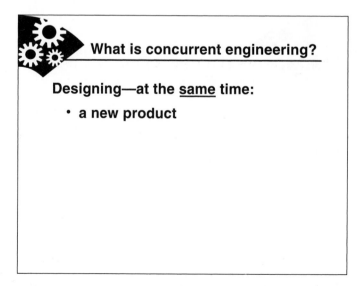

And so on.

Building a slide a piece at a time isn't limited to bullets. In Chapter 16, I said that the presenter actually used graphical images instead of bullets. This was her slide:

That's a lot easier to look at than a bullet slide with all the bullets showing at once, but it's still distracting to the audience. She actually presented the slide by first showing us only the title:

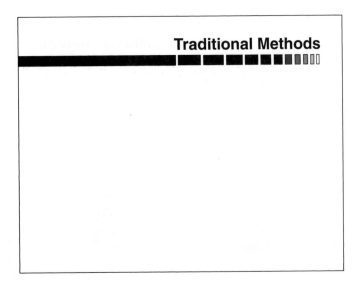

That told *her* what her next slide was, so she didn't have to memorize the slides in her presentation. She introduced the slide, and then she added the image of a restaurant, explaining that the restaurant needed to order more food from a vendor:

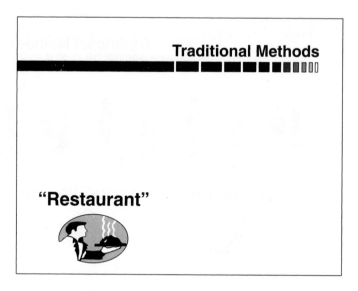

Next she added the image of the food vendor, explaining that it was the source of the food:

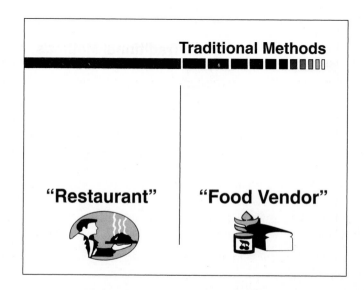

Then she walked the audience step-by-step through the process of ordering food, showing each step in the process individually while talking about it. This was the first of those steps:

So what could have been one slide—all visible to the audience at once—became more than 10 separate projected images during a computer presentation. Because each new image appears instantly—with just the click of a mouse—there's no distraction in moving from one to the next. The computer makes it easy.

Less Is More

Don't create distractions from your content.

You can do all kinds of incredible things with today's software. For most business presentations, "less is more." Use builds throughout, of course, but don't use flashy animation effects (zooms, spirals, swirls) without a good reason.

What are the advantages of projecting the images one at a time? Several:

1. Your slides look less busy. By building from almost nothing and adding incrementally, the audience isn't overwhelmed by seeing everything at once.
2. Your audience isn't distracted. There's nothing up there you don't want people to look at. The images you've already talked about don't distract them because they're looking at the new image.
3. The appearance of a new image on the screen draws the eyes of your audience to it, just when you want their eyes there. That replaces the need for a pointer.

And everything happens quietly, smoothly, instantly, seamlessly. It looks professional, and it's easy to do!

There's another advantage, one of the most important: Building helps you, the presenter, figure out in advance the best way to present a slide. Otherwise, you find yourself staring at a complicated slide and, while standing in front of an audience, having to remember how to walk the audience through it.

But when using builds, you've solved that problem in advance, in your office, just you and your computer. You've figured out the best order for building the elements on a slide and made it part of your presentation. All you have to do now is click the mouse and bring up the next element. This is not a small matter—it really takes the pressure off!

 For a quick lesson on this topic, go to http://www.professorbailey.com.

So what else can you use builds with? Almost everything. Remember this slide?

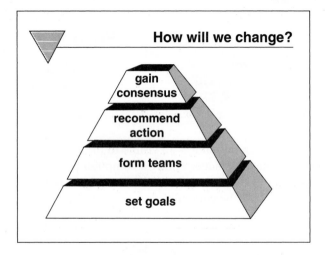

Why show it all at once? Show the title first, and then build it from the bottom up, like this:

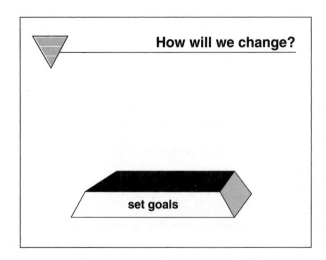

The same goes for time lines. Start with the title, then show just the time line, and then add your narrative, one element at a time. Here's what your *third* image might look like:

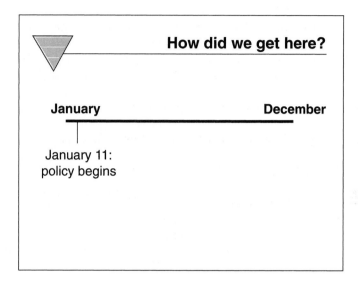

By the way, building slides an element at a time is especially helpful for graphs and other complicated slides.

Choose Your Transition Effects Carefully

Building a slide one element at a time is a terrific advantage of computer presentations. But what most people notice is the transition effects: one slide, for example, dissolving into another or a bullet flying onto the slide from the top or the left. Are transition effects useful? Or are they just flashiness?

They can be both, so the trick is to make them useful without being merely flashy. Let's look at two times for transition effects: when moving from one slide to the next and when moving from one element to another within a slide.

Transitions From One Slide to the Next

There are countless transition effects, and the more you work with computer presentations, the less you depend on them.

My Preferences

I prefer "Dissolve" for transitions from slide to slide and "Wipe from left" for all my bullets.

You've seen transition effects during the weather reports on television: For example, one weather map appears to roll up as another appears beneath it. You can do the same type of thing with each slide of your computer presentation. Blinds close covering the old slide and then open with a new slide showing; a checkerboard pattern appears and changes one slide to the next; curtains open to reveal a new slide; and so on.

Some transitions are obtrusive: One slide moves off the screen to the upper right while another appears in its place. Use obtrusive transitions only for special effects. Otherwise, your audience notices your transition instead of what you're transitioning to. That's normally not what you want to happen.

Other transitions are more subtle. I like Dissolve: One slide simply dissolves into another. There's no dizzying movement taking the eyes from one part of the screen to another. The eyes stay in the same place on the screen and a new image emerges. I use Dissolve for most of my movement from slide to slide. If you set the speed of the dissolve to "fast," there's really no distraction. Instead, there's a little movement on the screen that catches the attention of the people in the audience—alerting them that you've now gone to the next slide. That's a great visual cue, reinforcing your transition without distracting attention from your message.

"Transitions" Within a Slide—Animations

When you build a slide an element at a time, you don't have to have each element suddenly pop on the screen, without any transition effect. PowerPoint calls transitions within a slide "animations." For example, let's look at the complicated slide we've been working with:

How would you apply animation to these elements? Here's how you could do it (there aren't any "correct" answers):

- Have each graphical image dissolve onto the screen. Use the same animation each time or you'll distract your audience.
- Have the arrows wipe right across the screen. The arrow appears to draw itself from left to right. It's as though you uncover the arrow from left to right. In this case, the "Wipe from left" effect moves your audience's eyes from the image you've just talked about to the one you're about to talk about.

There are other choices for our sample slide. But be careful. If you have each graphical image drop onto the slide from the top of the screen, as though falling from the sky, you and your audience will tire of the effect quickly.

What about animation for bullets? Should the words just pop instantly on the screen? That's all right. But I prefer, again, the "Wipe from left" effect—as though someone is typing the words onto the screen. I think the movement helps alert people in the audience that the image on the screen is changing. They might miss a new bullet without an animation effect. One animation I don't like is when an entire line "flies" in from off the screen ("Fly from left"). The words get blurry, and the animation is distracting.

Play with animations to set the tone you want and to give proper cues to your audience. The effects can be *very* useful tools, not just useless flash, for a computer presentation.

Consider Using Special Features

Computer presentations can do even more:

- *Sound.* It's a lot easier to figure out how than when to use sound. If you have it happening too often—such as a "whoosh" sound with every bullet—you'll surely distract rather than amuse your audience. My suggestion is to use sound for its content (you want people to listen to a certain song or segment of a speech) if your presentation calls for it. Otherwise, if you must use sound just as an effect, use it once—and no more—in your presentation. Otherwise, I'll guarantee that you're irritating a significant number of people in your audience.

- *Video.* Video takes lots of computer memory. In short bursts, though, it can be useful. For example, if you want to show your audience who someone is, video may be better than a still picture. So if you're giving a presentation to job applicants you're courting, a brief clip of the CEO might work well.

- *Demonstrations of computer programs.* You can, without ever exiting your PowerPoint presentation, demonstrate another computer program. Want to show people the latest features in your word processing program? Go to it, demonstrate, and then exit it. You'll be automatically back to your presentation program, right where you were when you left it, ready for your next slide. Want to demonstrate the computer model you've been working on? You can. Want to jump to the Internet? Do it. You'll leave your presentation program seamlessly and return to it—again, seamlessly! But practice this first on the computer you'll actually be using. You need to know the links will work.

- *Narrated presentation.* This is a slide show with recorded words. Think of it as a "presenter-less presentation." Use it to go places you can't.

HOW SHOULD YOU GIVE YOUR PRESENTATION?

Little advice is necessary here, and most people succeed (if they've designed their presentation well!). That's for several reasons:

- You've done most of your work up front for computer presentations. Preparing the builds has solved, in advance, the order you want to use for presenting each slide.

- Graphics, transitions, and special effects can make a professional presentation you look forward to giving (and may even want to show off!).

- Your audience's attention is on the screen much of the time rather than on you.
- The audience is more likely to enjoy your presentation—setting up a good synergy where you feel better because they feel better.

I see nervous, ineffective speakers come alive all the time when they learn how to design a good computer presentation.

Here are my tips for giving a computer presentation:

- *Don't use a pointer very often.* By building each element, you draw your audience's attention to the screen at the right time—a pointer is superfluous. By holding a mouse in one hand and a pointer in the other, you can look pretty awkward. Reserve the pointer for emphasizing something (I'll use it to tap the important bullet or image on the screen).
- *Look at your audience most of the time.* Presenters who are new to using computer presentations often face the screen too much. Of course, it's a good thing to look at the screen when you're moving to the next bullet, the next image, or the next slide. Members of your audience will look at the screen then, too—which is what you want them to do.
- *Step toward the audience when you want attention on you.* Your audience will mostly look at the screen if you've done a good job designing your computer presentation. If you have times in the presentation when you want your audience's attention on you, you have to draw their attention to you. Otherwise, they'll be afraid of missing something on the screen. Just move a little. The movement will catch their eyes and get their attention.
- *Have fun!* If you've done a good job designing your presentation, this will come naturally.

EXERCISES

A. Explain how you'd build this slide and what transition effects you'd use:

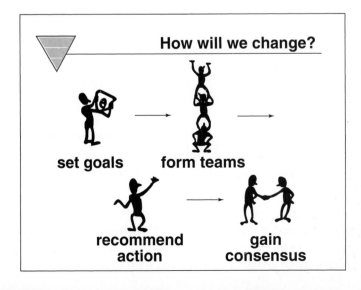

B. Give the presentation you prepared for Chapter 16 (defining a term) as a computer presentation. Follow the advice in this chapter about building almost every element and using transition and animation effects purposefully.

C. Give a 4- to 6-minute presentation that describes how to do something. A hobby is fine. For example, how do you swing a golf club? Draw a cartoon? Prepare an omelet? Or describe how to do anything you know something about that members of the class might not.

Or you can describe how to do something you've learned in your business courses. Have you learned something interesting about marketing a product? Managing a changing organization? Performing an accounting procedure?

A simple prop or two is okay, but the emphasis should clearly be on your slides.

Whatever topic you choose, your goal is to put together everything you've learned so far:

- Have a clear structure—one your audience can't get lost in. Follow the structure in Chapter 15 exactly.
- Design your visual aids as well as you can. Chapter 16 gives you suggestions.
- Follow the advice in this chapter for designing a computer presentation.

CHAPTER 18

Rehearsing, Setting Up the Room, and Overcoming Nervousness

There are important things to think of after you design your presentation and before you give it.

This chapter helps you finish preparing your presentation and take care of last-minute details so you'll be successful. Each of these three topics is important:

- rehearsing, rehearsing
- setting up the room
- overcoming last minute nervousness

Let's look at them more closely!

REHEARSING, REHEARSING

Why "rehearsing, rehearsing"? Because there are two types of rehearsal, each important.

Rehearse by Yourself

The simplest type of rehearsal is in front of a mirror, in your car, or in an empty room. The main purpose of this type of rehearsal is to go over the words you need to say to accompany your visual aids and to work on your techniques of delivery. And your best place to rehearse is, if possible, in the room you'll actually present in. The more you practice in that room, the more it will be *yours*—and you'll be comfortable in it when the day of your presentation arrives.

You don't want to memorize anything; you do want to rehearse enough that the approximate words come easily to you. The more you rehearse, the easier the words will come to you during your actual presentation.

During this rehearsal, also work on good techniques of delivery: pauses for those special moments and a little extra loudness or softness of your voice; a few planned hand movements at key times to show how big or small something is (but don't try this in your car!); eye contact (pretend the room is full).

Go through your entire presentation, preferably again and again. You may want to time yourself, too.

Rehearse in Front of Others

The second type of rehearsal is also important: in front of a small audience, usually of your peers. The goal of this rehearsal is to be sure your presentation makes sense—to make sure your words and slides get your message across efficiently and with the right emphasis and tone. Most writers wouldn't think of publishing a book without having others look at a draft first. Speakers shouldn't give important presentations without the same kind of review. This rehearsal is a good time, too, to try out any audience involvement so you can fine-tune it.

For this second type of rehearsal, you probably want to give your entire presentation at least once without interruption. People in your "audience" will probably want to stop you often to give you their ideas. Ask them to listen and take notes unless they get completely lost and need some explanation from you.

SETTING UP THE ROOM

Experienced speakers usually worry about this more than anything else. That's because setting up the room sometimes has to take place at the last minute and is often to some extent under other people's control. But only to *some* extent! If you're the only speaker, and you're speaking in a strange room, be certain to get there early (often an hour) to set up the room the way you like it.

What if you're not the only speaker? Well, the room has to be set up to somebody's specifications, so why not yours? If you know how to set up a room, you'll probably be doing all the other speakers a favor, anyway!

Let's look more closely at what you need to do to set up a room well:

- Position the screen.
- Set up the projector.
- Position tables and chairs.
- Adjust the lights.
- Adjust the temperature.
- Check the microphone.
- Eliminate distractions.

Position the Screen (If It's Portable)

Many places have a permanent screen. But sometimes the biggest presentations—for hundreds of people—take place in a hotel ballroom. Everything else in the room depends on where the screen is. Most screens you can't move. But if you have a portable screen:

- *Be sure it's not immediately under a light.* The light will wash out the projected image.

• *Be sure it's near you.* Audiovisual people—the ones setting up the screen—may have never given a presentation themselves. Often I see the screen in a corner of the room while I'm in the front of the room. I like the screen near me (that is, up front) so the audience can easily look back and forth between me and the screen.

Set Up the Projector

The projector is your crucial piece of equipment, so if there is a problem, you need to find out about it right away. Once you have a screen set up, get your projector ready to go!

For most places that hold frequent presentations, a computer projector is hanging from the ceiling, in a booth, or fixed in place. That's great. But if not, positioning the projector is the second thing you want to set up when you enter the room. Where you place the projector governs many other matters for setting up the room. You want to place it the right distance from the screen, for example, before you decide where tables and chairs should go. The right distance is usually where the projected image fills the screen as much as possible. That way, your audience will be looking at the largest image possible.

An image doesn't usually fill a screen completely from top to bottom. You want to use the top part of the screen as much as possible because everybody can see there. So set your image high on the screen rather than in the middle or low.

If you're using an extension cord, try to use an outlet on the side of the room you usually won't be on. That way the cord won't be a tripping hazard for you.

Position Tables and Chairs

Once the projector and screen are in place, you can position the tables and chairs for your audience. Set up the tables and chairs to get your audience as close as you can to you while giving yourself room to move about. That way you won't have to talk loudly for people in the rear of the room to hear you. A U-shape arrangement is ideal for audiences under about 25 people.

Adjust the Lights

Ideally, you'll have no light immediately over your screen but full light over your audience. Adjust as necessary. If you have to compromise—which usually happens—prefer a little more light, even at the expense of a slightly dimmer image on the screen. That way your audience is less likely to be sleepy. Do what you can to avoid a dark room!

Along these lines, close blinds and drapes. You don't want people looking out the windows while you're talking. If closing them makes the room too dark, try closing them part way.

Adjust the Temperature

Prefer slightly cool rather than slightly warm. That way, people will be less likely to get sleepy. Just a degree or two too warm can cause problems, no matter how good you are.

If the thermostat doesn't have a control you can use, get the building engineers to adjust the temperature. They'll usually want to crank it down 5 degrees or more just so you won't call them back. Be watchful.

Check the Microphone

Most of the time you won't need a microphone. But use one if you have to raise your voice a bit while talking. Although people may hear you if you simply raise your voice, you'll strain your voice and lose most of your inflection (which makes you hard to listen to).

When you do need a microphone, here are some considerations:

- *Prefer a wireless microphone.* A wireless microphone lets you move easily wherever you want. A microphone with a wire creates a tripping hazard and limits your movement. A microphone on a lectern traps you completely—avoid it whenever you can!

- *Check out the microphone in advance.* To check out the microphone, simply say something profound (like the alphabet) while someone else listens (preferably from several places in the room, including the very back). As you talk into the microphone, move around the room to all the places you expect to be during your presentation. That way, you can find out if there are any places in the room that cause feedback—that horrible high-pitched squeal that brings everything to a halt. If you're using a wired microphone, coil the wire so it will uncoil freely during your presentation. It will probably be a mess by the end of your presentation, but at least you can get off to a good start. If you're using a wireless microphone, be sure it has fresh batteries. Batteries may seem to last forever in a flashlight, but for a wireless microphone they need replacement every few hours of use.

- *Be sure you're dressed properly to use the microphone.* "Lapel mike" is another name for a wired or wireless microphone. But don't put it on your lapel—when you turn your head to the side away from that lapel, your voice will fade out. For men, put the microphone on your tie (as high as possible); for women, be sure to wear a blouse or suit jacket you can clip the microphone to.

- *Avoid wearing noisy jewelry.* Necklaces and badges on chains can clank against the microphone, causing a distracting noise your audience can hear but that you, as the speaker, probably can't!

Eliminate Distractions

Some distractions you can't control—such as the sound of cars outside your building or an air conditioner in it. Look and listen as you set up.

Is the ceiling speaker playing restful music? It won't seem so restful once you start talking and have to compete with it.

Will the doors be closed during your presentation? In larger rooms, there are usually several entrances. The one for you to worry about is the one at the back of the room. If it's open, audience members back there may hear outside noises that you can't while you're giving your presentation at the front of the room. Just before starting your presentation, close the rear door and ask someone sitting near it to be sure nobody coming in the room late leaves the door open.

OVERCOMING LAST-MINUTE NERVES

You've done everything you can to prepare: You have great visual aids, you've designed a few pattern breakers, and you've rehearsed several times to yourself and in front of others. In other words, there's nothing left to do but actually give the presentation.

Start Slightly Late and Finish On Time

In many speaking situations, especially formal ones with a number of people in the audience, not everybody will be there on time. If you start on time, people will be walking in during your carefully crafted beginning. Worse, all the seats at the back will probably be full, so the late arrivers will have to spend time hunting for a seat up front and getting people to move out of their way.

By starting a couple of minutes late (if you know some people are missing), you can lessen the problem. When people still walk in late, pause and help them get seated: "Hey, there's a seat way up front, right here by me!"

But starting late doesn't mean finishing late. Audiences hate that. If you go even a minute over your time, people will get restless.

Are you nervous? That's normal! Only the most experienced professional speakers avoid last-minute nervousness.

So how can you lessen the effects of that nervousness? There's no sure-fire solution that will keep you conscious and employed, but here are some tips that usually help:

- *Look over your slides.* If you've done a good job designing your visual aids, you'll probably feel reassured by simply glancing through them. You should be saying to yourself, "Oh, this is easy to give." And "The audience is really going to like this one!"

- *Start a conversation with someone who arrives early.* By starting a conversation, you not only distract yourself from feeling nervous, but you also normally get a friendly reaction that will help relax you.

- *Talk to a friendly face.* When your presentation is just beginning, find a friendly face and talk to that person. Often the friendly face will be the one you started a conversation with before your presentation began! Once you find that friendly face, you'll probably feel yourself start to relax.

 For a quick lesson on this topic, go to http://www.professorbailey.com.

EXERCISE

With the help of other people in your class, actually set up a room as well as possible for a presentation. After you have the room set up, point out to the class what is good about the room. And point out any things that aren't good but that you can't change (such as the size of the screen).

CHAPTER 19

Preparing an Annotated Presentation

Annotated presentations save time for you and your reader.

An annotated presentation is simply a printout of your slides, usually one per page, with your comments underneath. Figure 19.1 is an example of one page from an annotated presentation. And Figure 19.4, later, is an example of an entire annotated presentation.

Annotated presentations are replacing many reports. Often, people had to prepare a report and then give a briefing on it. That involved lots of duplication and extra work. Worse, who read the reports? Many reports went from the printer to an in-box to an out-box without ever passing through the brain cells of the person at the desk.

Why was that? One reason is that the reports looked like they had lots of words in them. And not many pictures.

An annotated presentation changes all that. Now you can have essentially one product: the presentation. Once you prepare your presentation, you simply print out each slide on a separate page: The top of the page has the image of a slide; the bottom has your explanation for it. For you, it's much easier than writing a report. For a reader, it's the next best thing to being at the actual presentation.

 For a quick lesson on this topic, go to http://www.professorbailey.com.

An annotated presentation has two important benefits:

- The annotated presentation can be useful to people who couldn't attend the presentation.
- It can also be useful to those who attended but want a reminder later of what they saw and heard.

Just as important, the capability of adding words to a page with the slides on it means the slides themselves don't have to stand alone. They can be simple, even pictorial.

You can easily learn how to create an annotated presentation in PowerPoint—just look at the Notes Page view.

An important consideration when preparing an annotated report is how you want your reader to read each page:

1. Do you expect your reader to study the image of the slide first and then look below and read the annotation?

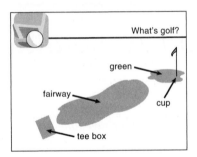

What's golf?

green

fairway

cup

tee box

Many of you are familiar with golf, but let's have a quick review:

- You start at the tee box and hit a ball toward the green. Your ultimate goal is to get the ball into the cup while hitting it as few times as you can.

- On most holes, you can't hit the ball far enough to get all the way to the green with one swing of the club, so you want to hit the ball in the fairway—a place where it's easy to find your ball.

Golf Academy/swedge@golfacademy.com   **3**

FIGURE 19.1 Sample Page from an Annotated Presentation

---

2. Or do you expect the reader to simply glance at the image of the slide and then read the annotation below?

3. Or do you expect your reader to go directly to the annotation first, read it carefully, and then look up at the image of the slide?

What did you do when you first looked at Figure 19.1? How long did you look at the image of the slide before looking at the text?

This is an important consideration because readers are used to starting at the top of a page of writing—such as a report—and reading down. But annotated presentations have most of the information—and the narrative flow—occurring at the bottoms of the pages. The image in an annotated presentation is equivalent to an illustration embedded in a report.

I think the answer to the question I posed is either number 2 or 3 above—but not number 1. I believe most readers will take, at most, a quick glance at the image of the slide and then quickly turn their attention to the annotation. Careful readers may then glance back up at the slide if the annotation refers to it. Some readers may even get into a flow of only reading the annotations below, glancing up at the slides only if necessary.

What does this mean for you as someone preparing the annotated presentation? Don't assume the image of the slide stands alone. Make the annotation below read like a narrative so a reader can turn from one page to the next, reading the narrative, glancing at

---

Landscape or Portrait?

There's no standard. Either format is fine.

Landscape format lets you print out your cover slide as it would normally appear.

Portrait format gives your readers the normal orientation they expect for a written document.

---

the slides, and getting all the information. Work to keep your annotations brief (bullets are great, of course!), and tell your story there.

For the annotations, I use a serif typeface (like Times New Roman) in somewhere around 12–14 points. If I'm using landscape format, I'm careful not to have the lines of text go all the way across the page. That would make the lines too long for the reader to read comfortably, so I move the margins in.

The rest of this brief chapter gives you suggestions on how to put together a good annotated presentation. Here's what we'll cover:

- cover page
- executive summary
- other slides

COVER SLIDES

You usually don't want to print your cover slide as a notes page. You want the cover slide to serve as the cover for your report, so just print the slide as a slide—so it fills the full page. However, since you're preparing an annotated presentation, you may well want to add some words to the cover slide. For example, suppose this is the cover slide for your presentation on keeping score in golf:

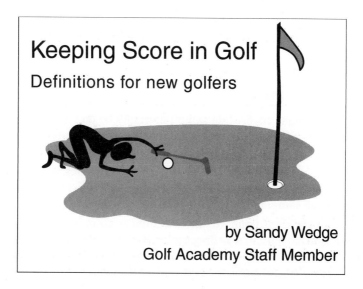

That's great for the presentation—simple, uncluttered. But for the annotated presentation, you may want to add, for example, your address, phone number, and e-mail address, like this:

Other things you might commonly include, depending on the circumstances, are the date and your company's logo. Figure 19.4, at the end of the chapter, shows you how a cover page fits into an annotated presentation.

What if you want notes to explain something about your cover slide? Perhaps, during your presentation, you made some important points while you were still showing the cover slide to your audience. Here's what I suggest:

- Start your annotated presentation with the cover slide as I've already shown (full page, unannotated).
- Then have an executive summary for your presentation (as I explain in the next section).
- Then print the cover slide again, but this time as a notes page (and annotate as necessary).

EXECUTIVE SUMMARY

The page after your cover slide should normally be an executive summary. An executive summary is the most read page in a report, so it's equally important to have one for an annotated presentation, which is a written document, too.

An executive summary is probably not one of your slides, so you'll need to create it. I normally do that using my word processor, but you can also do it in PowerPoint. Figure 19.2 is a sample executive summary.

You'll normally want your executive summary to be concise—rarely longer than a page, and shorter than that is fine, too. People reading an annotated presentation are usually in the mode of "tell it to me quickly!" They're not expecting to read lots of words on any page. So work to keep your executive summary brief.

Executive Summary

This short presentation tells you some of the important terms you need to know to keep score in golf.

As many of you know, the goal on each hole of golf is to keep hitting a ball until you can get it to fall into a small hole several hundred yards from where you started.

These are the three terms I'll cover:

- *Par.* The number of swings a good golfer would expect to take on a hole. Usually this number is a 3, 4, or 5—depending on the length of the hole.

- *Birdie.* One less than par (usually a 2, 3, or 4—again, depending on the length of the hole).

- *Bogey.* One more than par on a hole.

Golf Academy/swedge@golfacademy.com   **2**

FIGURE 19.2 Sample Executive Summary

Figure 19.4 shows you how an executive summary fits into an annotated presentation.

OTHER SLIDES

The rest of your annotated presentation simply consists of the rest of your slides printed as notes pages, as in Figure 19.4 at the end of the chapter. What should you say on these slides? Just say what you would if you were actually giving the presentation. You may, of course, want to be more concise. Remember, readers are ready to turn every page, so hit the main points on each slide and move on.

Here are some special considerations for this part of the annotated presentation:

- *Normally add page numbers and footers.* For example, you may want to add your company's name address, etc., in case someone copies one page from your annotated presentation to give to someone else.

- *Normally don't include certain slides in your annotated presentation.* Specifically, leave out these: the opaque slides (obviously!) and the slide saying "Questions."

- *Normally don't print out each separate animation on a separate page.* For example, don't print out a slide with only the first bullet, then print it out again on another page with the first and second bullet, then print it out again with the first, second, and third bullets, and so forth. That would be too many pages to turn for your reader. Just print the slide once with all the bullets on it.

- *But occasionally do print out each animation.* Suppose, for example, one of your slides has several photographs on it: The first photograph appears, then it disappears and a second one comes on in the same place, then it disappears and a third one appears in that place. . . . Imagine what the printout would look like. In cases like that, you'll need a separate printout for each time you show a new photograph. PowerPoint can handle that.

A final issue is how to handle blueprint slides. There are four blueprint slides for the actual presentation on golf (see Fig. 19.3).

I definitely recommend you include most of these—they're your "headings." Here's what I suggest:

- *Have very brief annotations.* For the blueprint slide, you could simply say something like this: "Today we'll cover these three terms: par (a good score), birdie (a very good score), and bogey (a common but not-so-good score). Let's start with the first one: par."
- *Don't include the first moving blueprint slide.* It's an unnecessary page.
- *Do include the second, third, and any other moving blueprint slides.* They're your "headings." Again, keep the annotations brief: "Now let's turn to our second topic: birdie. A birdie is a great score to get on a hole!"

FIGURE 19.3 Skip First Moving Blueprint Slide

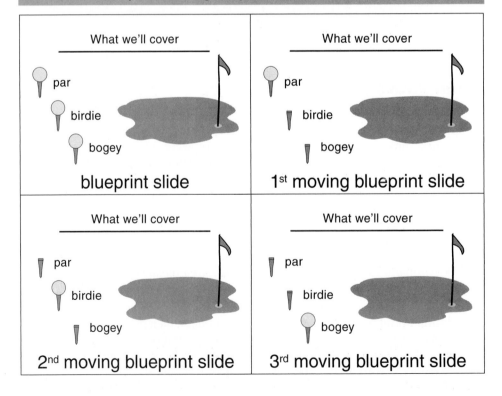

Keeping Score in Golf
Definitions for new golfers

1212 Mesa Ridge Drive
Mesa AZ 22222
(111) 222-3333
swedge@golfacademy.com

by Sandy Wedge
Golf Academy Staff Member

Executive Summary

This short presentation tells you some of the important terms you need to know to keep score in golf.

As many of you know, the goal on each hole of golf is to keep hitting a ball until you can get it to fall into a small hole several hundred yards from where you started.

These are the three terms I'll cover:

- *Par.* The number of swings a good golfer would expect to take on a hole. Usually this number is a 3, 4, or 5—depending on the length of the hole.
- *Birdie.* One less than par (usually a 2, 3, or 4—again, depending on the length of the hole).
- *Bogey.* One more than par on a hole.

Golf Academy/swedge@golfacademy.com   2

What's golf?

green

fairway

cup

tee box

Many of you are familiar with golf, but let's have a quick review:

- You start at the tee box and hit a ball toward the green. Your ultimate goal is to get the ball into the cup while hitting it as few times as you can.
- On most holes, you can't hit the ball far enough to get all the way to the green with one swing of the club, so you want to hit the ball in the fairway—a place where it's easy to find your ball.

Golf Academy/swedge@golfacademy.com   3

Purpose of presentation

to teach you the *names* of scores for a hole

My purpose today is simple—to let you know the different kinds of scores you can make on a hole. You've undoubtedly heard some of these terms before.

What do you think—is a birdie good or bad?

Golf Academy/swedge@golfacademy.com   4

What we'll cover

par

birdie

bogey

Today we'll cover these three terms:

- par (a good score)
- birdie (a very good score)
- bogey (a common but not-so-good score)

Let's start with the first one: par.

Golf Academy/swedge@golfacademy.com   5

What's a par?

the number of strokes a good golfer should expect to hit a ball from the tee into the cup

As you can see, a par is the number of strokes a good golfer should expect to get from the tee to the hole. Only the very best golfers can make a par or better on *all* 18 holes on a golf course. An average golfer will be happy to have several pars during an 18-hole round.

Most golf courses have three kinds of holes: par 3, par 4, and par 5. Let's look at each of those now.

Golf Academy/swedge@golfacademy.com   6

Example: par 3 hole

one swing and two putts

par 3 holes average 165 yards

A par 3 hole is the shortest one in golf:

- Good golfers expect to hit from the tee to the green in one stroke.
- Then they expect to get the ball into the hole from there in two more strokes.

Golf Academy/swedge@golfacademy.com   7

Example: par 4 hole

two swings and two putts

par 4 holes average 380 yards

The most common type of hole on a golf course is a par 4:

- Good golfers expect to take two strokes to get from the tee to the green.
- Then they expect to take another two to putt the ball into the hole.

Golf Academy/swedge@golfacademy.com   8

FIGURE 19.4 Sample Annotated Presentation

FIGURE 19.4 (Continued)

EXERCISE

Prepare an annotated presentation for the presentation you gave on defining a term (see Chapter 16).

Final Project: Learning Computer Techniques

Overview

Business professionals today depend on being up-to-date with the computer revolution. The goal of this exercise is for you—as a speaker or as a listener—to learn practical skills that can help you communicate better.

For example, if you know how to make flowcharts easily and well, you're more likely to use them in reports you write and in presentations you give. And flowcharts typically communicate far more effectively than several paragraphs full of words covering the same material.

This project will teach you not just flowcharts but many other techniques that are ready and waiting for you in your word processor and in your presentation program.

For this project, then, you and a partner will do two things:

- Give a 10- to 20-minute computer presentation that teaches students how to do something important on the computer. Each presentation should include some audience participation.
- Prepare an annotated presentation following the advice in Chapter 19.

Important note: You must go beyond simply showing the class how to use the computer. Instead, show the class *how to do good things on the computer*. For example, if your topic is flowcharts, bring in examples of creative, interesting, effective flowcharts; explain what makes them good; and show the class how to do them. By the end of such a presentation, the class should know lots about what makes for good flowcharts and how to do them on a computer.

Topics

Here are the topics you can choose from (only one group per topic):

- *Creating flowcharts in PowerPoint and Word.* Find good examples of flowcharts in publications and tell the class what makes for a good flowchart. Look over any pertinent Help items in Microsoft Office. Teach the class the characteristics of good flowcharts and show how to make them in PowerPoint and Word.

- *Creating tables in PowerPoint and Word.* Find good examples of tables in publications (books, newspapers, and magazines) and tell the class what makes for a good table. Look over all Help items in Microsoft Office. Teach the class the characteristics of good tables and show how to make them in Word.

- *Using Custom Animation in PowerPoint.* Look over all Help items in Microsoft Office. Teach the class how to use a key feature or two of Custom Animation.

- *Creating bar and pie charts in PowerPoint and Word.* Find good examples of bar and pie charts in publications and tell the class what makes for good ones. Look over all Help items in Microsoft Office. Teach the class the characteristics of good bar and pie charts and show how to make them in PowerPoint and Word.

- *Drawing in PowerPoint and Word.* Look over all Help items in Microsoft Office. Be sure to include AutoShapes.

Teach the class how to draw (including curved lines) and how to use a few AutoShapes.

- *Using sidebars and drop caps.* Find good examples of sidebars and drop caps in publications and tell the class why they're effective. Look over all Help items in Microsoft Office for text boxes (the way to create sidebars and drop caps). Teach the class the characteristics of good sidebars and the function of drop caps. And teach the class how to create them in Word.

- *Using Custom Animation in PowerPoint.* Look over all Help items in Microsoft Office. Teach the class how to use a key feature or two of Custom Animation.

- *Finding and editing clip art.* Look over all Help items in Microsoft Office. Show the class how to get and edit Microsoft Clip Art. Show how to get clip art from the Web and other sources. Teach the class how to edit clip art—such as combining part of one image with part of another image.

- *Finding and editing photographs.* Show the class how to find high-quality photographs. Look over any Help items in Microsoft Office. Show the class how to use most items on the Picture toolbar.

- *Using WordArt, 3-D effects, and shadows.* Look over all Help items in Microsoft Office. Find examples of these effects from publications and be prepared to tell the class when these effects can be useful. Teach the class how to use WordArt and how to create 3-D effects and shadows.

- *Using "clip sound," recording your voice, and using Record Narration in PowerPoint.* Look over all Help items in Microsoft Office. Teach the class how to acquire clip sound, how to record a voice and edit it using Sound Recorder, and how to use sound in PowerPoint.

- *Demonstrating another useful program.* If you know another relevant program, such as Photoshop, FrontPage, Dreamweaver, or Illustrator, demonstrate it to the class. The goal is to let students know what capabilities their graphics shop almost certainly has in a corporate or business setting.

Final Project: Creating Reports

Overview

This appendix is an exercise that replicates an extremely common business situation: looking into something important, giving a presentation on it, and writing a report. The topic of this project should be useful, too: how to prepare one element—such as a table of contents—of a good report.

Much of the writing in an organization is correspondence: e-mail, memos, letters. However, important projects often require a report. Chapter 19 covered one important type of report—the Annotated Presentation—and showed you how to prepare one. Here are a few other types of reports:

- *Ad hoc reports.* These can be on anything. The director of facilities of a company might ask an architectural firm to suggest a redesign for the interior of a building. Or the vice president for marketing might ask for a report on how to market a new product. Or the chief executive officer might ask for a report on what the competition has done for the past year. Or a middle manager might ask for a brief report suggesting a better process.
- *Audit reports.* Auditors are people who inspect something to see if people are following laws, rules, and procedures. When they finish their inspection, they issue a report on their findings.
- *Research reports.* Many scientific and other research organizations consider their reports to be their main products. These organizations, for example, might look into a better way to launch a satellite and then report on their findings.
- *Annual reports.* Companies prepare a report each year to the shareholders who own the company. The top companies put a lot of energy and resources into these.

If you're in business and have to prepare such a report, people reading it expect it to be a professional product.

Just as there are countless formats for memos and letters, so are there countless formats for reports. However, most reports have cover pages, tables of contents, and other elements to make them look professional and be easier to read. This project asks you to choose one element of a report, such as the cover page or the table of contents. Then you'll:

- Work with one or two other people and give a polished presentation to the class on how to do that element well.
- Then work by yourself and write a report on how to do that element well. Your report will have to include all the elements of a report that the rest of the class has given presentations on: cover page, table of contents, graphs, sidebars, and so forth. These are easy to do with today's word processing programs.

You don't need to do any traditional research, such as finding articles on good ways to prepare tables of contents. Instead, just look at several dozen tables of contents. You may have trouble finding a lot of reports. But annual reports are easily available. And magazines and books often do a good job. Popular publications typically use the elements of a business report, often creatively and effectively. Are there techniques in these publications that reports could use?

What do the popular publications have, for example, in their tables of contents other than title and page number? Pictures? Summaries? You'll see. And what layout techniques do they use?

As a result of this project, you should learn some exciting things about how to prepare a professional-looking report. A side benefit is that much of what you learn can apply to papers you write for your other college courses.

Group Presentation

Work with one or two other people in the class and look closely at one element or characteristic of a report. For a group of two, give a 12- to 18-minute presentation to the class; for a group of three, give an 18- to 24-minute presentation. The purpose of your presentation is to give practical tips to help the people in your class do a good job writing their final paper.

Here are the specific topics to choose from:

- cover page
- table of contents
- first pages of chapters or sections
- title, subtitles, and headings
- eye catchers (limit yourselves to sidebars, pull quotes, and drop capitals)
- bar and pie charts (only these two)
- illustrations other than graphs
- elements unifying a report

The final papers must include all the items in the list you just read. So your group presentation, in effect, teaches the other students how to do those papers. The other students expect you to do a good job because they will have to use the information you give them. For that reason, you can expect an attentive (and demanding) audience.

Here are some requirements:

- Give the class a one-page handout that summarizes your key suggestions. Students should be able to refer to this when they write their final papers. Please keep this handout short and practical (and, of course, in Plain English!).
- Stay within the time limit.
- Don't just give a book report. If your topic is, for example, bar and pie charts, most of your research should be looking at (and analyzing) bar and pie charts—not reading a book about them.
- Include audience participation: Group competition, demonstrations, class exercises, and other techniques keep the class alert. Be sure the audience participation teaches something important about your topic. Chapter 14 may give you some ideas on audience participation.
- Use visual aids. The second section of this book tells you how to choose and use them.
- Remember that you're teaching the class something, so don't just show the class (for example) one heading and then another heading and then another heading. Each example should be there for a reason. Your recommendations are a very important part of this exercise.
- Be sure each member of the group participates equally in the actual presenting. One person shouldn't do all the talking while the other simply passes out an exercise.
- Tell the class the important sources you used to prepare your presentation (if any). It's often helpful if you bring your sources to class and show them to the class during your presentation.

- Rehearse, rehearse, rehearse. This should be a polished, thoughtful, informative presentation.

Final Paper

The final paper is an individual—not a group—project. Work by yourself.

Write a 5- to 8-page paper (not including cover page, table of contents, and attachments) based on your presentation. It should be a written version of your group presentation, a way of teaching your topic in writing. Assume that your paper is to people who did not see your presentation.

Use all the elements that the group presentations covered (cover page, table of contents, eye catchers, bar charts, sidebars, etc.).

Key suggestion: Don't forget to include examples in your paper to make it commu-

nicate independently of your presentation. You can use the ones from your presentation, if you wish.

Be sure to document all borrowed material. Internal documentation is fine. Chapter 12 covers the basics of documentation.

When you're through, you'll not only hand in your paper—you'll also present it to the class. Using transparencies or the paper itself, show us how you did all the things the presentations were about. That is, show us your cover page and explain it to us; show us your table of contents and explain it to us; show us your graphs and explain them to us; and so on. Give an informal, unrehearsed presentation that lasts about 3 or 4 minutes: something thorough but not rambling. The class should be "oohing" and "aahing" the entire time at the neat things you're showing!

Formats for Letters and Memos

With businesses today relying on e-mail, letters and memos are not nearly as important as they used to be. That's why this is an appendix!

There are no standard formats for letters or memos. Each organization comes up with its own, and many variations are possible. Still, most formats follow some conventions. This appendix discusses common practices.

Letters

Unlike a memo, a letter is normally to people outside your organization. You want your letter to look inviting. If you can make your first page look good, your readers will more likely pick up your letter and have a good first impression. So, within the formats your organization may prescribe, use white space, especially on the first page, to get the proper effect.

Let's look at several common formats for letters. The first example (Fig. C.1) is loaded—it has just about every possible element:

- *Writer's address.* The writer's address is at the top of the letter (in the "letterhead"—preprinted on the stationery). Most organizations have letterhead stationery. The letterhead address is usually at the top or bottom, though some do put it on the left margin. You may want to include the nine-digit zip code instead of the five-digit one in the example.
- *Date.* The date is on the far right. Other common places for the date are at the far left or at a point halfway across the page (that's not quite the same as centering it on the page). Also, there's no standard space for the date to go

below the top of the page. Nor is there any standard space between the date and the inside address. Adjust to have a nice-looking page. With a very short letter, add more space after the date and possibly widen the margins a little.

- *Inside address.* This is the same address you put on the envelope. Consider putting a little extra space between the inside address and the salutation ("Dear Joe"). That extra space is optional. If you put space there, also put it between the last sentence of your letter and the signature block.
- *Salutation.* The salutation sets the tone. There's a range of formality (the list here is from most formal to least formal):

    Dear Mr. Elm:
    Dear Joe,
    Joe,

Use someone's first name only if you're on a first-name basis with that person. The traditional convention is to use a colon if you use the person's last name but a comma if you use only the first. Today, though, you often see a wider range than in the past (again, from most formal to least formal):

    Dear Mr. Elm:
    Dear Mr. Elm,
    Dear Joe:
    Dear Joe,
    Joe,
    Hi, Joe!

As you can see, the colon still sets a more formal tone. If you're writing to a woman and aren't sure how to address her, use "Ms." before her last

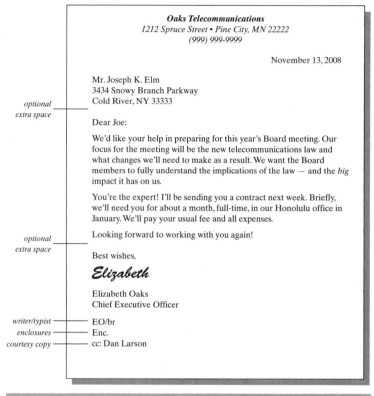

Oaks Telecommunications
1212 Spruce Street • Pine City, MN 22222
(999) 999-9999

November 13, 2008

Mr. Joseph K. Elm
3434 Snowy Branch Parkway
Cold River, NY 33333

optional extra space

Dear Joe:

We'd like your help in preparing for this year's Board meeting. Our focus for the meeting will be the new telecommunications law and what changes we'll need to make as a result. We want the Board members to fully understand the implications of the law — and the *big* impact it has on us.

You're the expert! I'll be sending you a contract next week. Briefly, we'll need you for about a month, full-time, in our Honolulu office in January. We'll pay your usual fee and all expenses.

Looking forward to working with you again!

optional extra space

Best wishes,

Elizabeth

Elizabeth Oaks
Chief Executive Officer

writer/typist — EO/br
enclosures — Enc.
courtesy copy — cc: Dan Larson

FIGURE C.1 Common Format for Business Letters

---

name. What if you don't know the name of the person you're writing to? The old "To whom it may concern" is an invitation to send your letter on a quick and permanent trip to the trash can. Instead, consider using the person's title as the salutation: "Dear Director of Human Resources." Or just leave the salutation off entirely.

- *Body.* Use Plain English, including headings (for longer letters) and bullets. Your headings for letters should not be overly dominant (such as a huge point size), or they'll overwhelm the format of the letter.

- *Complimentary close.* Common closes are "Sincerely," "Best wishes," "Regards," "Warmest regards," "Respectfully," and

"Yours truly." Capitalize only the first letter of the first word. Occasionally today you'll see a very short paragraph, followed by a comma, serve as the complimentary close:

Looking forward to seeing you,

That can be effective.

- *Signature block.* As with the salutation, there's a range of formality for signing your name. Suppose your name is William Spruce and your friends call you Bill. Mr. Spruce would use one of these signatures:

William Spruce
Bill Spruce
Bill

Use the full name for strangers and for official documents (like proposals and invoices) that require a legal signature.

- *Writer/typist.* This information is usually only clutter. Use it only if you must document it.

- *Enclosure.* Also usually clutter. If the body of the letter makes it clear what you've enclosed, leave this line out. Use it only to add information the body doesn't have. For example, actually list the enclosures ("1. Report from the staff, July 7," etc.) if the body of the letter refers to them only vaguely and if circumstances (such as legal matters) require such documentation.

- *Copies.* Usually helpful. In years past, "cc" meant "carbon copy." When carbons disappeared (thank goodness), it came to mean "courtesy copy." Basically it says who else got copies of

the letter. Today, the second "c" sometimes disappears ("c: Fred Spruce"). Even better is just to say "copy: Fred Spruce." A related abbreviation is "bc," meaning "blind copy." Use it to send a copy to someone without letting the original addressee know. Obviously, the initials "bc" don't go on the original letter you send to the addressee—they go only on the appropriate copies. Use "bc" judiciously—unless you want to appear to be going behind someone's back.

- *Reference line.* Traditionally, letters didn't have "subject" or "reference" (or "regarding") lines. These lines are helpful for organizations that prepare or receive a lot of correspondence. Don't hesitate to use them if they serve a purpose (see Fig. C.2). Today, the reference line

FIGURE C.2 Letter with Optional "Re:" Line

Birch Debt Collectors
6767 Maple Street • Dogwood, MN 22222
(999) 999-9999

June 23, 20xx

Ms. Tina Pixel
Overnight Computers
5656 Plywood Street
Knothole, MN 22222

Dear Ms. Pixel:

Your company's check bounced. I'm returning it and asking for cash by Friday. If I don't hear from you by then, you'll be hearing from our lawyers.

Sincerely,

Lira Franc

Lira Franc
Chief Financial Officer

Spruce Computer Integration
7878 Masonite Street • Cottonwood Grove, MN 22222

FIGURE C.3 Another Common Format for Business Letters

sometimes comes after the salutation but before the body of the letter.

Consider starting the date and signature block half way across the page. This is not the same as centering them on the page. For short letters, place the body in the middle of the page (vertically) or slightly higher (see Fig. C.3).

Figure C.4 shows how to put the writer's address on a letter that doesn't have that information preprinted on the stationery. An alternative is to simply create your own letterhead format on your word processor. The space between the writer's address and the date is optional.

Memos

The memo is disappearing. E-mail has all but taken its place!

A memo is a format for corresponding within an organization. Figure C.5 is a typical format.

There's no standard order or format for the "To," "From," "Subject," and "Date" lines, so it's important to check the preferred style at your organization. Writers often write their handwritten initials after their name in the "From" line as a way of signing it. Some formats put the word "memorandum" on the top of the page.

3434 Snowy Branch Parkway
Cold River, NY 33333

November 21, 2008

Ms. Elizabeth Oaks
Chief Executive Officer
Oaks Telecommunications
1212 Spruce Street
Pine City, MN 22222

Dear Elizabeth:

I'd be glad to help with your Board meeting. I'm tied up the first week
of January, but I can be in Honolulu for the next four weeks.

I'm sending you a summary of the key points of the new
telecommunications law—just for your background. Could you have
your folks send me a copy of the recent report they wrote on the
implications of the law for your company?

Thanks!

Sincerely,

Joseph K. Elm
Consultant

FIGURE C.4 Common
Format with No Letterhead

To: Department Heads
From: James Bond, Department of Security and
          Administrative Services
Subject: Review of security procedures (by Wednesday)
Date: February 2

Please personally review the attached draft of suggested
changes to our security procedures. I need your comments
by Wednesday.

Here's some background: In January, Jason Brown asked us to
review the security procedures we use for storing sensitive
material. As you know, our corporate success depends on our
technology: we have to be first, and we have to be ahead of the
competition. Other companies would have a significant
advantage if they could get hold of much of the correspondence
we consider routine.

We are concerned not just with correspondence and other
material on paper but also with anything in computers or on
disks. The attached draft gives my department's approach to
solving this important problem.

FIGURE C.5 Common
Format for Memo

APPENDIX D

Sample Papers

This appendix includes three sample papers:

- The first two sample papers were in response to Exercise E, Chapter 2. That exercise asks you to describe your job in Plain English.
- The third sample paper was in response to Exercise H, Chapter 6. That exercise asks you to define a term in Plain English.

After each paper, you'll see the results from running the paper through a grammar checker.

Sample Paper: "Working in Thailand"

To: Dr. Bailey and students

From: Nattawat Sattaworakul

Subject: Working in a garment factory in Bangkok

Date: March 11

I grew up in a business-oriented family in Thailand. From an early age, I lived and breathed the realities of operating a business—giving me a direct exposure to the rewards and difficulties of the business world. My mother's family owns and operates a small garment factory in the very busy and highly commercialized area of Bangkok. My father and his partners distribute jewelry and gems.

I can remember as a young child witnessing my parents' hard work. I have always admired that about them and hoped I would be able to maintain what they worked so hard to build.

Immediately after graduating with my Bachelors Degree in Law, I joined my mother's family's company as an Assistant General Manager. My mom and uncle decided that instead of hiring a new person, they would train me. Here is the structure of the company and where I fit in:

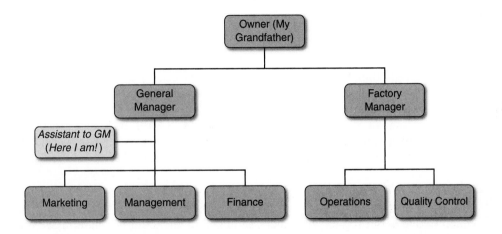

The factory is small, producing many types of garments—including uniforms for students and companies. The business was at its annual peak when I started, so the job was very busy from the first day. Generally, March to June is the busiest time of the year for the factory.

As a newly hired assistant to the general manager, I had to learn every little thing about almost every part of our company. At the beginning of my job, my primary responsibilities included:

- taking orders
- shipping and handling products
- developing our products

Let's start with my first important duty.

Taking Orders

My first responsibility was to take orders from customers. This was not very difficult because I already knew our regular customers who had been doing business with us for years. My mother always said it was important to maintain good relationships with our customers. If they believe in our capability to make them good products with reasonable prices, they will be loyal to us. She said taking orders is where it all begins. Most customers placed orders by phone. But new customers and customers who wanted specially tailored products came to our store.

The process of taking orders from new customers required a little more time than normal. I recall an example from my first week on the job. A new customer came into the store to place an order for 500 jackets. The jackets were for their salespersons, and they wanted us to put their logo on the jackets. Because he was a new customer, I took him around our factory to see the process of manufacturing—from picking the material to the packaging the final product. We negotiated the price and talked about the entire manufacturing process. He signed the contract!

Shipping and Handling Products

After packaging the final product, I was responsible for coordinating the shipment to our customers. Shipping can be directly to our customers or via a shipping dealer. The latter was usually the case in the event that our customer's location is too far.

Typically, the shipping process was as follows:

1. First, I checked the inventory. This was very important so we'd know we were delivering the right thing. It also told us how many products we had left in our stock.
2. Next, I gave the products and the order form to our employees so they could load them onto the company's truck.
3. Last, I accompanied our employees to the customer's location. Sometimes I helped our employees reload the product in the customer's stock room. Afterward, I received payment and the customer's signature showing he'd received the order.

Developing Our Products

My job also included development and strategizing. A good example: When I delivered our products to one of our regular customers, he talked to me about the material we used to make our jackets. He suggested that we use a particular type of fabric. He said that it would extend the life of the jacket and be cheaper to produce. When I got back to the factory, I offered the idea to my mother. We did a lot research on this new material, starting with asking the other customers what they thought, talking to our distributors, and comparing the price from different dealers. A few weeks later, we started to make the jackets from this material and it truly did cost less to produce and had greater durability.

Overall, I completely enjoyed working for my family's business. I was able to experience many aspects of the manufacturing and sales process. I also saw the satisfaction of bringing a product to the marketplace and making our customers happy.

Here are the results from running Nattawat's paper through a grammar checker:

	Results
Words per sentence	14.9
Characters per word	4.6
Passive sentences	0
Flesch Reading Ease	56.9
Flesch-Kincaid Grade Level	9.0

Sample Paper: "Managing a Pizza Parlor"

To: Classmates in MGT 503

From: Michael Day

Subject: Describing my job

Date: February 3

I was a pizza restaurant manager for over five years. During my time with the company, I had many responsibilities. After over five years of experience and several months of absence from the fun, I have pinpointed the most important responsibilities for that position. They are:

- marketing for my store
- controlling store costs
- staffing my store

Marketing for My Store

Marketing at this level included handing out coupons to the residents in our delivery area, running promotions with area businesses, and increasing involvement with elementary schools and kids—anything needed to increase sales.

Handing out coupons seemed easy enough: Schedule drivers to walk through the neighborhoods and place coupons on the doors of potential customers. My supervisor told me that drivers wanted to door hang because it increases business, increases deliveries . . . which increases tips. Simple. Not so fast. Drivers do not want to waste their valuable time door hanging. They can sit in their cars listening to music until a delivery order comes in. Why work when you can sit and do nothing?

I interacted with local businesses by giving out free pizza coupons, discount buffet coupons, and VIP coupons to managers so they could give them to customers of their choice. One time a health club opened, and I invited the employees to come to my store and eat dinner. I wanted to show them that I offered a good selection of food to those who were fitness conscious. I served vegetarian pizza, salad, and spaghetti.

I increased sales by promoting Kid's Night. I had employees decorate the store with balloons and streamers, and I hired a clown to come in for two hours per week to hand out balloon animals to all the kids. To increase involvement in schools, we had a school lunch program. We offered large pizza for $6 to the private schools in our area.

Controlling Store Costs

I was solely responsible for monitoring and achieving the profit goals in my store. To reach the lofty goals set, I had to control costs. The three types of costs that were important to me were:

- cost of sales
- cost of semivariables
- cost of labor

Controlling costs was the most important part of my job. I counted every pound of all products used in making a pizza. How much cheese did the cooks use? How much beef, pork, and other toppings did they use? Can you believe the cooks are supposed to count how many pepperoni slices are on a medium pizza? If my food costs were out of the standard of .2%, I had to explain why to my boss. If $20 was missing on $10,000 of sales, my boss had to know where, why, and what I was going to do to make sure it didn't happen again.

Controlling semivariables was also hard. I had to monitor the use of plates, forks, straws, and napkins. My boss had me speak with a waiter because he gave a table too many napkins. I lost points on an inspection because the waiter gave a customer a straw for a cup of water. I lost points on a major inspection because of a one-cent straw!

Controlling cost of labor was a lot easier. I was able to control my labor by accurate forecasting. I used historical information to forecast, and I was able to set up an accurate schedule. The schedule covered the business during normal times, and if it was slow, I sent people home early.

Staffing My Store

The most interesting part of my job was hiring and training. I spent 40% of my time hiring and training employees on their jobs and company standards. I had to hire people I thought would be able to stay calm and focused during our dinner rush. I had to sort through hundreds of applications every two months to find qualified applicants—this meant no felony convictions. After the long search, I would set up interviews. If the interview went well, and I felt the applicant would follow the rules, I would offer that applicant a job. How many interviews does it take to find someone who wants to measure cheese in a cup and count pepperoni for minimum wage?

When applicants became employees, I trained them. I had tapes and manuals to teach the new employee what to do. I spent hours showing them how to make pizzas and wait tables. When they were comfortable with the job, they had to pass a written test to become certified. I had to certify cooks and wait staff before they could work a shift alone. The final part of training is follow-up and feedback. Every pizza made and every table served, I evaluated. When I noticed something wrong, I corrected the mistake.

I believe my employees knew I wasn't giving them a hard time because I wanted to. Why would I care if *32 pepperoni slices* were on a medium pizza?

Here are the results from running Michael's paper through a grammar checker:

	Results
Words per sentence	14.4
Characters per word	4.4
Passive sentences	0
Flesch Reading Ease	65.8
Flesch-Kincaid Grade Level	7.6

Sample Paper: "360-Degree Feedback"

To: Classmates in MGT 503
From: Liz Wood
Subject: 360-degree Feedback
Date: March 11

No matter where you work, you probably hear a lot about the importance of feedback. However, can you think of any recent examples of receiving quality and timely feedback on your performance from your boss or anyone one else? Most likely, your answer is "No!"

In this memo, I introduce the concept of 360-Degree Feedback. In effect, 360-Degree Feedback (or "multirater" feedback) is an assessment that lets everyone you work with evaluate your performance. Most often, you get feedback on performance only from your boss. But this narrow view usually doesn't reflect the knowledge or opinions of everyone else. So 360-Degree Feedback gives you an accurate picture of your work performance from all directions.

Let's look at the assessment in greater detail, as if you were getting ready to go through the process. But remember, the assessment is a developmental tool, not a formal performance appraisal; the assessment identifies known and unknown strengths and weaknesses without impacting your salary, job status, or permanent record. It's hard enough to receive so much feedback from so many directions without the added stress of losing your job!

How Does the Process Begin?

360-Degree Feedback is intimidating. As your feedback "coach," I meet with you before the process begins, and I talk to you about what you can expect. In this meeting, I ask you to start thinking about who you want to evaluate your performance. To get accurate feedback on your performance, I ask you to nominate several people (in addition to your supervisor), called "raters," from every aspect of your work life. This diagram shows your supervisor and the different groups of people you should select from:

To keep the results anonymous, I need you to nominate at least:

- three customers
- three peers
- three subordinates

If you have at least three people in each rater group, it is harder for you to figure out how each person individually rated you. An important part of 360-Degree Feedback is ensuring anonymity and confidentiality, and therefore the process involves a lot of people!

You may be thinking, "What if I don't have subordinates or a designated customer base? Can I still do a 360-degree assessment?" The answer is *yes*. However, then the assessment is not 360-Degree Feedback but rather "multirater" feedback.

What Are People Rating Me On?

It depends on what assessment you are using. There are several different 360-Degree Feedback instruments on the market. The most commonly used assessments have 80–160 questions and assess performance satisfaction on a scale from 1 to 10. Each question correlates to a skill area. For example, there may be eight questions on the assessment that relate to conducting effective meetings. Most instruments will allow you to customize the skill areas you want to assess.

How Do You Interpret My Results?

After your raters turn in their assessments, I generate a report. Depending on the assessment you use, most reports have several sections, which may include:

- *A report summary.* This section gives you an overview of your results.
- *Identified strengths.* This section highlights the skill areas that you received the highest results on.

- *Developmental needs.* This section identifies areas for improvement.
- *Individual question results.* This section breaks down each question so you can see the average score of each group that rated you. For instance, it shows your peer group average, your subordinate group average, your bosses' average, and the score you gave yourself.

How Do I Deal with the Results?

Before you get your results back, you attend an interpretation workshop in preparation for reading the report and dealing with the feedback. Some of the feelings you may experience include rejection, denial, frustration, elation, or surprise. Once you get your results, you meet with me again, and I coach you through interpreting your results. As your "feedback coach," I help you look for trends or patterns in your results. For example, let's say for the question, "when listening, gives full attention to the speaker," you receive the following averages:

- boss: 10
- peers: 9.2
- customer: 9.1
- subordinates: 6.5

As your coach, I might ask you to consider why your subordinates are rating you far below the scores of your boss and peers. Hopefully, seeing these results will make you realize that you are not giving enough attention to your subordinates when listening to them. After we talk about this result, we then discuss action plans to help correct the behavior.

So 360-Degree Feedback is an excellent tool; it helps you get a clear picture of your work performance from a variety of perspectives. It also serves as a good metric for success. You can later retake the assessment and measure your new results with past results to gauge your progress!

Here are the results from running Liz's paper through a grammar checker:

	Results
Words per sentence	14.0
Characters per word	4.8
Passive sentences	0
Flesch Reading Ease	57.5
Flesch-Kincaid Grade Level	8.5

Commonly Confused Words

affect / effect

Affect is almost always a verb. *Effect* is almost always a noun.

correct: Warm ocean temperatures can *affect* the weather dramatically.

correct: One *effect* of warm ocean temperatures is a greater possibility of hurricanes.

alright / all right

Alright is nonstandard. *All right* is the correct choice.

alot / a lot

Alot is nonstandard. *A lot* is the correct choice.

among / between

Between refers to two items. *Among* refers to more than two items.

correct: The meeting went well *between* Ralph and Geraldine.

wrong: The meeting went well *between* Ralph, Susan, and Geraldine.

complement / compliment

A *compliment* means saying something nice about somebody. A *complement* is something that goes well with.

example: She paid him a nice *compliment* about his recent project.

example: His tie nicely *complemented* his suit.

desert / dessert

A *desert* is a dry place. *Dessert* means something good to eat at the end of your meal.

discreet / discrete

Discreet means circumspect or trustworthy. *Discrete* means individual or able to stand alone.

example: Their conversation was very *discreet* so nobody else would hear.

example: They had to perform 12 *discrete* tasks.

disinterested / uninterested

Disinterested means impartial. *Uninterested* means bored.

example: The players respected the referee because he was completely *disinterested*.

example: The players were furious with the referee because he was completely *uninterested*.

farther / further

Farther usually refers to distance. *Further* means more or additional.

example: The town was *farther* than we thought.

example: *Further*, it was much bigger than we thought.

fewer / less

Fewer refers to things we can enumerate. *Less* refers to things we can't.

example: There were *fewer* people in the town.

example: The town had *less* information available than we'd hoped for.

imply / infer

A speaker or writer *implies*. A listener or reader *infers*.

example: Her e-mail *implied* this would be an easy job.

example: We *inferred* from reading her e-mail that this would be an easy job.

irregardless / regardless

Irregardless is nonstandard. *Regardless* is the correct choice.

it's / its / its'

It's means "it is." *Its* is possessive. *Its'* doesn't mean a thing.

example: *It's* in your interest to do the job right the first time.

example: We put the toner back in *its* box.

principal / principle

Principal means "main" or the person who ran your school. A *principle* is a strong belief.

example: The *principal* reason you succeeded was your hard work.

example: He stuck to his *principles* and left anyway.

Theirs / theirs'

Theirs' is incorrect.

Your / you're

You're means "you are." *Your* means belonging to you.

example: *You're* absolutely right.

example: You left *your* coat at the restaurant.

Index